AF412161

DEMOCRATISING CAPITALISM?

Manchester University Press

LILIANA POP

DEMOCRATISING CAPITALISM?

The political economy of post-communist transformations in Romania, 1989–2001

MANCHESTER UNIVERSITY PRESS
Manchester and New York

distributed exclusively in the USA by Palgrave

Published by Manchester University Press
Oxford Road, Manchester M13 9NR, UK
and Room 400, 175 Fifth Avenue, New York, NY 10010, USA
www.manchesteruniversitypress.co.uk

Distributed exclusively in the USA by
Palgrave, 175 Fifth Avenue, New York, NY 10010, USA

Distributed exclusively in Canada by
UBC Press, University of British Columbia, 2029 West Mall, Vancouver, BC,
Canada V6T 1Z2

British Library Cataloguing-in-Publication Data
A catalogue record for this book is available from the British Library

Library of Congress Cataloging-in-Publication Data applied for

ISBN   0 7190 7094 5 *hardback*
EAN   978 0 7190 7094 5

First published 2006

15 14 13 12 11 10 09 08 07 06   10 9 8 7 6 5 4 3 2 1

Typeset in Minion with Lithos
by Action Publishing Technology Ltd, Gloucester
Printed in Great Britain
by Biddles Ltd, King's Lynn

CONTENTS

To my parents

*A*CKNOWLEDGEMENTS

Countless acts of kindness and generosity from more people than could be mentioned here gave me sustenance over the years and made this book possible.

The research for this book started as a doctoral dissertation in the Centre for the Study of Globalisation and Regionalisation, at the University of Warwick, under the stimulating and effective supervision of Richard Higgott and Jan Aart Scholte. I also owe a debt of gratitude to the organisations who have provided financial support: the Ministry of Education of Romania, The University of Warwick, the Committee of Vice-chancellors and Principals, the Centre for the Study of Globalisation and Regionalisation at the University of Warwick and the Central European University in Budapest.

Special thanks to Radu Baltasiu, Claudiu Degeratu, Brîndușa Fecioru, Daniela Gârleanu, Anca Manoliu, Elena Morariu, Adrian Neculau, Brîndușa Palade, Daniel Pop, Dumitru Sandu, Alexandra Stănescu, and Conțiu Șoitu for their help with my empirical research in Romania. I am grateful to my interviewees for their interest in my research and their willingness to answer my many questions. Many colleagues and friends have read drafts of various chapters of the book. I would like to thank Judy Batt, Corneliu Berari, Thomas Christiansen, Randall Germain, Peter Katzenstein, Bogdan Micu, Mihaela Miroiu, Adrian Miroiu, Helen Nesadurai, Anastasia Nesvetailova, Mădălina Nicolaescu, Minerva Ocolișan, Paola Robotti, Stuart Shields, Timothy Sinclair, Stelu Șerban, Fernanda Tuozzo, Michael Waller and the anonymous reviewers of Manchester University Press for their comments and encouragement. The support of colleagues in the International Politics Department at University of Wales, Aberystwyth and in the School of Politics and Sociology at Birkbeck College, University of London is also appreciated.

Finally, I am grateful to the staff of Manchester University Press for their patient and gentle guidance during the publication process.

*A*BBREVIATIONS

AGA	*Adunarea Generală a Acţionarilor* (General Meeting of Shareholders)
ANP	*Agenţia Naţională de Privatizare* (National Agency for Privatisation)
ARD	*Agenţia Română de Dezvoltare* (Romanian Development Agency)
BNR	*Banca Naţională a României* (National Bank of Romania)
BVB	Bursa de Valori Bucureşti (Bucharest Stock Exchange)
CDR	*Convenţia Democratică din România* (Democratic Convention of Romania)
CEE	Central and Eastern Europe
CMEA	Council for Mutual Economic Assistance
CNFSN	*Consiliul Naţional al Frontului Salvării Naţionale* (National Council of the National Salvation Front)
CNVM	*Comisia Naţională a Valorilor Mobiliare* (National Commission for Securities)
CPUN	*Consiliul Provizoriu al Unităţii Naţionale* (Provisional Council of National Unity)
CURS	*Centrul pentru Sociologie Urbană şi Regională* (Centre for Urban and Regional Sociology)
EBRD	European Bank for Reconstruction and Development
EC	European Commission
EC-GDE	European Commission – General Directorate for Enlargement
EECR	*East European Constitutional Review*
EU	European Union
FDSN	*Frontul Democrat al Salvării Naţionale* (Democratic National Salvation Front)
FPP	*Fondul Proprietăţii Private* (Private Property Fund)
FPS	*Fondul Proprietăţii de Stat* (State Ownership Fund)
FSN	*Frontul Salvării Naţionale* (National Salvation Front)
GR	*Guvernul României* (Government of Romania)
IFI	International Financial Institution
IMF	International Monetary Fund
ISPA	Pre-accession Structural Instrument
MEBO	Management-Employee Buyout
MOR	*Monitorul Oficial al României* (The Official Monitor of Romania)

NATO	North Atlantic Treaty Organisation
NPAA	National Programme for the Adoption of the Acquis
OECD	Organisation for Economic Co-operation and Development
PAS	*Programul Acţiunilor Salariaţilor* (Employees Shares Programme)
PCR	*Partidul Comunist Român* (Romanian Communist Party)
PD	*Partidul Democrat* (Democratic Party)
PDA	*Partidul Democrat-Agrar din România* (Democratic Agrarian Party of Romania).
PDSR	*Partidul Democraţiei Sociale din România* (Party of Social Democracy of Romania)
PER	*Partidul Ecologist Român* (Romanian Ecologist Party)
Phare	Polish-Hungarian Aid for Economic Restructuring
PNL	*Partidul Naţional Liberal* (National Liberal Party)
PNL-AT	*Partidul Naţional Liberal – Aripa Tînără* (National Liberal Party – Young Wing)
PNŢCD	*Partidul Naţional Ţărănesc, Crestin şi Democrat* (National Peasant Party – Christian Democratic)
PRM	*Partidul România Mare* (Greater Romania Party)
PSAL	Private Sector Adjustment Loan
PSD	*Partidul Social Democrat* (Social Democratic Party)
PSDR	*Partidul Social Democrat Român* (Romanian Social Democratic Party)
PSM	*Partidul Socialist al Muncii* (Socialist Labour Party)
PUN	*Partidul Unităţii Naţionale* (National Unity Party, changed name of PUNR)
PUNR	*Partidul Unităţii Naţionale din România* (Party of Romanian National Unity)
RFE/RL	Radio Free Europe/Radio Liberty
SAL	Structural Adjustment Loan
SAPARD	Structural Adjustment Programme for Agriculture and Rural Development
SIF	*Societate de Investiţii Financiare* (Financial Investment Fund)
SOE	state-owned enterprise
UDMR	*Uniunea Democratică a Ungurilor din România* (Democratic Union of Hungarians in Romania)
USD	*Uniunea Social Democrată* (Social Democratic Union)

Currencies

ECU	European Currency Unit
Lei	Romanian Dollar
$	United States of America Dollar

Introduction

The defeat of communism in Central and Eastern Europe (CEE) marks the end of an era in world politics. The collapse of the bi-polar security structure opened up new questions for the stability of the international state-system, while economically the failure of planning to withstand the increased competitive pressures in the world economy, and its subsequent disintegration, spurred a new wave of capitalist expansion in the form of globalisation (Herman 1996). For the countries of the former Soviet bloc, the crucial issue was twofold: their bid to establish an alternative economic and political system was judged a disaster and they were eager to leave it behind; at the same time, they needed to find acceptable terms for joining an international community whose dominant norms, liberal democracy and market economy, were the opposite of their own: the plan and the political monopoly of the communist party.

Initially, the answers to these dilemmas seemed self-evident: transition or, as it later came to be called, transformation. The prestige of the western norms seemed so unquestionable, the abandonment of communist ideals so complete, that the CEE nations hardly paused to consider their choices. Democracy and market economy were the only game in town and one that seemed easy to play. Confidence that these models would deliver where the old ones had failed and that the enduring, historical developmental gap between the east and west of the European continent could be bridged quickly, created great momentum for democratisation and marketisation throughout CEE. In Romania, as elsewhere in the region, the dominant neo-liberal ideology and its supporters, both inside and outside the country, played a crucial role in shaping the course of the economic and political reforms. How this happened and why is the topic of this book.

The argument

The dominant account of post-communist transformations explains the success in the reform of the economy as the direct result of the commitment of CEE governments to neo-liberal precepts for reform. In the case of Romania, this kind of explanation goes like this. The governments of 1990–96 were neo-communist, and this was the reason for the delays in democratisation (Crăiuţu 1996; Linz and Stepan 1996) and marketisation, as well as the lacklustre economic performance (EBRD 1999, 2000; IMF 2000, 2001).

Significant steps towards economic and political reform were taken only after the democratic coalition – *Convenţia Democratică din România* (Democratic Convention of Romania – CDR), which had stronger neo-liberal convictions, recognised as such by the international financial institutions (IFIs) – came to power, at the end of 1996. Even under this government, however, due to a degree of ideological half-heartedness and practical incompetence, and in spite of significant advances, Romania did not become a fully-functional market economy. It was the last among a group of ten CEE countries negotiating accession to the European Union to achieve this status, in October 2004 (EC 2004).

This book challenges this orthodoxy on two levels. Empirically, the reformist record of the 1990–96 governments appears to be more substantial than initially thought. Equally, the efforts of the Democratic Convention, while misplaced in certain areas, such as the severity of the 1997 stabilisation programme, which induced a steep three-year recession, represented significant breakthroughs in the marketisation of the economy. More substantively, the performance of both governments is evaluated from within a conceptual framework that takes account of structural and institutional constraints. Thus the pre-1996 governments faltered for at least two non-ideological reasons. Structurally, the economy was biased towards heavy industry and was, for this reason, less likely to respond well to market-based strategies for reform. Second, no institutions able to shape and channel change were in place; there had been no attempts prior to 1989 to liberalise the economy or to make the administration of the plan more flexible or sensitive to market mechanisms. At the same time, without denying CDR's commitment to reform, the advancement of reform during the latter part of the 1990s cannot be understood without taking into account the institution-building efforts of the previous governments.

The assessment of reform in Romania has been dominated by the preoccupation with evaluating success in terms of the speed with which compliance with the western models was achieved. This exercise was bound by rather simplistic assumptions about how system-wide change can occur. Most studies of post-communist transformations ask questions about institutional change, but institutional analysis on its own is not sufficient. This becomes apparent when an attempt is made, for instance, to articulate a basis for the comparison of democratisation and marketisation across different periods or types of countries: CEE, Latin America, Southern Europe, etc. In order to construct a comparison, a case has to be made that in spite of the differences between these cases, they are, at some level, instances of a same kind. To define the level of commonality, in spite of sharp and deep-running institutional differences, this analysis proposes that at this underlying, systemic level, CEE countries can and should be considered cases of state capitalism in transition towards a market-based form of capitalism. Thus, while this study shares with others an empirical emphasis in the gradual institutionalisation of politics as democratic politics, of the market as main mechanism for economic co-ordination, and the separation between politics and the economy itself, it also seeks to interpret and assess these institutional changes as the means through which a particular form of capitalism emerges. In this case, the argument will be made that some of the institutional configurations of property rights justify the question whether the form of capitalism that is emerging in Romania might not be described as 'democratic'.

These assumptions have immediate methodological consequences. The premise that what we are witnessing is a process of reconstitution of politics as democratic politics implies and requires that political events, actions and reactions be evaluated through their longer-term impact on the constitution of the rules of the political game. As political actors try to fashion and project particular identities and programmes, as they run the state or represent the political opposition, they negotiate explicitly the shape of the new political institutions and at the same time they create new boundaries around the political field itself. Within the field, the transition is from a relatively short period of fluidity, of 'void of power' when anyone can take part to a stage where this population of political actors and their rules of engagement become relatively stable towards the end of the decade. In the process this circle of insiders also develops a set of practices and norms about how it relates to the public as a whole and refashions the symbolic repertoire of politics. In the immediate post-revolutionary period the tropes of communist political language and understanding of conflict dominate. Obsession with state control, the role of the security services, generalised suspicion and prolific production of threats, aspirations for complete transparency of the political process and the belief that only direct democracy can guarantee the integrity of this process, permeate all political acts. There is sharp, irreconcilable conflict between radical ideas of democracy and moral renewal on the one hand and fear that there is no 'real' change and that some ubiquitous force, either the government run by neo-communists or the old *securitate,* is still in control. All governmental acts are experienced as painfully ambiguous and none, even those most obviously leading to change, such as the law on political parties, elections, a new constitution, can truly reassure that the break with the past is irreversible.

Over time, significant changes in the symbolic repertoire of politics take place. Personalised attacks against opponents still occur, but there are fewer attacks that engage the integrity of the political process itself. The conventions of the democratic political game – that popular supremacy is assured by parties, through representation and elections – become accepted. Thus, new implicit, unspoken rules of political behaviour protect the myths of democracy, and reassurance and threat are experienced on much more moderate terms. From managing the fears over the role of the state as a great invasive force, as was the case under communism and in the early 1990s, the political process shifts onto the more mundane concerns to do with economic struggles and the provision of a degree of social justice. Increasingly, political debates are about concrete policies and the major, emotionally-charged symbols of national interest, democracy, and Euro-Atlantic integration are mobilised in relation to well-defined, concrete policy measures.

Parallel to this process of reconstitution of politics as democratic politics, the rules of the economic game change as well. In Romania the abandonment of the plan as the main mechanism of economic co-ordination was part of the wave of changes that occurred very early in 1990 by way of revolutionary fiat. The first declaration to the population, on the evening of 22 December 1989, after the flight of the communist dictator, Nicolae Ceauşescu, made by the self-appointed, transitional, revolutionary government, included a promise that the plan would be abolished. The declaration did not spell out how this was to take its place, but allowed enterprises to take initiative in the running of their own affairs. The new, overwhelming and poorly-defined freedoms bestowed on the enterprises and their managers simply meant initially that enterprises continued to operate out of inertia within the established production chains, until a new legislative framework, including corporatisation, liberalisation of prices, trade, and exchange, and privatisation was put in place in the subsequent years. However poorly managed, this delegation of power by the new political authorities to economic agents was gradually incorporated in institutions that recognised and made durable the autonomy of the economic sphere and created a new mechanism for economic co-ordination: the market.

Within these institutional changes, it is also possible to trace the systemic shift, i.e. the slow emergence of capitalism: the capital relation, the commodification of labour, money and land and the consolidation of the regime of private property rights. To a certain extent, the socialist political economies, even though dominated by collective property, nominally owned by the whole people but in fact entrusted to one agent, the state, can be characterised as forms of state capitalism. The communist state had mobilised society to achieve a degree of primitive accumulation of capital. These assets were transferred to private owners after 1990 and began to function as capital proper; the ensuing patterns of ownership are more diffuse than tends to be the case in Western economies, but the capital relation functions nonetheless. Also, the commodification of labour existed under the communist regime as well since the whole of the labour force was salaried. At the same time, the extraction of surplus labour was a process to which the workers were presumed to have acquiesced. The historical necessity of socialist accumulation – accumulation by the state, on behalf of the people – was the basis for the development of the whole society. This ideological justification for commodification and exploitation, the principle of 'assumed necessity', was abandoned after the collapse of the communist regimes and replaced by the capitalist principle of the freedom of workers to sell their labour power.

Thus, the careful delineation of the systemic and institutional levels of analysis and the emphasis on the parallel processes of re-constitution of the political and economic spheres autonomously and in relation to each other constitute the premises and analytical frameworks that distinguish this analysis from others. In addition, I seek to take account of the fact that economic and political changes of this scale are also opportunities for observing cultural change. None of the events presented and analysed here can be isolated from the meaning and significance given to them by those directly involved and this account seeks to convey to the reader some of the flavour of how this period of tremendous change has been experienced, within the Romanian culture and how the frameworks of understanding and the particular shaping of affects legitimatised by the communist regime gradually changed.

The breakdown of the old order caught all actors unawares. The avowal of a radical shift to new values and economic and political freedom occurred without preparation, and the consequences, meaning and implications of this shift were poorly understood initially. In the early 1990s, there was a persistent feeling that all actors were struggling to grasp what exactly had happened; in the process of doing so they were deploying tentatively a whole set of inherited discursive expectations and learned emotional responses as though they were seeking to establish whether these would still hold. The alienation that had pervaded life under the communist regime, a certain sense of 'lack of reality', as often expressed and confessed to in works of art, meant that individuals were often conscious of being split between two contradictory levels of reality, both of which were experienced as surreal. One was the bureaucratically controlled, external reality, in relation to which they could experience themselves only as automatons. The other was a private life/space that had to remain secret and whose contours had to shift permanently, in response to arbitrary aggression from the official sphere; this perpetual self-surveillance and self-interruption of spontaneous acts led to a sense of powerlessness and ultimately lack of reality.

From this perspective, the end of the communist regime was a particular form of societal reaction of self-defence against this personal cost imposed by the socialist project. And indeed, the great promise and opportunity of this historical juncture was that this extreme form of estrangement and alienation might be toned down, that the dissonance between the private and external realities might be reduced. At the same time, it is understandable that the cultural bedrock of social life – the assumptions and norms and the associated emotional tones and dominant shaping of affects that constitute the glue of society – entered a period of revaluation and restructuring in which the significance of acts was fluid and uncertain. That the sweeping changes of the 1990s could be contained at all is perhaps testimony to the continuance of cultural frames that had been inculcated by the communist regime. There was no question about the need for a democratic state, social order, privatisation, the construction of market institutions, etc., even as the question of what legitimate forms these might take remained, for a time, open-ended.

Cultural change in this case means that gradually the sphere of what the political regime could define through formal, bureaucratised prescription was redrawn. Ever greater areas of social life were extracted from the realm of surveillance of some kind of ubiquitous, malevolent eye and relegated to the discreet, relatively autonomous private sphere.

Privatisation as a strategic research site

This book considers the course of economic and political reforms in Romania as a whole, and it is based on a review of evidence regarding all the major developments of the 1990s in these areas. However, not all of these reforms can be presented in equal detail within the limited space available. Seeking to strike a balance between countrywide generalisations and the need to illustrate more closely at least some of the major phenomena involved in post-communist transformations, I have focused the analysis on privatisation, which becomes the main testing ground for the more general explanations offered here.

Privatisation is a suitable research site for this broader investigation of the political economy of post-communist transformations in Romania because it cuts across all the major dimensions of domestic systemic change: the reconstitution of politics as democratic politics, the construction of the market as the principal mechanism of economic co-ordination, the separation between economy and politics, and changes in public perceptions about property rights and legitimate action in the public sphere. Thus, all the major political actors recognised privatisation as fundamental to their interests and fought over its content, methods and pace. Domestic neo-liberal advocates of privatisation, keen to show their commitment to the set of norms of macro-economic management designated as the 'Washington consensus' (Williamson 1994; Yeaple and Moskowitz 1995), insisted on the link between privatisation, marketisation and growth. In theory, immediate privatisation of state-owned enterprises could kick-start the creation of a market economy by promoting competition, improving corporate governance and stimulating growth. Privatisation could attract foreign investors, know-how and technology, and it could solve some of the financial problems of the cash-strapped CEE governments (Blanchard et al. 1991; Blanchard et al. 1993; Sachs 1993). For social-democrats, privatisation was a means for the co-opting of various groups into the political and economic system, through redistribution. Concerned about political stability, they considered acceptable both state intervention and market-based measures as the means for reform (Ionete 1993; Pilat 1993b, 1995; Dăianu 1996b). The development of privatisation policies over time illustrates the main patterns of interaction and contest between these political actors; it is an opportunity for the development of their identities and practical alliances. Privatisation is also at the core of a vast process of economic redistribution and it involves directly all citizenry. International partners have similarly looked at progress in privatisation as a significant indicator of reform progress and political credibility.

Second, choices about privatisation touch upon crucial questions about the significance of institutional variations in property rights within capitalism. The redistribution of the results of the primitive accumulation engineered by the socialist states has far-reaching consequences for the patterns of emerging property relations. These new patterns affect corporate governance and the extent of commodification of labour. It is one of the key contentions of this book that in CEE capitalism is potentially democratic at least in two senses. First, the capitalist economy is supported, subsidised and to an extent limited and modified by a vast infrastructure of non-market economic relations: subsistence agriculture, informal economy based on self-employment and widespread land and housing ownership. Second, following vast mass privatisation programmes, virtually every household in the country owns equity and shares. Even though the dividends earned in this way may not represent a high percentage of household income, and, as minority shareholders individuals can exert little direct control over management, owning shares has become a significant form of participation in the capitalist economy. It has, however, an important socialising role as it makes practical and immediately relevant the logic of the market, and creates familiarity with the institutional embodiments of this new economy.

The term 'privatisation' can apply to related, but slightly different, activities. Bennett (1997) has identified three forms of privatisation. *Divestment* is the transfer of property rights from the state to the private sector. *Delegation* refers to the transfer of certain functions and activities to the private sector, while the actual property rights remain with the state. When the private sector replaces the public sector in certain economic activities, *displacement* has taken place (Bennett 1997, 4). The number of sales and their total proceeds as a percentage of GDP gives an indication of the scope of divestment. Displacement and divestment are measured by the percentage of the private sector in the GDP. This is a relative measure since not all activities created by privatisation are recorded in the national statistics. For this reason, it is very difficult to quantify displacement other than by comparing the values of these indicators at different points in time (Bennett 1997, 5–6).

In Romania, privatisation has mainly taken the form of divestment. The state-owned assets sold off or given away by the end of 2000 comprised the whole housing stock, 80 per cent of agricultural land, over 8,500 state-owned enterprises (SOEs), four banks, and others. The sale of state housing and the restitution of agricultural land proved relatively straightforward politically. Tenants could buy the state-owned apartments in which they had lived at discount prices and spread the payments over five to fifteen years. By 1994, almost all of the estimated 2.3 million flats were sold (Stan 1995a, 430). Similarly, in agriculture the land reform of 1991 returned to the former owners or their successors the plots conscripted into co-operatives during the communist campaign of 1948–62. Over eight million hectares were repossessed by 1994, although the actual issuance of property certificates lagged behind (Stan 1995a, 430). Although the process of implementation of this reform was arduous, by the end of the 1990s all claims were resolved, and the number of court cases on this issue dropped (Stan 1995b; Verdery 1999).

This analysis focuses on the divesting policies for the privatisation of SOEs. The land reform and the sale of state housing are an important part of the overall process of privatisation and their role in the creation of a specific 'socialist' infrastructure to the capitalist economy will be evaluated as well, but do not require extensive presentation, as they were less contested politically. In the early 1990s there was universal recognition of the injustice done by communists to peasants and there was little political opposition to these measures. In the case of state housing, the beneficiaries of privatisation included the majority of the population and thus the measures had a wide political base.

By contrast, the privatisation of the industrial SOEs was much more complicated. Unlike with the land, potential claims over industrial property were less clear cut. The size of the properties to be privatised was much greater and, in contrast to state apartments, there were no obvious buyers. Additionally, the industrial base of the country was the one great achievement of communism and had been produced 'by the people and for the people'. How these collective claims could be dis-aggregated so as to create a transparent and fair process for the privatisation of industrial SOEs proved a question with vast political, economic and social consequences.

Thus, one of the points of contention and political struggle throughout the 1990s was the scope of the privatisation programme: which SOEs to sell. As SOEs embodied the work of the whole population over several decades and a big chunk of the accumulated national wealth, it was important to ensure that privatisation would enhance rather than undermine this wealth. Initially, only about 50 per cent of SOEs were to be privatised. Gradually, this mandate was extended to sectors that were more sensitive politically, such as public utilities, banks and telecommunications.

Chapter outline

In this analysis, the content and pace of economic reforms in Romania are linked to four factors. These are (i) the cultural gap between the expectations of the public and the requirements of a market economy; (ii) the fragile political consensus around reform; (iii) the structural power of industrial interests and their ability to co-opt factions of the political elite; and (iv) the slowness of institution-building processes. The first chapter introduces in historical detail the communist experience across these dimensions up to the end of that regime in December 1989.

The economic and political processes of transformation analysed here are embedded in processes of cultural change that have their own logic, as argued in Chapter 2. The culture of resistance that emerged under the corrupt and oppressive communist regime contained norms of social solidarity, and notions about acceptable behaviour and success (Verdery 1996; Kligman 1998). After the collapse of the regime, in a social context where most reference points, organisations, institutions, and social roles disappeared or changed dramatically, these norms continued to exert an influence. For instance, reactions to the reform process were shaped to an extent by expectations of political and economic achievement derived from the heroic model of communism and by mistrust of the ruling elite and the state.

The strong polarisation of politics after 1990 is discussed in Chapter 3. The main political party was *Frontul Salvării Naţionale* (The National Salvation Front – FSN),[1] which took power in December 1989 and then won the elections of May 1990 and September 1992. Some of its leaders, such as President Ion Iliescu, had held important positions of authority under the former regime. The FSN was spurned as 'neo-communist', anti-democratic and conservative. Its legitimacy was challenged because it was tied to the past and seemed unable and unwilling to carry out radical reforms (Călinescu and Tismăneanu 1992; Tănase 1993, 1996; Andreescu 1998).

The most vocal opposition parties were the 'historical parties', that is parties that had been active on the Romanian political scene before 1938, and briefly between 1944 and 1947, before they were outlawed by the communists. These were *Partidul Naţional Ţărănesc, Creştin şi Democrat* (National Peasant Party – Christian Democratic – PNŢCD), *Partidul Naţional Liberal* (National Liberal Party – PNL), and *Partidul Social Democrat Român* (Romanian Social Democratic Party – PDSR). From 1991 they co-operated under the umbrella of the *Convenţia Democrată din România* (Democratic Convention of Romania – CDR). They had the advantage of inheriting a distinct political profile, derived from their non-communist roots. Thus they could claim to know the meaning of democracy and presented themselves as the embodiment of democratic principles and values. An important number of their leaders – such as Corneliu Coposu, Radu Câmpeanu, and Sergiu Cunescu – had been political prisoners under the communist regime and strongly rejected anything 'communist' (Almond 1990; Tismăneanu and Pavel 1994).

This polarisation of politics made compromise and a process of consensus building very difficult in post-1989 Romania. The political class was thus weakened in its confrontation with conservative industrial interests. Under stringent attack from the opposition, and in recognition of the social-democratic inclination of the electorate, the FSN looked for allies elsewhere. Its conservative wing together with the dominant industrial interest groups took Romania through the first stages of reform. After 1996, the Democratic Convention pursued reform more aggressively, but faltered in the face of opposition from the same interests, and ultimately lacked the confidence to capitalise politically on the advances they did push through (Aligică 2001).

Chapter 4 shows how structural conditions in the economy strengthened the hand of industrial interests. There was a strong bias towards heavy industry, with production concentrated in a relatively small number of huge enterprises. Also, the idea that the market would by itself restructure the relationships between enterprises and between sectors had fewer supporters in Romania compared to other CEE countries (Dăianu 1996b, 1999). Rather, it was thought that only gradual exposure to the conditions of competition, through liberalisation of prices and the exchange rate, would allow enterprises in metallurgy, petrochemicals, and machine building to restructure (Ionete 1993). The expectation that enterprises would use this slack to restructure of their own accord looked realistic in 1993 and 1994, when external demand stimulated growth. During 1995–96, however, it became apparent that, instead of restructuring, the heavy industries were trying to keep the momentum of increased production by relying on subsidised domestic demand (National Bank of Romania (BNR) 1997a, 1997b). The public utilities, whose prices remained controlled until 1997, the banks and agriculture were the main avenues used by the state to subsidise the heavy industries. Other economic policies, such as the control of inflation, exchange and interest rates and taxation, also protected the interests of the rust-belt sectors (OECD 1998). In privatisation, this policy orientation led to the selective targeting of the enterprises to be sold. The small and medium-sized enterprises were privatised first, while the public utilities and the banks were not included in the privatisation programme initially since they were considered of 'national interest' and thus too important to be left to the vagaries of private ownership and the market (OECD 1993).

After 1996, increased institutional capacity, the uneven but significant restructuring that had taken place in industry, and increased commitment to reform on the part of the Democratic Convention converged to make possible a number of significant changes. Liberalisation policies freed the banks, the public utilities and agriculture from their role in channelling subsidies to the heavy industries and stimulated their restructuring. At the same time, many big state-owned enterprises in the heavy industries continued to exert strong pressure on the government through strikes and other forms of public protest (OECD 1998).

The slow pace and the unevenness of reforms in Romania are also explained by the weakness of the Romanian state, a factor discussed in Chapter 5. Reform of the public administration did not become an explicit objective until the last few years of the 1990s (Nunberg 1999). Examples of misplaced effort, such as the revision of legislation in order to remedy inadequacies of implementation and the politicisation of the bureaucracy, were common during this period (World Bank 1998b). This weak institutional basis in the public sector was mirrored by the weakness of market institutions in Romania. Stock and commodities exchanges were slow to develop. After they were set up in the mid-1990s it took several years before they began to play a significant role in economic transactions (National Commission for Securities (CNVM) 2001). Banks had to build institutional capacity under conditions of exponentially increasing demand and an unstable policy environment (BNR 2000).

Finally, these cultural, economic, political and institutional dimensions are explored in the context of the relationship between successive Romanian governments and the IFIs and the EU, between 1989 and 2001 in Chapter 6. In fact, it is only through a careful consideration of events and decisions across all of these dimensions that the complexity of these relationships can be fully brought out and the common stereotypes of interpretation, that attribute to these organisations the role of the only consistent promoters of neo-liberal reform, can be questioned and corrected.

In sum, this book argues that the neo-liberal ideological reading of political and economic reforms in Romania shared, for reasons that will be explored later, by both domestic and international actors, obscures the role of the different governments, pressure groups and interests in shaping the reform process. The course of the reforms and their relative success are better explained as the result of the combination of political, economic, institutional and cultural factors outlined above.

The evidence for the questions discussed here comes from a variety of both primary and secondary sources. Chapter 2, on culture, is based on interviews with opinion makers and academics in Bucharest and an extensive survey of the Romanian press. The press participates in the biases of the culture of which it is a part, which makes it a suitable source of this enquiry into post-communist culture. After the fall of communism, in particular, the mass media in CEE countries were slow to evolve a professional role based on specific rules and standards, and a position of impartial scepticism towards the authorities. Instead, they claimed that in the absence of solid political institutions they had to take a leading role in setting democratic standards. This and the lack of autonomous sources of information encouraged the politicisation of the press, which became predominantly a site for political struggles. Newspapers were explicitly 'for' or 'against' the government or the opposition (Gross 1998).

Among the sources sampled for this analysis were the major broad sheets *Adevărul* (The Truth), *Romania Liberă* (Free Romania), *Bursa* (The Bourse), *Curentul* (Current News), *Cotidianul* (The Daily), *Ziarul Financiar* (The Financial Newspaper). Specialist periodicals dedicated to political and economic matters, *Capital* (Capital), *Adevărul Economic* (The Economic Truth), *Economistul* (The Economist), *Sfera Politicii* (The Political Sphere), and *Polis*, were also consulted. This survey has focused on the second half of the period under study, from 1997 to 2001, when the post-communist trends can be supposed to have stabilised to a certain extent. The patterns in question are confirmed through other sources, such as the extensive parliamentary debates on the privatisation laws covered in chapter 3 and indirect accounts in the foreign press, especially the *Financial Times, Radio Free Europe/Radio Liberty* (RFE/RL) and the *East European Constitutional Review* (EECR).

In Chapter 3, the information on events, the activities and positions of the main political parties comes from secondary scholarly literature, the RFE/RL *Transition Report,* entries on Romania from the EECR, other local and international media. In addition, this research is the first to use records of the parliamentary debates around the privatisation laws of 1991 and 1995 to identify the arguments and values that supported the decisions on the design of the process.

Chapter 4 draws on aggregate statistical information on macro-economic developments that comes from official sources, such as *Comisia Naţională a Valorilor Mobiliare* (National Commission for Securities – CNVM), *Banca Naţională a României* (National Bank of Romania – BNR) and the IFIs. In addition, the opinions of policy-makers were traced through some of their publications, such as the specialist review *Oeconomica* whose contributors occupied positions in the cabinet, central administration, and parliament. In regard to privatisation in particular, public notices in the *Monitorul Oficial al României* (Official Monitor of Romania – MOR) allowed the author to trace the reaction of the different governments to practical problems encountered in privatisation. The abundance of primary and secondary legislation published in the MOR reflected a prominent feature of governance in Romania, where problems tended to be tackled through legislation or executive orders at the highest level.

The analysis in Chapter 5 builds on operational documents from the World Bank, *Agenţia Naţională de Privatizare* (National Agency for Privatisation – ANP) and *Fondul Proprietăţii de Stat* (State Ownership Fund – FPS) that have restricted circulation in the public domain. The access to these sources was facilitated by interviews with members of the governmental bureaucracies in Bucharest.

As well as providing a rich empirical account of institutional and cultural changes in politics and the economy, this book is an attempt to trace the development of capitalism in Romania. Implicitly, this is an illustration of how capitalism is articulated on the bedrock of cultural understandings and social relations inherited from socialism.

Notes

1   Brief presentations of the political personalities and parties mentioned in the book are
     given in the Glossary and biographies.

1

Communist legacies

The December 1989 regime breakdown was a moment of rupture and radical discontinuity in Romania's economy and politics: the rule of the party-state was removed and the plan was abandoned. The agenda for change that emerged amidst popular unrest focused around the construction of a democratic political system and a market economy. To appreciate just what this transformation agenda entailed, it is useful to review the main features of the economy, the institutional underpinnings of the role of the state in the economy and the cultural notions about action in public sphere as they were crystallised towards the end of the communist regime. Similar to other Central and Eastern European countries, in Romania the tasks of the post-communist transformations were overwhelming in relation to the strength and credibility of political actors, and the final section of this chapter explains how political leadership and a new political system emerged in the wake of the revolution.

Structural imbalances in the Romanian economy at the end of 1989

Romania was a late developer politically and economically. The modern Romanian state was created in 1859 through the election of one prince for both Moldova and Vallachia, hitherto autonomous principalities under Ottoman protection. In 1881, Romania won its independence from the protectorate of the 'Great European powers' and became a kingdom under a German prince, Carol I of Hohenzollern. State building went hand in had with the gradual modernisation of the economy. The agrarian reform of 1864 eliminated completely the serfdom of the peasantry (Durandin 1998, 121) and state-assisted industrialisation, through investments in infrastructure, direct purchases for the military and intermittent protectionism (Hitchins

1994, 183–195, 359–376), began at the end of the nineteenth century.[1] National markets for industrial products and capital began to emerge, but the development of agriculture was hampered by the ownership structure of the land: with the exception of a few major landowners, most households owned barely enough land to support themselves and the mechanisation and chemicalisation of agricultural production were modest.

This conservatism in agriculture was a form of social protection of the peasantry, whose potential for political turmoil was feared by the political class of the time (Ioniţă 1996, 157). It reflected a type of insertion in the capitalist world-economy that was not uncommon for that part of the world, which specialised in extensive agricultural production, exporting mostly cereals and other agricultural products and importing industrial goods (Wallerstein 1979). The peasantry dominated the social structure numerically while economic power was concentrated in the hands of a handful of big landowners and industrialists; the narrow middle class was dependent on state employment and opportunities for smaller-scale economic enterprise were monopolised by foreigners. The long-term consequence of this unbalance was a deepening of the 'abyss between urban and rural Romania' (Dobrogeanu-Gherea 1910, 5). This was seen by some as a failure of the liberal political class to do more than to import from the West the institutions of a modern state and economy without ensuring, however, that they were integrated in such a way as to stimulate the development of the country. Instead, these institutions remained superimposed 'forms without content' (Weber 1965, 514; Roberts 1951, 337).

After the first world war, Romania's territory and population doubled in size; the union of Transylvania, hitherto part of the Austro-Hungarian empire, and Bassarabia, part of the Russian empire, also compounded the diversity and complexity of administrative, economic, political and cultural systems in the new state (Livezeanu 1998). Thus, tenuous political organisation and unfavourable international economic conditions did little to shift the economic or social structures. In spite of significant successes in the development of a national industrial base, the interwar economy remained dominated by agriculture. At the end of the Second World War 74.3 per cent of the working population were still employed in agriculture (Earle and Săpătoru 1994, 89).

This was to change significantly through the policies introduced by the communist regime. The year-plans for 1949 and 1950 established the developmental priority of the state: the building up of a diversified industrial structure, based on technologically advanced heavy industries. Investment in industry amounted to 48.3 per cent of total investment in 1950 (of which consumer goods received 41.9 per cent) and 57.5 per cent in 1951–55 (of which 50.2 per cent went to consumer goods) (Montias 1967, 25).

To develop the economy, the communist regime sustained remarkable levels of investment growth throughout the 1960s and 1970s. In the first half of the 1970s, for instance, the average annual increase in investment was 11 per cent, reaching 15 per cent growth in 1975. Industry took 57.2 per cent of net investment, with most of the funds going into the energy-intensive heavy industries – steel, chemicals, and refining (Linden 1986, 352, 354). As a consequence, the gross industrial output increased annually on average by 10.6 per cent in 1950–55, by 9.5 per cent in 1955–58, 15.4 per cent in 1958–60, and 12.2 per cent in 1960–63, some of the highest rates of growth in the region (Montias 1967, 56, 68; Shafir 1985, 107).

This was an extensive pattern of development as planners focused on increasing steadily the range of new and technologically advanced industrial products. It was also balanced: until 1963, consumer goods and heavy industries contributed in equal measure to the total industrial product (Montias 1967, 15). This was made possible by the fact that although capital investment was channelled towards the heavy industries, a comparable pace of production growth was achieved in the consumer goods industries through the large-scale absorption of cheap and relatively low-skilled manpower and this compensated for the relative scarcity of capital. The structure of international trade also reflected this equilibrium between industrial sectors. Compared to 1948, in 1965 the share of raw materials, fuels, and semifabricates in imports increased, while their share in exports decreased. Advanced industrial products represented about 50 per cent of all exports in 1965, a significant increase from 1948 (Montias 1967, 156–160). For the longer term, however, this meant that Romanian industry was dependent on imported raw materials; the balance of payments equilibrium depended on the capacity of the industry to compete in the world markets and increase exports (Montias 1967, 82–83).

Thus, during the first three decades of communist rule, the development of the Romanian economy was largely self-sufficient. The agricultural labour force was mobilised to take employment in industry, and the investment in heavy industries was undertaken at the expense of restricted domestic consumption. The balance of payments was in relative equilibrium and there was little need for foreign borrowing (Linden 1986, 352–353).

Towards the end of the 1970s, this self-sufficiency was lost as the regime chose to maintain its policy priorities even as the trade-offs that had sustained the development of the heavy industries were coming under increasing pressure. Internally, the reserves of labour and raw materials, especially petroleum, were becoming exhausted. Externally, the conditions for oil imports and the demand for Romanian exports deteriorated: the quadrupling of oil prices in 1973 and 1974 increased production costs while the recession of Western economies shrunk markets (Cojanu 1994). As a consequence, Romania began to develop trade deficits in both hard currency and roubles and had to borrow from abroad to balance its balance of payments. Total debt grew rapidly, and when in 1982 the servicing demand rose to $2.6 billion, this proved more than the country could manage. The government asked for a rescheduling of payments and, in a fateful political overreaction, the communist leader Nicolae Ceauşescu made a commitment to pay the total foreign debt of about $10 billion before it was due. This target was achieved in 1989 (Ben-Ner and Montias 1991, 164–165).

Other countries of the former Soviet bloc began to experiment with more liberal forms of control over the economy in response to these external shocks, such as decentralisation of management and increased economic incentives for the labour force, but in Romania the opposite was the case. As a consequence, in Romania, the controls over the economy were tightened to insure a 'dramatic compression of imports' and a 'brutal compression of living standards' (OECD 1993, 11–13). This led to an increase in rationing of basic foodstuffs, queuing, and power cuts to households. At the same time, the scarce resources available for investment in Romania in the 1980s were increasingly used in grandiose building projects whose economic rationale was dubious: a new civic centre in the capital, a canal to link Bucharest to the Danube, and the 'restructuring' of villages. The return to invested capital decreased from 1.51 lei of value added for each leu invested between 1976 and 1980, to only 0.69 lei of value added in 1981–86 and 0.21 lei in 1986–90 (Dijmărescu 1993a, 59).

Reduced technological imports in the 1980s thus led to the deterioration of the nation's industrial base. In addition, the Romanian industry had a number of other features that were to complicate the reform process in the 1990s. It was dominated by large enterprises, with 49 per cent of production taking place in firms of 3,000 employees or more (OECD 1993, 11). Many of these, especially in the heavy industries, were the sole producers for at least some of the products in their portfolio and sometimes had only one or two domestic customers. In other words, for many products, the industry was monopolistic and monopsonistic. The trade links between firms were organised along closed, vertically integrated chains of production (Ben-Ner and Montias 1994; Pilat 1996).

Romanian industry was also energy intensive. In 1989, for every $1 million of GNP about $317,250, i.e. more than a third, represented energy costs. Metallurgy produced only 9.8 per cent of industrial output and 5.4 per cent of GDP, but consumed 23.4 per cent of the total energy used in the economy. Similarly, the chemical and petrochemical industries consumed 41.5 per cent of all energy inputs but generated only 21.3 per cent of industrial output (Dijmărescu 1993a, 59). The gross primary energy intensity of the Romanian economy was in 1990 approximately 1.9 tons of oil equivalent for $1,000 of GDP. This was about three times the average in OECD Europe and one of the highest in Central and Eastern Europe (World Bank 1994a, 1).

This subsidisation of the heavy industries by the other economic sectors became even more difficult to sustain following the trade shocks in the early 1990s: the disappearance of the Council for Mutual Economic Assistance (CMEA), the Gulf War and the war in Yugoslavia. CMEA trade had provided both relatively cheap energy imports and export markets for the heavy industries. It was the destination of 45.3 per cent of industrial exports in 1989. The discontinuation of the payment systems within the CMEA raised the costs of imports of gas and oil; for instance, for twelve months in 1990/1991 the increase was by 61.8 per cent for oil and 32.5 per cent for gas (Dijmărescu 1993a, 60). The Gulf War and the embargo on Iraq deprived Romania of oil shipments already paid for to the value of $1.5 billion.

Thus, in spite of early successes and the considerable contribution to the modernisation of the country, by the end of the 1980s, the communist regime of Romania was deemed to haven fallen short of its own ambitions and expectations and could not meet effectively the rigours of international competition. Domestically and in international opinion, the feeling was one of 'unmitigated disaster on all fronts' (Ronnas 1991, 61). The economy was dominated by a run-down industrial sector, and within this sector the large energy-intensive enterprises played a major role. The sheer size of this sector meant that the amount of restructuring required was very high and the onus on the rest of the economy to absorb the costs of such restructuring considerable (Dăianu 1996b, 1999). But it was not only industry that suffered from lack of investment in the 1980s. This was a period of regression in many areas of social life. The compression of living standards was severe with consumer goods shortages, queuing for basic foodstuffs, lack of heating in winter, and power cuts becoming an everyday reality for all but the most privileged of Romanians. How this austerity was experienced will be discussed in the third section of this chapter, after a short detour to outline the institutional and organisational forms that constituted the mechanism of co-ordination in the economy, the plan, which also changed after 1990.

Corporate governance under the plan

As is well known, within the socialist political economies of CEE the plan was the mechanism for centralised, bureaucratic co-ordination of the economy by the political centre (Kornai 1992, 110–130). Ideally, the ambition of the planners was to create by way of bureaucratic control and know-how a perfectly efficient market which would become the incarnation of the law of demand and thus bypass all the waste and failures that beset markets based on free actions by firms and individuals and the signalling function of prices. Bureaucratic ambition aside, through the plan the ideological aspirations of the regime about the finality of economic activity – the construction of a particular type of economy – shaped the activity of enterprises, their links, and managerial priorities. This allowed the regime to meet its developmental targets quickly and efficiently and indeed economic growth until the early 1970s, as shown earlier, was impressive. As the internal resources for development became exhausted and the external equilibrium with the world economy became harder to sustain, however, the costs and tensions of the plan itself became more and more apparent. Anomalies, such as shortages, as well as dysfunctional adaptive responses, such as hoarding of resources, became all pervasive and the system itself entered into crisis.

To understand the post-1990 transformation process that is our focus here, it is important to appreciate in more detail the nature of the plan and the relation between the plan and market, between the inherited and the emergent orders. Thus, some of the institutions that underpin market co-ordination in a modern economy did not exist under the communist regimes at all: the functions of stock markets, competition, bankruptcy, exit and entry of economic agents into the economy were realised by the plan thorough administrative decision. After 1990 these institutions would have to be created from scratch. But other major economic institutions that are part of the market mechanism existed under the communist regime as well: prices, money, trade, banks, and firms. Embedded in the socialist economy, however, the functioning of these institutions was very different (Iancu 1994, 33). Administered prices reflected bureaucratic judgements not only about the relative costs of certain products, but also their social importance: luxury goods were overpriced while basic foodstuffs were sold at below production price. Trade between enterprises took the form of planning allocations, and in spite of the introduction of fiscal planning the role of money as expression of value was very weak: the economy was only semi-monetised (Kornai 1992, 130–159). Even though prices had a residual signalling function and differences in prices led to the emergence of very limited trade and markets outside the command economy (Olson 1992), this informal economy was parasitic on the state sector.

Thus, at one level, the plan can be seen as the attempt to reconcile and make perfectly harmonious on paper a vast array of representations about and measurements of economic activity. The freeing up of prices, trade, money and managerial decisions in early 1990 thus entailed initially a sudden and radical shift in the meaning and significance of what had been the categories of information created by the plan, in the form of prices, total production value, trade etc. They became concrete figures whose significance was to be derived from a new set of market-based relationships yet to be established and the inherited system of interconnected prices was a very weak guide for decision making at all levels (Şerbănescu 1994, 1–13).

In any modern economy, the accounting system incorporates and implements the core assumptions about the relationship between state and firms. It is the basis for taxation policies, and for the data used in the generation of macro-economic indicators that in turn serve as the basis for policy-making at governmental level. In command economies, to make the plan workable at all, simpler measures of economic activity were used, such as quantitative targets for production, and the rules for profit formation and depreciation assumed no inflation. After 1990, a new accounting system was necessary, introducing categories of information that reflected a more distant relationship between enterprises and government and different mechanisms of macro-economic management (Coşea and Vlăsceanu 1993; Antohi 1995).

Thus, when the plan was abandoned in 1990, both the government and the economic agents were information-poor. For the government, the data generated by the planning bureaucracy was almost useless and this was a handicap for the elaboration of industrial policy. For enterprises, the economic signals were confused (Ionete 1993). The sudden elimination of the plan, and the pressure for survival, created uncertainty. For the government, the immediate priority was to keep the economy working and so received priorities, based around the need to protect energy supplies, persisted.[2] Both government and enterprises fell back upon the information embedded in established networks of exchange between enterprises (Pasti 1995, 106–116).

The structuring effects, the horizontal and vertical linkages between enterprises created by the plan persisted and were to have an enduring impact on managerial strategies. The chains of production had historical depth and the blueprint of past relationships between enterprises was already encoded in their product portfolios, the size and structure of the demand for their products, the number of their labour force and the associated labour legislation. Thus, even though freed from bureaucratic control, the decisions of the firm managers could not depart very much from earlier patterns. Some Western neo-liberal advisers hoped that markets would emerge quickly and spontaneously, as international trade was liberalised, citizens became consumers, new enterprises emerged and the state-owned enterprises actively sought new customers, restructured their production in the face of competition and pursued profit (Sachs 1993). In practice, the motivation and ability to change varied widely among enterprises in the same country and in different countries. In Romania, the fact that most enterprises had some kind of monopoly at least in some product markets sheltered them from competition on the one hand and gave them ammunition to resist active efforts by the state to close or restructure them by pleading national interest on the other.

Thus fundamental differences existed in institutions, between the plan and the market, direct control over the economy, and more distant macro-economic management. But the complexity of the post-1990 transformation cannot be understood without taking into account the social networks fostered by the plan and the politicisation of economic information within them. Knowledge of the production capabilities, output, labour force, and raw material requirements was sensitive for enterprises. There was considerable pressure to report great successes in the completion of the plan, because this was rewarded politically: the regime had an interest in the success of its projects and tended to reward success with greater allocations in subsequent years. At the same time, enterprises had to avoid becoming hostages to fortune, as, in spite of plan allocations, shortages were in fact endemic and underreporting of supplies or production was a necessary protective cushion: enterprises had an incentive to hoard their resources. Thus the information produced by the planning system for the centre was not reliable even within its own conventions. At the level of the enterprise, there was little information on the system as a whole and little basis for independent planning or action (Botez 1997, 56–67).

The plan worked within a unified bureaucratic structure, where enterprise managers liaised with civil servants in the line ministries who centralised information across the various sectors. These networks themselves were affected by the change and in turn channelled the implementation of policy. The plan required the subordination of enterprise management to the centre. The party-state set targets, controlled, and punished; the planning decisions had the force of command. Although the subaltern levels of the bureaucracy had to fulfil these obligations, and were assessed on that basis, ultimate responsibility rested with the centre. It was its duty to provide supplies, outlets for production, and money transfers to keep the SOEs working and solvent. To reconcile the reality of production on the ground with the prescriptions of the plan each superior bureaucratic level could take advantage of instruments that were also part of the plan and could be interpreted to their advantage: soft subsidies, prices, credit, and taxation (Voslenski 1984, 137–141; Zinoviev 1985, 256–280).

Thus, bargaining between the different levels of the bureaucracy played a crucial role in the practical implementation of policy. This mixture of formal rigour and practical arbitrariness put a premium on the development of personalised networks between bureaucrats, on connections, and the practical skills of making resources 'fungible'. After 1990, as SOEs had to change their focus from meeting production targets to actually selling their products, the required managerial skills also changed. Judicious emphasis on product quality, the ability to relate to a mass of unknown potential customers, and willingness to cut costs to increase productivity became more important, and constituted a substantial shift of priorities.[3]

At the same time, there also intervened a separation in this unified bureaucratic structure between managers and civil servants. The bureaucrats at the firm level, the managers, became responsible for the performance of their firms, and the firms were encouraged to act to pursue their own interests, to look for suppliers and markets, and increase performance. Managers' reaction to these requirements was variable. One possibility was to reorient their behaviour according to the new ethos, and engage constructively with the new risks and challenges. On the other hand, they could judge their chances rather more conservatively and attempt to delay restructuring and perpetuate access to soft financing (Iancu 1994, 27). Individual circumstances no doubt influenced such decisions. Crucially, however, in some sectors, especially the heavy industries, the structural conditions – high concentration of assets in one factory, dependence on one or two suppliers and end-users –

exacerbated the tasks of restructuring and provided managers with a strong negotiating position for setting the pace of the change (Coşea 1993).

The civil servants, i.e. the bureaucrats in the line ministries, lost after 1990 their traditional role as minders for the SOEs. Just as it was not obvious to the managers of the enterprises how they were to redefine their roles in the new economic and political conditions, the employees of the ministries were also uncertain about their position. It is safe to assume that their willingness to embrace new policies depended on the prospects such policies offered them for finding a new role for themselves. As will be shown in subsequent chapters, in fact there is no 'efficient action' in the direction of reform until/unless significant groups within this army of bureaucrats realise that they can use the opportunities opened by the creation of market institutions to maintain or enhance their life chances; in fact, it can be said that the pace of institutional construction is given by the ability of incumbents – members of the state administration – to reorient themselves in the new environment and to convert their inherited advantages, in terms of specialised knowledge, access to the policy-making process and social networks, into legitimate, relatively advantageous and secure economic positions in the new order.

Out of this unified economic-political bureaucracy will emerge three distinct institutional areas: the politics of the state proper, based on the autonomy of the political sphere; the state bureaucracy, which will be in charge of defining and exercising the role of the state in the economy; and the economic management per se, which will be increasingly bound by the rules of the market. At this level, the post-communist transformations entail a triple differentiation through the distinct institutionalisation of politics, the economy and the role of the state in the economy.

This conceptualisation contradicts the expectation of the neo-liberal technopols who in early blueprints for reform envisaged a clean and decisive break with the old and assumed that bureaucrats at the firm and central levels were ready to change their roles very quickly. Perhaps such change would have been eased by a complete change in the circumstances for economic activity, in the form of a 'big bang' reform strategy. Consistent signals about the new rules of the game might have provided clearer motivation for change. But even in Poland where this was attempted, the restructuring of the state and the construction of market institutions remained a protracted process that depended on the effectiveness with which the political sphere itself became autonomous and provided direction for economic reform. As Orenstein (2001) shows, both in Poland and the Czech Republic, reform was successful because changes in government brought about by elections led not to radical policy discontinuity but to significant policy corrections between successive governments.

This conclusion is also valid for Romania. Until 1996, gradual reform under a democratic and relatively weak government led to the co-existence, for a time, of the old and the new institutions. For instance, the co-existence between liberalised and controlled prices, between a liberalised exchange rate and controlled access to foreign currency, reinforced the utility of pre-existing connections, economic and social networks. Additionally, the design of the reform programme in Romania, and privatisation in particular, was unclear about the distribution of property rights, leading to a perpetuation of the stand-off between the government and some of the SOEs. However, even during this period it is possible to discern evidence that the corrective pattern identified by Orenstein, a pattern that would become stronger after 1996, was already at work. When the accumulated inflationary effects of the liberalisation of prices, introduced in November 1990, led to popular protests and a change of government in late 1991, the broader lessons were not lost on the political leadership. It became apparent that the government had to build effective macro-economic mechanisms to control inflation, and to strengthen the institutions that had a role to play in this area, such as the national central bank.

This section traced some of the most important lagging effects of the plan after the plan itself was abandoned. The structures of the socialist economy remained effective in the orientation of enterprises, of their managers and the central administration, especially the line ministries. Without political and ideological backing these structures ceased to exert the overriding influence that had been characteristic of the planned economy. Nonetheless, given the initial conditions in the early 1990s, increased uncertainty, the dramatic decrease in levels of production and the external trade shocks, it is understandable that all economic actors fell back to a certain extent on these old strategies and practices. At the same time, it has been suggested that new market institutions, such as stock exchanges, banks, and instruments for governmental macro-economic policy, began to emerge, with some delay, only as actors within the state bureaucracy began to see their usefulness as part of their own strategies of survival and adaptation to radically changed economic and political conditions. These observations also help qualify the expectations about swift and radical change so prevalent at the beginning of 1990. Within democratic forms of government, the best hope for a successful reform scenario was in fact represented not by the shock tactics proposed by the neo-liberal technopols but the corrective and complementary policy decisions taken by successive governments.

Authority crisis and the dissolution of the communist social pact

As Huntingdon (1968) observed, communist parties in the former soviet bloc were successful in the modernisation of the economy and politics. Centralised political power was deployed effectively to develop the economy and standards of living improved substantially. But this concentration of power and the mobilisation of the population to achieve economic and ideological aims had an undermining effect on the autonomy of society (Burawoy 2003). This section traces the most salient aspects of the lasting influence on public culture of the attempt by the regime to control both social reality and its representation. In spite of its monopoly over the state, the authority of the communist party was in time undermined by its visible failure to meet the expectations it had created. Moreover, these expectations, the scaling up of values and their increased role at times of change was intensified even more by the communist cultural patterns, which encouraged an overemphasis of values over realistic constraints. As will be shown later in this chapter, the political choices made by the emergent parties also contributed to this atmosphere of effervescence, instability of frames of reference and radicalised political activity.

Thus, it is common knowledge that in post-World War II Central and Eastern Europe communist parties extended the domain of the political beyond anything known before. They used political power to implement a 'systemic' revolution (Bauman 1992). The communist regimes attempted to create a new type of society and a 'new man' (Lifton 1963; Zinoviev 1985; Goldfarb 1989). The subservice of individuals was secured by eliminating individual property rights and through comprehensive forms of social integration and mobilisation (Nodia 1996, 24–27). Political legitimation rested on the priority of goals over means or law (Rigby 1982), on Marxist claims about the objective trend of history and the revolutionary character of the Party (Berki 1982; Brunner 1982; Heller 1982; Markus 1982), on paternalism (Fehér 1982), and the cult of the leader (Gill 1982).

To mobilise and integrate their populations, the communist regimes created a world-view in which the Party was the hero who transcended the political instability and the painful economic and political backwardness of the previous era and developed a society based on justice, equality and a superior standard of living for all its citizens. The Party was portrayed as a superior political agent which derived its strength from its use of the scientific method, which guaranteed that the Party's aims and strategies were objectively justified and correct. Limitations in achieving its aims were temporary. In Kornai's words, these claims amount to a curious process of self-legitimation:

> Whether the ruling group expresses the desires and interests of the majority, and whether the majority of the people supports them are not measured by whether this support is manifested in some tangible form (for instance a ballot). The possessors of power have appointed themselves as the manifest expression of the people's interests and the repository of a permanent public good. According to the elliptical thinking described, one can almost say they have legitimated their power 'by definition'. (Kornai 1992, 56)

This inclination towards 'elliptical thinking', which buttressed the position of impregnable right of the Party, became an important frame in the public culture as a whole, a way of organising the arguments and rhetoric in support of any objective deemed desirable by the Party.[4] In the fragment below from a propaganda work on the Romanian economy, typical for the style of communist official pronouncements, the sense of heroism, charisma and exceptionality, envelops the goal of industrialisation:

> The development of the industry, and especially of the heavy industry, is considered as *the only way* of raising Romania to the level of the economically advanced countries through *the harmonious and balanced* development – on *a constantly ascending line and at a rapid rate* – of *the whole* economy, the *constant increase* of social labour productivity, the *intensive and complex* development of agriculture and the *systematic advance* of people's living standard. Industrialisation ensures in fact national independence and sovereignty. (Lupu 1968, 17)[5]

A variety of positive attributes are presented as guaranteed features of this desired reality, in this case industrialisation. That the 'harmonious' and 'balanced' and 'constantly ascending', 'at a rapid rate', development of all sectors in the economy might not be possible, or what the trade-offs might be between these different objectives are, at best, marginal concerns. The implicit beliefs about action, what is desirable and possible, communicated by the official culture are also evident here. The imperative is indeed absolute: the Party (the state, the individual, etc.) has to and can achieve perfection. In such magical, incantatory pronouncements, what is desirable becomes confused with what is possible: the meaning and the outcome of the Party-inspired actions seem to flow un-problematically and without any significant resistance from its special identity.

At the same time, Lupu is careful to invoke many of the possible facets of industrialisation. Consideration and refutation of opposing arguments is an important device for the construction of rational argument in European culture (Goodwin 1997, 14–15). In this case, different aspects of the process of industrialisation are acknowledged, but they are simply enunciated and are not given explicit consideration. In spite of its elliptic character, this is a gesture towards the rationalism and scientific spirit that the Party also represented. The ability to forge together elements that would normally be incompatible, in this case 'individual heroism' and 'organisational impersonalism' was the main feature of the 'Leninist (communist) Party' (Jowitt 1992, 8–12).

This synthesis was an unstable ensemble, however. Its survival depended on the identification of and war against enemies: class enemies, the backwardness of the peasantry and any 'negative attitudes' that stood in the way. The reign of terror in the early phases of the regime realised the political ambitions of the Party; it was also crucial for the maintenance of its organisational integrity. The vast social restructuring operated by the Party gave it huge opportunities to reward materially social groups, particularly the formerly dispossessed, while violence was used against opponents (Pop 1993; Jela 1997; Tănase 1997). In later years, purges inside the party, and the campaigns to achieve various planning targets, served the same objective (Sampson 1982; Lefort 1986; Zilber 1997). Thus strong emotional overtones became attached to these heroic agents and objectives (Heller 1982, 59–60; Bar-On 1999; Neculau 1999), all the more so since the hero/villain dyad could be projected by the regime onto any actor, in relation to any goal.

These excessive ideological claims of the communist party impacted variably on society, depending on resistance by different groups, and the extent to which they were enforced.[6] Even when the concrete promises of the regime were no longer believed, what endured was a commitment to certain values, such as equality, economic development and national self-reliance in certain areas. Also enduring was a set of extraordinary expectations about the effectiveness of action in the public sphere and a tendency towards absolutist, all or nothing, evaluations of success. Metaphors of war and struggle became the normal frame for understanding social action, and 'storming', periods of frantic activity followed by slackness, became the typical manner in which objectives were achieved (Jowitt 1992, 79; Verdery 1996, 42, 54).

At the same time, informal arrangements were important for meeting the everyday needs of people since the state regularly failed to deliver the promised basic goods and services. *Blat*, 'favours of access' to resources, granted by people who had official, immediate access to certain scarce goods, to others, under the guise of friendship, or family 'help' were common (Ledeneva 1998, 34–37). In Romania, they were so widespread that the acronyms of the Romanian Communist Party (PCR) were said to stand for three words that were synonyms of *blat*. Thus, *pile* (a 'file', a tool that smoothens metals), *cunoştinţe* (acquaintances), and *relaţii* (connections) represented the main strategies for survival under the rule of the PCR.

In spite of the efforts from above to eliminate them, informal practices corroded and corrupted the 'organisational integrity' of the Party (Jowitt 1992, 121–158). In time, the Party became unable to sustain the tension at the core of its identity, the tension between the heroism of its expectations and the impersonalism of its bureaucratic means. It could not find new objectives on the revolutionary scale of its first two decades in power and it could not discipline its own officials, who became much more interested in pursuing their own private agendas than in subordination to the Party (Voslenski 1984, 188–240; Botez 1997, 87–116). The ideology itself ceased to represent the 'truth' in which citizens had to believe and became simply something they had to be seen to agree with (Havel 1991; Michnik 1993). Cynics became more numerous than true believers (Poznanski 1993).[7]

The Party often made the existence of this informal realm the explicit focus of its repressive policies. Press campaigns attacked the character and integrity of groups such as sales assistants, doctors, and other service providers that were at the core of *blat* networks and practices. These groups were blamed for shortages (Jowitt 1992, 62–87). But this additional attempt to control only intensified a sense of 'lack of reality' among the population.

The ideology of the Party was so obviously part of everyday life, from the architecture of the cities and living spaces to the availability of basic foods and services. And yet the 'normalcy' of everyday life and even physical survival rested on informal practices that were de-legitimised and prosecuted.[8]

The difficulty created by this clash between descriptions and claims that seemed to come from separate and contradictory levels of reality was sometimes resolved in the form of black humour.[9] Self-actualisation was 'situationally determined', 'people could say one thing in one context and another in another context and not be judged deceitful, or forgetful, or mad' (Verdery 1996, 96). This, in turn, created a 'fundamental reflex toward micro-experiences of solidarity and opposition' (Verdery 1996, 96). Similarly, for Kligman 'living in two interrelated "realities" – a stagnant official public sphere and a dynamic informal one – defined the habitus of socialism in Ceauşescu's Romania' (1998, 40).[10]

Such splits within the self, to use Kohut's terminology (1971), are not unusual. Indeed, there is a vast literature on alienation in capitalist societies, not least that of the Frankfurt School. The persistent awareness of this double reality and the politicisation of this situation is however distinctive in the way in which such splits were experienced by people living under the communist regime. Since the party-state assumed such a great role in the construction of reality, both material and ideational, it was also made responsible for this dissonance and pronouncements about its final, abysmal failure as a system of economic, social and political organisation were often formulated in exact terms. The consequences of this expansion of consciousness or indeed ability for dissimulation for the democratic reconstitution of politics after 1990 are difficult to pin down, but it can be surmised that the fractious fragmentation of political allegiances and the difficulty in creating the sense that a robust democratic political regime is in place, even though they did not lead to dramatic political instability, are more or less direct legacies of this cultural set-up.

The attempt by the communist party to control social reality and the knowledge about it also stunted the development of specialised reflection on social affairs and of social sciences in particular. The truth claims of the Party were so radical and far-reaching that there was little room left for explicit, open, scientific debate. In a sense, the autonomy of scientific research was never completely extinguished since, although the institutional bases of these activities were severely restricted, they were not completely absent. Additionally, intellectuals and scientists tried to assert the autonomy of their spheres and to escape official censorship. However, in Romania, where the regime remained ideological to the end, the closure of some social science departments and the politicisation of others disabled to a greater extent than elsewhere in the region the production of knowledge about social affairs. Professionalisation in the already marginal social sciences depended on strategies of avoidance of current affairs through a return to classical texts or abstract thought (Verdery 1991).

Participation in the official discourse, embracing certain themes, such as nationalism, that were crucial to the claims to legitimacy of the communist regime, was to a certain extent compulsory (Verdery 1991). This inhibition of the scientific understanding of social issues fuelled the sentiment of 'lack of reality' already created by the encroachment of formal, official prescriptions on a variety of realms of experience and by the peculiar relationship between official and informal practices. Helplessness, the impossibility of creating an opening in official discourse and of even imagining a practical way of breaking free from the grip of the regime were expressed in fictional form (Buzura 1974; Sîrbu 1992), in interviews and letters broadcast by Radio Free Europe, and diaries (Antonesei 1995; Jela 1997).[11]

Thus, the attempt by the communist party to control both discourse and reality, the material conditions of existence and the minds and the sentiments of its citizens, made the reconciliation, through cultural work, of the contradiction between the claims of the party and the everyday experience more and more difficult. This tension might have been felt most acutely by what Eyal, Szélenyi and Townsley (1998) have termed as the 'underground elite': members of the secret police in particular. Enlisted to do the dirty work for the regime – agents of terror, disinformation, and manipulation of all kinds – their loyalty was forged out of a heady and perverse mixture of beliefs and material benefits. Their status as the elect, above the law, was shrouded in secrecy, which added both a thrill and a sense of unlimited power and impunity to their actions. With this insider status also came, however, subjection to ideological controls that were much more stringent than those exerted on the population at large. Thus, their moral and emotional situation was extraordinary even by the standards of the communist regime: they were people who had had to assimilate and take to heart the myth of the exceptionalism of the regime and that of their own. This exceptionalism justified in their own eyes their role in carrying out the morally reprehensible work of oppression, while cynicism was also a necessary accompaniment of their situation. Overall, the depth of their concomitant identification and dissociation from the regime, through black humour and cynicism, was greater than that of the population at large.

These groups were also the most vulnerable in the wake of regime breakdown. Bereft of institutional guarantees for their survival, they were also likely scapegoats within a society exhausted by decades of ideological oppression. In the event, as it will be shown later, they were also the major, and natural, carriers, of the cultural frames and patterns described here, especially since in Romania the exit of the communist party from the political scene was particularly abrupt and difficult to politicise.

This was the cultural legacy of the communist regime in Romania. The communist party had socialised not only claims about itself but, more broadly, beliefs about the possibility of action in the public sphere and its purposes. To count, actions had to be crowned by extraordinary achievement and to transcend objective limitations. Extreme terms of evaluation also applied to the failure to oppose it actively and this became another persistent theme in the Romanian culture: a predilection for absolute negative evaluations of all things Romanian.[12] Symbolically, had the behaviour of the Party or its claims changed towards the end of the 1980s, this might have freed up the hold on the public imagination of these frames of understanding. As it was, the ignominious exit of the Party from the political scene and the absence of any other agent with sufficient moral authority to restate these boundaries, meant that the cultural process of change was initially chaotic and a new consensus around the norms that should define political action or effective action in the public sphere more generally was slower.

Members of the former underground elite have been suspected of indulging in making spurious accusations against prominent politicians and there is certainly a public for a peculiar discrediting game aimed at making all values relative. Informal practices and social networks of yore persist but are now labelled as corruption or incompetence. While there are no doubt ample opportunities for corruption within the vast post-1990 processes of economic redistribution, the generalisation of accusations of corruption and the assumption that all public servants are corrupt only serve to create a climate where it continues to be difficult and even dangerous to take responsibility for particular acts. Paradoxically, it is also the perfect cover for those who are in a position to appropriate wealth and exert influence with impunity.

Governing the weak state: hatred of the past and fear of the future

Romania's communist regime remained totalitarian to its end on 22 December 1989 (Shafir 1986; Fischer 1989; Tismăneanu 1989; 1996a). It had been imposed on the country, after World War II, as in the rest of the Eastern European bloc, under Soviet influence (Halpern 1993). Its history is punctuated by changes in the political leadership at the very top which coincide with phases in the establishment and the consolidation of the regime. Between 1944 and 1953, the coming into power of the communist party and the beginning of the restructuring of the economy, society and politics were executed under the close supervision of Soviet advisers and in the presence of Soviet troops by leaders such as Ana Pauker, Teohari Georgescu and Vasile Luca who had been exiles in the USSR. With Stalin's tacit approval, they were removed from power in 1953, by Gheorghe Gheoghiu-Dej, a homegrown communist leader, who sought to obtain a new legitimacy for the regime through a nationalist programme of relative independence from Moscow. The most visible achievement in this direction was the withdrawal of the Soviet troops from Romania, in 1953, and the rejection, in 1964, of proposals made by the USSR to use the CMEA as a framework for implementing a certain division of labour across the Eastern Bloc, according to which member states were to capitalise on their existing strengths and specialise in certain kinds of agricultural or industrial production. This would have locked Romania into the position of a mostly agricultural producer and would have hampered its ambitions to develop its industry. Gheorghiu-Dej continued to use state terror in carrying out the nationalisation of productive property in industry and commerce, the reorganisation of agriculture, the army, the police, the state administration, and the launching of the first economic plans. It was not until the regime was consolidated, in the early 1960s, that a certain amount of political liberalisation, in the form of a greater tolerance for non-ideological forms of culture and public life, culminating with the release from prison of all political detainees in 1964, took place.

This relative opening up of the regime to a degree of experimentation in the economic sphere, freer access to alternative sources of information, and the development of trade links with Western Europe was continued by Nicolae Ceauşescu, who replaced Gheorghe Gheorgiu-Dej in 1964. The most dramatic gesture that confirmed Ceauşescu's relative independence from Moscow and brought him widespread domestic and international support was his public condemnation of the Soviet invasion of Czechoslovakia in 1968. Having thus attracted the wrath of his Soviet patrons, and fearing that he would be removed through an internal coup, Ceauşescu grew anxious to secure his hold on power. He took inspiration from Asian communist dictatorships and gradually eliminated all competition within the higher echelons of the communist elite (Comisso 1986). He also appointed members of his family to key positions creating a totalitarian cum *sultanistic* regime (Linz and Stepan 1996, 349–356). Legitimate opposition to the regime was not possible, and there was no forum for a peaceful negotiation of its dissolution.

Instead, the political transition from communism took the form of breakdown (Batt 1991), a revolution whose organisation, events, actors, and general character were necessarily fluid and contested (Ratesh 1991). Unrest flared up first in Timişoara, a major city in Western Romania, and spread to Bucharest, on 21 December 1989. A huge rally organised by the communist government in the capital to show support for the regime span out of control as members of the crowd heckled the dictator. That evening, members of the public gathered in some of the major squares in the city protesting against the regime; they refused to disperse even when military units were deployed to intimidate them. On the morning of December 22, the army was required by Ceauşescu to shoot and arrest the demonstrators. The defence minister refused to obey this order and shortly afterwards committed suicide. The news of his act, portrayed as an acknowledgement of guilt and betrayal of the regime, was broadcast on national radio that morning. This was a turning point for the army units already deployed on the streets of Bucharest who joined the anti-regime demonstrators. In what turned out to be the definitive breaking point of their hold on power, however, Ceauşescu and his wife, Elena, faced with angry demonstrators about to enter the party headquarters, fled by helicopter from the top of the building. As it turned out, none of the exit solutions they might have planned for worked out: they were captured within hours and two days later they were put on trial in a makeshift 'revolutionary' tribunal that sentenced them to death without right of appeal. They were shot dead on December 24.

Thus the change of regime was pronounced in the streets of Bucharest and broadcast to the whole of the country from the studios of the national television station. It was the result of grass roots mobilisation; the political channelling of this uprising and the emergence of new political institutions were fraught with uncertainty and conflict. The first political grouping to offer leadership in post-communist Romania was *Consiliul Naţional al Frontului Salvării Naţionale* (National Council of the National Salvation Front – CNFSN). In its month-long existence, the CNFSN presented itself as a broad, non-partisan group that was taking over the exercise of power as a transitional government, until free elections could be organised. In the first public announcement of its constitution and principles CNFSN also formulated the programme of the revolution: the dissolution of the party-state, democratic government and free elections, and free enterprise (Iliescu 1990). CNFSN also tried to resolve some of the most pressing governance issues: redirecting foodstuffs from export to the domestic shops in order to put a stop to shortages; ending the rationing of energy supplies to the population to provide heating in winter; co-opting the military and the security forces; and running the day-to-day business of the country. Most significantly, by passing emergency decrees that gave the appearance of due process to economic, social and political demands already imposed by grass roots direct action, CNFSN averted political chaos or civil war.

The grass roots mobilisation of a great number of social interests pressing for immediate repeal of some of the most outrageous policies of the communist regime was overwhelming. Existing newspapers and other media outlets were taken over by newly-established associations of employees and became fora for the expression of the new-found freedom of all and sundry. New publications were established overnight and street demonstrations in the capital were daily occurrences. In the absence of a negotiated political transition, the breakdown of the communist rule was taken as permission for the more or less automatic fulfilment of pent-up demands. Professionals wanted jobs in cities and the ban that had prevented non-city dwellers from taking employment there was removed; farmers wanted their land back and in many places co-operatives were disbanded; many wanted to travel abroad – the borders were opened and every citizen gained the right to have a passport; workers obtained shorter working hours and better pay; abortion was legalised; and there were many other examples of reform.[13]

Powerful, and conflicting, emotional needs were expressed publicly and vocally for the first time, through the newly-freed media and in public demonstrations. For some, the need to assign responsibility for the communist regime and to make the break with communism irreversible was paramount. For others, these demands were too radical and represented a direct threat or a source of instability in an already fluid political situation (Băieşu 1990). The members of the military and the security forces feared for their safety, as they faced the real possibility of becoming scapegoats for the outgoing regime. More than 3.5 million people had been members of the PCR. While the sheer magnitude of this figure diluted the ideological importance of being a party member, it also meant that a huge number of people were sensitive to accusations of collective guilt. Thus, the need for some sort of framework for what was going to happen next, for stability, was also important (Tănase 1993; Gheorghe and Huminic 1999).

It is difficult to exaggerate the urgency of these issues in Romania in the first few months after the revolution (Verdery and Kligman 1992; Tismăneanu 1993). The communist regime was utterly compromised. It was seen as a complete failure, a mistake of historical proportions that had brought Romania to a dead end from which it would be very difficult to retreat (MOR 177/1991, 22). It had put its citizens through huge deprivations. It had done violence to individual and collective aspirations of freedom and human dignity (Antonesei 1995; Breban 1997; Jela 1997). The lack of active opposition to the regime caused a catastrophic loss of collective self-esteem (Neculau and Curelaru 2000). The painful awareness of the lack of ideas and self-confidence about how society could be taken forward was visible in the insistent search for leaders who were 'morally clean' (Pleşu 1990, 1).

In contrast to Hungary, Czechoslovakia and Poland where open opposition to the regime had allowed the articulation of a stance for society in relation to the state and the options available to political action (Michnik 1993) and some recuperation of trust and self-esteem (Ash 1983), in Romania the political programme for change was formulated ad hoc and lacked a clear societal mandate. Even though the ability of anti-communist resistance to dent the power of the communist regimes in the region was limited, and the latter kept control on the major levers of power, such gestures of courage and self-affirmation had an important symbolic value for the society as a whole (Brandys 1984). They redeemed some of the humiliation and deprivation inflicted on these societies by their arbitrary regimes (Ost 1990).

In post-communist Romania, the two sets of conflicting needs outlined above – for a sense of stability and for certainty that the break with the communist regime was irreversible – were politicised in an antagonistic fashion. The CNFSN, an ad hoc umbrella organisation that lacked cohesion, and its successor, *Frontul Salvării Naţionale* (National Salvation Front – FSN), appealed to the more conservative sections of the public (Kideckel 1992, 75; Mihuţ 1994, 414) while the historical parties,[14] supported by the humanistic intelligentsia, proposed a radical moral stance, condemning the communist regime and offering themselves as guarantors of a new democratic order (Morgan 1994). They saw a process of moral healing as the basis for a democratic society and put the issue of culpability for the communist regime at the top of the political agenda for the rest of the decade. This included the request that former communist activists should be banned from public office for at least eight years (Călinescu and Tismăneanu 1992).

But the link made by the historical parties and the humanistic intelligentsia between experience of democracy and participation in political life, which would have excluded some of the leaders of the CNFSN and later FSN, was not the only source of mistrust between these two political forces. There was very little give and take in the evaluation of each other's actions and often assumptions of bad faith and misunderstandings accentuated their differences. For instance, when the Front passed constructive measures, such as the law that allowed private enterprise and the establishment of political parties, this was seen as an attempt by the Front to obtain political capital from doing what anyone in their position would have done. When the Front hesitated in legislating radical economic and political reform, it was accused of harbouring the intention of returning to a communist regime (Mary Ellen Fischer 1992; Carey 1996).

The Front seemed intimidated by this criticism. In any case, some facts could not be denied. For instance, its leader, Ion Iliescu, had been a member of the Central Committee of the PCR before 1971 and had held lower positions of authority in the party until 1989, although he was known as a dissident to the personal rule of Nicolae Ceauşescu. Unfortunately, the FSN failed to deal with this issue directly by encouraging a public debate about the character and consequences of the communist regime. Instead, the Front exploited the fact that the claims of the opposition were politically sensitive and maintained silence over the question of its relationship with the past regime. The FSN also fuelled speculation about its role in the revolution. Some of its members claimed that the Front existed prior to the revolution and played a role in bringing it about. In other declarations, the Front was presented as the 'emanation of the revolution', an ad hoc organisation (Brucan 1998b, 228–294).

The emergence of the FSN as a political party, distinct from the CNFSN, the temporary government, in late January 1990, also fuelled speculation about the Front's commitment to the rules of the democratic game and fair competition in the elections. Public support for the revolutionary government was significant in the early months of 1990. There were few institutional checks on its power, as there lacked a clear institutional framework for the coming elections, and the numerous political parties that sprung up in early 1990 had a weak presence outside the capital, Bucharest. Against this background, the intention of organising the FSN as a political party was reminiscent of the practice of confusing state and party that had characterised the communist regime (Bârlădeanu, quoted in Betea 1997, 236–237). On their part, under pressure to contain the volatile political situation, the CNFSN leaders also perceived the relative freedom of the historical parties to organise and take part in elections as unfair competition. In the event, after negotiations punctuated by heated public debates on national television, and street demonstrations, the CNFSN was replaced with *Consiliul Provizoriu al Unității Naționale* (Provisional Council of National Unity – CPUN) on 1 February 1990 until a new government was elected in May. Twenty-seven new parties that had emerged in January 1990 held half of the seats, while the other half and the presidency went to the FSN (Câmpeanu 1990).

The Front's neo-communist and anti-democratic orientation also seemed confirmed by the events of June 1990. Shortly after their victory at the polling booth, in May 1990, the Front was seen to have encouraged the vigilante activities of the Valea Jiului miners who came to Bucharest to resolve what should have been a mere public order incident. On 13 June, the police moved to clear *Piața Universității* (University Square) of protestors who had occupied it for several months, but were met with resistance that later escalated into arson attacks on the TV station building and the police headquarters. The police were unable to contain the unrest and before army units could be brought in, thousands of miners from Valea Jiului descended on Bucharest to defend the newly-elected government. The miners vandalised the headquarters of some of the opposition parties and attacked some of their members. The government tried to contain the miners by asking them to avail themselves of particular facilities – food and accommodation – before they could be sent back. President Iliescu met with them and thanked them for their contribution in what he presented as an attempt to convince them to leave the capital. At a minimum, this incident proved the weakness of the police and the diffidence of the government in the face of well-organised social groups. Politically, by seeming to give political cover to this vigilante action, the reputation of the Front as neo-communists and non-democrats became entrenched and their efforts in the following years to build the institutions of democracy received little credit from their opponents (Marga 1993).

The Front also made compromises in order to obtain the acquiescence of the army and the former Securitate. This meant that the role these organisation played in the events of the revolution was never fully accounted for, which further intensified the distrust of the opposition in the Front's commitment to transparency and a break with the practices of the former regime (Ionescu 1992d, 1994d, 1994e). A more confident party might have claimed that the co-opting of the former Securitate into a legitimate regime of law and order was a success. Instead, the ambiguity of the Front over this issue gave credence to the claims of their opponents. The Front became associated in the eyes of the democratic opposition and various foreign commentators with extremist nationalist groupings whose search for political models included a revisiting of the pro-fascist cultural movement of the inter-war period (Shafir 1992d; Tismăneanu and Pavel 1994). This compromised further the attempts of the Front to portray itself as a democratic force as it became unable to distance itself from nationalists (Schwarz 1997).

Given the political uncertainty and volatility created by the sudden break-down of the communist regime, the actions of the Front could, in principle, be explained without branding them as neo-communists. At the same time, the intransigence of the historical parties and their allies, the humanist intelligentsia, is understandable. After all, these groups had been, in different ways, at the receiving end of state terror and were most keenly aware of the dangers of unchecked power. Their perception at the beginning of the transition was that the Front had a monopoly on the means of real power (access to state resources, the national media, etc.), while their own position was one of extreme weakness and vulnerability. Additionally, they might have felt more keenly than the FSN, who were already in the limelight, the danger of having their message drowned out by the multitude of parties that emerged after December 1990: there were more than one hundred officially registered political parties in June 1990. In the circumstances, the historical parties did not have the confidence to appreciate that their symbolic political capital was in fact extremely important in a situation where political capital of any sort was very scarce. Thus they were unable to take a pragmatic, rather than principled, position.

Their role as 'true democrats' and opinion makers was recognised by the international media and international organisations. For instance, their assessment of the progress of reform in Romania influenced crucial decisions such as the postponement in 1991 of the admission of Romania to the Council of Europe (Andreescu 1998, 12–14).[15] The role of 'true democrats' positioned these groups as gatekeepers for a number of Western aid programmes, at a time when the ideological import of the changes in CEE was paramount and commitment to democratic values was rewarded by significant economic opportunities (Mungiu 1996; Wedel 1998).

Thus, the historical parties chose to operate according to an ethic of principled conviction (Weber 1994) in their political activities. This was a means to counterbalance what they perceived as their weak position as new parties without immediate access to the resources of the state. The FSN, on the other hand, coming into power in the wake of the revolution, used an ethic of responsibility. Although this orientation had the merit of being pragmatic, it was also useful in evading some embarrassing questions about past affiliations. None of these parties could reach out to appeal to other than their 'natural constituencies'. The Front failed to reassure those who feared a return to the past, while the historical parties ignored the security needs of the former 'communists'. Thus, the weakness of agency in post-communist transformations (Elster, Offe and Preuss 1998) was compounded in Romania by the polarisation of the political system. The compromise between those who hated the past and those who feared for their future was very tenuous indeed.

As a consequence the 'democratic pact' (Stepan 1986, 79) between the political parties included a commitment to democracy as the only game in town. But the distrust between the parties was reflected in overcautious institutional design. Proportional representation led to minority governments dependent on shifting coalitions of voting in the parliaments. In addition, in parliament, the two chambers replicated each other's functions and delayed the passing of legislation (IIDEA 1997). Lack of trust between parties was also reflected in the duplication of reform measures, which was to be a major factor delaying the implementation of economic reform. It also created the perception that the different parties were unwilling to commit to economic reforms. Their ability to do so was undermined by their fragility and their fear of the assumed conservatism of the population and the attacks from their rivals (Dijmărescu 1993b, 77). Similarly affected was their willingness to take responsibility for the inevitable costs of the reforms (Dijmărescu 1993a).

Notes

1 Political unification is often a pre-requisite for the industrialisation of backward countries according to Gerschenkron (1992, 113).
2 See for instance the many 'appeals' in the national press in January 1990 for workers to return to work (Iliescu 1990).
3 This process of re-skilling is amply documented by interviews in the Romanian economic press as well as interviews conducted by this author.
4 Some of the policy priorities of the Romanian Communist Party (PCR) and their institutional consequences were reviewed above. The working class and the heavy industries were the most common functional substitutes for the Party in this cultural scheme, the most likely to be cast in the heroic role.
5 Emphasis added.
6 For instance, Kubik (1994) and Batt (2001) made the argument for the distinctiveness of the regional cultures of Cieszyn Silesia in Poland, and Banat in Romania respectively.
7 It is not possible to explore here the complex emotional and moral predicament of individuals or groups held in captivity. These phenomena belong to a wider category of social and personal traumas, such as domestic violence, holocaust, apartheid and war. See for instance Herman (1994), Tal (1996), and Bar-On (1999). Mihaela Miroiu (1999) also noted in a study of post-communist Romanian culture the similarity between the situation of women in a patriarchal culture and that of people living under totalitarian regimes. Common features are the prevalence of fear, the internalised constraints to self-development and the peculiar complicity between victim and perpetrator that is the price for survival in such extreme circumstances (Miroiu 1999, 135–162). In these situations gestures of self-mutilation by women, such as abortion, could be seen as strategies of political resistance (Băban 1996).
8 The 'cultural work' of reconciling certain formal claims in the culture with realities that might belie these claims is not, of course, unique to the communist regimes. Edelman (1964) noted this tension in his study of symbolic politics and Scott (1990) analysed the coexistence of official and hidden codes of behaviour and meaning at work in the relations between the dominant and the dominated social groups. In a study of grass roots democratic activity in a community in the USA, Eliasoph (1997) showed that the belief in the worthiness of democracy and civic engagement and the

sense of impotence of individuals in influencing national policy were reconciled through a stratagem of 'avoiding politics'. This consisted in professing interest in democracy but restricting militant action to local issues over which the activists felt they had some control.

9   This was captured well in the black humour of the times. As an example, here is a stanza from *Istorya SSSR v Anekdotakh: 1971–1991* (Riga: Everest, 1991, p. 188), quoted in Ledeneva (1998, 72): 'No unemployment but nobody works./Nobody works but productivity increases./Productivity increases but shops are empty./The shops are empty but fridges are full./ Fridges are full but nobody is satisfied./Nobody is satisfied but all vote unanimously.'

10   Kligman adapted Bourdieu's notion of habitus to describe the 'socialist habitus' of Ceauşescu's era. Habitus is the internalised, taken for granted ways of seeing and being, whose acquisition through early socialisation ensures the 'fit' between individual perceptions and strategies for action and their cultural environment (Kligman 1998, 15). See also Bourdieu (1990, 52–79) and Thompson (1991, 12–14).

11   Many of these works, although written before 1990, were published after the revolution.

12   The TV station PRO-TV broadcast in 1998 a series of programmes whose title, *Există şi români fericiţi* (Happy Romanians exist as well), challenged this common perception.

13   See for instance *Financial Times*, 2 January 1990, 'Romania prepares for sweeping moves towards democracy', and *Financial Times*, 3 January 1990, 'Generations come together to revive political life: Freedom's chaotic rebirth in Romania'.

14   See 'Historical parties' in Glossary and biographies.

15   Andreescu was one of a handful of members of the opposition invited by the Council to make representations on this issue. Romania was invited to become a member of the Council in 1993.

2

Cultural factors in the economic and political transformations

This chapter considers how cultural notions about action in the public sphere changed during the 1990s in Romania.[1] From a near complete dominance over debates and practices, the heroic model of action, outlined in the previous chapter, was slowly replaced by more pragmatic and limited evaluations of success and failure. This process is parallel to that of the constitution of politics as democratic politics and the consolidation of democracy. In fact, only when expectations about the role of the government and the actual rules of the political game – for insiders and in the relation between insiders and the public – normalise, is the reconstitution of politics along democratic lines complete. The first section of this chapter documents this process by looking at changes in the language and framing devices used to describe and engage opponents in politics, to construct the identity of political parties and to articulate political programmes.

The following sections explore how conceptions about economic reform and the role of the state and other institutions evolved during the 1990s, with a particular emphasis on privatisation and private property in section three. Here, the markers of cultural change, expressed as changes in the tone of assessments and criteria by which performance is judged, also reflect the increased institutionalisation of the separation between state and the economy. Increasingly, it is understood and accepted that although the state continues to play a role in the economy, a relatively autonomous economic mechanism, the market, is also at work and that economic decisions, even though they are not rational in any absolute sense, do have to be coached in rational terms. Finally, the last section in this chapter evaluates briefly the development of technical knowledge about society and the gradual filtering through in public debates of these, more restrained, terms of evaluation and judgement.

The changing language of politics

It has been suggested here that the reconstitution of politics as democratic politics is also a process of dissolution of the communist political vocabulary and the emergence of a new set of narratives and metaphors able to represent and explain the process of change, to offer a vision for the future, and, ultimately, to reassure and integrate the citizenry into the new political order. As Edelman (1974) alerts us, symbols arise as complex crystallisations of shared experience and retain the power to mobilise the emotions and passions that engendered them. For this reason, any change within the symbolic repertoire of politics is an intense emotional experience, matching significant shifts in economic and social conditions. In the case of post-communist transformations, the extent and depth of this change is indeed remarkable but in Romania in particular it was made even more dramatic and prolonged by the sudden disappearance from the political scene of the communist party, which had been its central, stabilising anchor.

The majority of scholarly analyses characterise the Romanian transition as a neo-communist takeover of power from inside. But this position overestimates the extent to which the continuity of some of the state structures amounted to the reproduction of communism as a social and political project. The party structure that had shadowed the state administration was in fact removed at one stroke and most of the personnel that had been part of the nomenklatura either lost their jobs or were assimilated as far as possible into equivalent positions in the state administration. As an ideology and a societal project, communism was dead even though its structural and institutional foundations in the economy and politics would take time to change. As long as these foundations survived, they could be and were regarded as a potential power base for a neo-communist political project, but there was no active political force able to mobilise, or interested in mobilising, this potential: the loss of legitimacy of the communist regime was irretrievable even for its nominal supporters, the members of the communist party and the nomenklatura.

Thus, it would be reasonable to expect that in the absence of institutional support, the relevance of old models of understanding politics, especially the heroic model, would begin to diminish. However, these models continued to exert a certain fascination in the early 1990s and were played out in the politics of the time for a number of reasons. The absence of a concrete political actor that would incarnate these values caught the would-be opponents and/or successors of the communist regime by surprise. They had judged any effective action against the government beyond their own means. Barring unexpected fortuitous events in international politics or a palace coup, Ceauşescu's position was accepted as enduring and impregnable. And indeed the hold of the hypnotic ritual that had substituted for public life in Romania in the 1980s seemed unbreakable as late as November 1989 when the XIVth

Party Congress re-elected Ceauşescu as General Secretary, without the slightest sign of dissent within its ranks.

Thus, the sudden breakdown of the regime exposed the misjudgement and failure of these opponents to act effectively and to challenge Ceauşescu's reign. In retrospect, their behaviour appeared even more shameful and difficult to explain especially since the brittleness of the façade of self-confidence and drive mounted by the communist regime was exposed by the smallest gesture of defiance: instead of cheering on cue, the crowds amassed in front of the Party Headquarters on 21 December 1989 heckled the dictator. Within hours, what might have been a mere irritation, snowballed into a real challenge to the legitimacy of Ceauşescu's clan, and ultimately a revolution, as the heckling of a few demonstrators was followed by equally surprising failures to act by the supposed enforcers of the regime: the police, the army and the *Securitate* did not intervene to protect their leader, and Ceauşescu could not get a grip on himself and the situation (Câmpeanu 1999, 42–46).

The manner in which the vulnerability of the regime was exposed shed a negative light on the would-be opposition, and undermined the justifications it had offered itself for its earlier inaction. Rather than acknowledge and accept this error, the opposition became stuck in an attitude of disbelief that a real change of regime had taken place and continued to make strenuous efforts to cast the new revolutionary government in the role of the villain. Unwittingly, it gave a ghostly kind of substance to the old ideals, by refusing to believe that the political force that had embodied them had disappeared. By resurrecting its old enemy, however, the opposition also provided itself with a belated opportunity for a fight that should have taken place and that was in fact crucial to its claims to represent the true ideals of democracy. The democratic opposition thus gave itself a political identity and a role to play in the post-communist transformations.

This post-hoc struggle against communism was also a shrewd political move in another sense, as the historical parties became able to capitalise on more general aspects of the political climate in the country. The sudden collapse of the regime exposed the chasm between the staged high politics of the party-state and a society that had become passive and atomised. In the void left by Ceauşescu's death and the dissolution of the communist party, there was spontaneous civic and political activism, a first step towards the reconstitution of civil society. In content and tone, though, these public activities – demonstrations in the streets, free expression of opinions in the media, reorganisation of trade unions and civic associations – seemed to be opportunities for collective acting out of long suppressed attitudes of defiance, opposition, derision or sometimes adulation and submission to the old regime even though the object on which these passions had been invested had disappeared.[2] It was as though by giving expression to these emotions, various actors needed to check out for themselves that the disappearance of the communist regime was real. Equally, they were also trying to gauge the extent to which old habits and modes of reasoning and comprehension, what might be thought of as the imprint of decades of totalitarian control over society, were still appropriate.

In the effervescence created by the sudden collapse of the authority of the party, the meaning and significance of current and past political events came under intense scrutiny. The events of the revolution, so publicly played out on the television screens, were the first to attract feverish interpretation, and numerous scenarios occupied the attention of the media and the public for years (Ratesh 1991; Verdery and Kligman 1992; Tismăneanu 1996b). In addition General Antonescu, King Michael, ethnic minorities, Romanian prisoners in Soviet Russia, Romania's participation in the Second World War, the beginnings and meaning of the communist regime, anti-communist dissidence and the lack of it, were at the centre of acrimonious debates in the 1990s. Competing claims for compensation or punishment related to long-suppressed grievances and historical wrongs were re-politicised in the 1990s and they were gradually settled while the political system as a whole was taking shape. These phenomena were common in the whole region, but in Romania their resolution was particularly protracted (Gallagher 1995; Breban 1997, 108–154; Tismăneanu 1998; Paler 1999).

Even though for their opponents it was simply impossible to believe that a regime – whose hold on power seemed so secure and complete – could collapse and that its successors would not want or be able to capture the state to promote their own interests, for their part, the members of the transitional, revolutionary government seemed to feel most keenly the need to fill the void of power left by the disappearance of the Ceauşescus and the communist party as political actors, so as to avert wide scale unrest and disorder. While for the emerging democratic opposition it was inconceivable that any political force sanctioned by revolutionary fiat would not be somehow linked to the previous regime and that it would not attempt to reproduce itself as far as possible, for CNFSN the immediate fear seemed to be that the ebullience and mass enthusiasm that accompanied the downfall of Ceauşescu would spill over into uncontrollable economic and social demands and political instability.

Throughout the 1990s, the most potent political signs, the signs most likely to release energy and passion 'out of all proportion to the apparent triviality of meaning suggested by its mere form' (Sapir 1934, in Edelman 1974, 116), were 'democracy', 'nation', 'communism' and 'moral responsibility' for its excesses, decay, and corruption. There was sharp rhetorical confrontation between parties, each seeking to demonise the other. The democratic opposition was keen to extol its symbolic capital, i.e. its supposed moral purity, direct, authentic knowledge of democracy and commitment to swift change, to compensate for what it lacked in terms of organisation and grass roots appeal. Having branded their opponents as 'neo-communists' and thus having taken an essentialist view of political identity, their rhetoric was matched in fervour not so much by the FSN but the right-wing, nationalist parties, especially Romania Mare.

Politicians themselves often displayed lack of care in managing their own image and that of their party. Confrontation was the style of engagement throughout the 1990s in Romania. The initial positioning of the main parties and especially the choice of the Democratic Convention for an ethics of 'ultimate ends' were at the core of this. The political debate before 1996 was shaped by the conviction that the actions of the governments can be explained directly by their assumed, 'neo-communist' identity. The refusal to engage in a more circumscribed debate over what was possible and how, perhaps fears that their own identity would be somehow damaged by association, translated into consequential decisions, such as the refusal to co-operate in the government in 1992. Văcăroiu's subsequent dependence on the support of the nationalist parties delayed its reform agenda and had economic costs. A measure of political stability was bought at the expense of serious economic imbalances in 1995–96.

Once in power, the Democratic Convention and their allies had a chance to implement their ideal of transparency, a test the previous government had presumably failed. In the name of transparency, the interest in projecting an image of coherence and purposefulness to the public took second place, in a situation where managing a fragmented coalition was going to be a difficult political task in any case. Disagreements between the coalition members were played out in public. To his credit, Prime Minister Ciorbea tried to make it a rule that his ministers should not announce policies without prior debate in the cabinet, and that they should not express views that were in contradiction with the official policy.

Within a year of his term in office he was confronted by four major crises of Cabinet management. Three of his ministers were supposedly conned into signing a declaration in support of constitutional monarchy, thus breaching the Romanian constitution. Two Hungarian ministers threatened to leave the cabinet over changes in the education bill but rescinded after a compromise was found. The foreign affairs minister, Adrian Severin, a member of the Democratic Party (PD), made accusations of espionage against some politicians. The accusations were later found to be baseless and he had to resign. Another PD minister, Traian Băsescu, was forced to resign by Ciorbea after publicly criticising the cabinet.

Ciorbea's successor, Radu Vasile seemed less preoccupied with the consequences of appearing to lead a divided cabinet. He candidly told the *Financial Times* that he would have liked to sack Sorin Dimitriu, the Minister for Privatisation, but that unfortunately he could not do it because Dimitriu had significant political backing (Marsh 1998, 1). The IMF and World Bank criticisms at the time – that more attention should be focused on tax collection and increased revenue from privatisation – were promptly transformed by Vasile into opportunities to attack publicly his privatisation and finance ministers, both of whom subsequently resigned (in September and December 1998 respectively). His own departure from office was the cause of a minor constitutional crisis, since President Emil Constantinescu pre-empted his resignation by firing him. After some debate, Vasile agreed to submit his resignation.[3]

The process of transition from revolutionary, intemperate passions and evaluations that occurred between political parties and leaders, is paralleled in the way in which politicians as a class begin to be seen by the media and the public at large. As late as 1997, it is still possible to find examples of the short-shrift treatment even from serious publications. For instance, one influential journalist, the editor-in-chief of *Adevărul Economic*, Viorel Sălăgean, a Senator and an economics PhD, addressed Prime Minister Ciorbea in a series of 'open letters' throughout 1997 (Sălăgean 1997a, 1997b, 1997c, 1997d). 'With great difficulty, you [the PM] desperately tried to push the cart of the reform again, without achieving very much,' said Sălăgean and warned that the 200 day deadline the government had given itself to deliver on its electoral promises was approaching. His evaluations and attributions were not backed by facts or reasoning; they seemed to rely entirely on rhetoric. Thus, talking to the man responsible for delivering on these promises, Sălăgean said that 'whoever thinks that a government can realise the wonders of the kind stitched together in the "200 day programme", is either naïve or completely alien to the world in which he lives'.

> Although I am almost certain that you will not be able to control your pride, honourable Prime-Minister, and you will lay out a report to the country, which you will certainly present in front of the nation, on prime time TV, about the 200 day programme, looking to convince Romanians that if the nature has turned green this spring, this is due, of course, to the reform of the government, you will only succeed in falling into ridicule and embarrassment. (Sălăgean 1997b)

This form of direct address did not leave much room for response. The actions of Prime Minister Ciorbea were not assessed on their own merits, but were derived from a view of his identity. The appraisal consisted of unreasoned and unjustified attributions, stemming from an auctorial position with shifting, contradictory and absolute requirements and expectations. Such evaluations, however were not seen as transgressions in the post-communist public culture, a testimony to the fact that they were echoing, at least at the time, accepted norms.

Of course, all of these actors were entitled to have their concerns taken seriously. At the same time, the cultural style of their public airing was characterised by an intemperate emotional tone, and the sense that problems were great and resources nearly non-existent. The mood seemed to be one of exasperation, fear and despair. The abundance of such messages can create the impression that all problems are of the same order, and priorities are impossible to establish.[4]

It can be surmised that the meaning and uses of this 'wailing' depends on the sensibilities of those involved. For the savvy operators, this could be simply part of the ritual of establishing trust and getting on with the business of requiring and accepting favours. For some journalists this type of discourse has become a matter of professional reputation. For the unwary (foreign) observer, if inclined to assume that people say what they think and think what they say, the effect can be bewildering indeed. Changes in language were in time made possible by substantial learning on the part of politicians, who began to acquire the conventional skills that also reflected a certain structuration of the political field.

Reform and other actors

Observers of Romanian politics often despair of making sense of its seeming lack of consistency and coherence. Romania was in danger of becoming the 'land of perpetual potential', according to David Garner, the head of Citibank's operations in Bucharest (Wagstyl and Marsh 1998, 1). A prominent Romanian political analyst also believed that the first ten years of post-communist transformations told the story of 'how to succeed in blocking reforms' (Şandor, 1999), while another found it necessary to ask: 'can the vicious circle be broken?' (Şerbănescu 1999).

Such statements reflect the sense that Romania failed to achieve swift progress in political and economic reform. As knowledge claims about reality, their truth could be, in principle, evaluated to see whether they match the facts. Here, the interest is to note that through their style – the affirmations are not qualified but rather absolute – they participate in the cultural patterns described above. And indeed, the presence of such patterns can be easily documented. At every stage of the reform process, each of the measures described at length in chapters 3–5 were adopted in a 'storming' style. The main elements in this scenario were a long delay in dealing with an issue, a sudden sense of imminent crisis, heroic mobilisation, new opposition from 'intractable enemies', and finally, a degree of success in implementation.[5]

But although these crises were resolved as well as could be expected, this was rarely seen as a success, albeit a relative one. Instead, the overwhelming sense of dissatisfaction fuelled by unreasonable expectations would be temporarily resolved by a sort of retreat from dealing with issues. After a while, as problems became urgent again, the cycle would start anew. In other words, for many of the local public actors – politicians as well as journalists, unions, and other interest groups, 'revolutionary politics' is 'politics as usual'. The old frame – of absolute imperatives, heroic efforts, and ultimate failure seemed to creep in more often than not.

Metaphors of war and destruction, danger and imminent dissolution abounded in accounts of political and economic affairs in the national press.

'An aggression without precedent against the small private enterprises' was the headline for an article about a meeting of private entrepreneurs at the Romanian Chamber for Commerce and Industry (Rus 1997). The main points of complaint were recorded in the sub-titles: 'artificial taxes in a legislative disorder impossible to describe'; 'where can we go? Nobody gives us any facilities'; 'an aberration: to borrow in order to pay taxes'; 'let the minister come to our door, it is us who keep the country running'; and 'everybody is right, but nobody takes any action' (Rus 1997).

Other alarmist titles read: 'the policy of destroying the Romanian economy continues: Now it is the turn of the producers of machinery for the oil industry' (Pârvu 1997); private entrepreneurs found that 'the business world [existed] between political demagoguery and entrepreneurial pragmatism' (Dimofte 1997). In a survey of opinions in the private sector, it was concluded that 'the management of small enterprises [was] in turmoil'. It was said that: 'the private entrepreneurs are destined to disappear'; the entrepreneurs and the government are in 'a dialogue of the deaf'; and 'the indifference of the administration kills private initiative' (*Adevărul Economic* June 6–12, 1997).[6]

The National Bank of Romania also attracted a fair amount of heated controversy. A new law on banking supervision supposedly gave the BNR *'puterea să taie şi să spânzure'* ('the power to cut and hang' – the power to do anything it pleases). Although these powers were normal for a central bank, the other bankers were said to be afraid that sanctions would be applied 'subjectively' (Constantin 1998, 33). Frequent communications by the BNR sought to restore some calm in the face of claims by newspapers that 'the banks are empty', prompted at one point by cash-flow problems at one of the smaller banks, Albina (BNR 1999b).

Not only the general public, but the banks in difficulty seemed prone to blame the BNR for not rescuing them, as was the case with Albina, Dacia Felix and Credit Bank (BNR 1997b, 105–108; Vasilescu 1999). The whole of the banking system came under 'tough' criticism from the Liberal Party in June 1999. Its vice-president, Dinu Patriciu, thought that the banking system was 'structured wrongly, in the form of a pyramid', with the BNR as its 'apex'. The BNR was the 'mother' that smothered the rest of the banks because it combined two functions: supervision of the banking system and control over monetary policy. In his opinion, the two functions should be separated. Others in the meeting, while not contradicting this view, also explained that banks have to take responsibility for the loans they grant (quoted in Vasiliu and Vasiliu 1999, 12).

Ownership and privatisation

The contradictions and inconsistencies produced by the maximalist, heroic mode of thinking of the communist ideology also impacted on the area of ownership. The generic norms related to ownership shaped expectations and behaviour about the possession of and responsibility for material goods as well as feelings and desires. The communist ideology had portrayed ownership as shameful. It was also dangerous and layers of deception and social gamesmanship protected it. The ability to disown one's feelings, intentions, and deeds was crucial to survival in an environment where the acceptable norms of being were the concern of state ideology. Equally, the communist culture gave prominence to the role of moral prosecutor. Initially the monopoly of the Party, this role became a device for social conformity, as individuals learned to police themselves and each other (Kharkhordin 1995). After the communists lost power, the appeal of this role remained and it added to the usual collective action problems, as will be illustrated for the political scene in the 1990s.

These intractable dilemmas created by maximalist moral expectations were reflected in uneasy juxtapositions of perceptions and facts in opinion surveys.[7] In the crucial matter of social self-perception, for instance, the great majority (63 per cent) of respondents to a nationally representative survey conducted by the Centre for Urban and Regional Sociology (CURS) in 1997 said that they belonged to the middle class.[8] Only 2 per cent believed they were upper class, 28 per cent believed they were lower class and 7 per cent did not know the answer to this question.[9] The most common criterion used in making this choice was monthly family income (46 per cent), followed by own income (17 per cent), profession (13 per cent), home possessions (11 per cent), education (7 per cent) and connections (3 per cent) (CURS 1997, 46–7). Home ownership did not feature as a distinct option, although 89 per cent of those interviewed owned a house and 5 per cent owned two houses. 53 per cent of respondents also owned a piece of land, although the majority of these (67 per cent) were small plots up to one hectare. Thus, social class was not understood in relation to material possessions but the older status symbols.

Given the importance afforded to monthly income, it is perhaps understandable that the respondents to this survey found government performance at its lowest when it came to salaries. Only 13 per cent were satisfied, while an overwhelming 85 per cent were dissatisfied (CURS 1997, 32). At the same time the self-perceived social status did not seem directly related to another set of answers, to the question of 'How do you appreciate your family income?'. The majority (40 per cent) of those interviewed, thought that they had just enough for the basic needs. Only 22 per cent had enough for a decent life (a standard one might think describes the middle classes), without being able to buy expensive goods. Even fewer, 5 per cent in June 1997 (with a highest number of 9 per cent in March and September 1997), were able to buy expensive goods, if they saved for it. At the highest end, those who were able to buy anything they needed without any effort, represented 1 per cent of the respondents, while the lowest category, those whose income was not sufficient even for their basic needs represented about 30 per cent of the population (CURS 1997, 17–18).[10]

There were a number of other inconsistencies in the responses, which testify, perhaps, to ambivalence in the attitudes and behaviours of the population. For instance, to the question of what they would do if they came to possess a great sum of money, many chose saving in a bank (35 per cent) (CURS 1997, 48). At the same time, the banks were the institutions that received the lowest vote of trust. Only 23 per cent of those interviewed had some trust in banks, while 61 per cent had little or very little trust (CURS 1997, 30). It seems that the public tolerated the contradiction between a certain picture of social and economic circumstances, usually quite negative, and their personal strategies of survival (Bulai 1999). This was confirmed by the reverse situation: the institutions and values they gave lip service to were not necessarily adhered to in practice. For instance, the army was trusted by 83 per cent and the Church by 85 per cent of the respondents, while the national political institutions received scores between 10 and 20 per cent. But although the Church enjoyed the top position in the confidence vote, only 21 per cent of the respondents went to church often and only 7 per cent went very often. The percentages for those who went rarely and very rarely, were much higher, 39 per cent and 31 per cent respectively (CURS 1997, 45).

Similarly, Mungiu-Pippidi (2001) found that measures of 'subjective corruption' and measures of direct experience of corruption diverged significantly. Subjective perception of corruption was widespread. Thus 79 per cent of the Romanian respondents thought that most or almost all officials were corrupt (a statement given by 62.9 per cent of Bulgarians and 54.3 per cent of Slovaks surveyed). By comparison, only 13.7 per cent of Romanians always bribed in order to get things done (compared to 1.3 per cent in Bulgaria and 8.2 per cent in Slovakia). Occasional bribes were more common (53.4 per cent in Romania, 28.3 per cent in Bulgaria and 47.7 per cent in Slovakia). She also found that the most important determinant of the subjective perception of corruption was the lack of trust in the public administration and that most of those questioned did not demand fair treatment from the administration (Mungiu-Pippidi 2001, 2–7).

This conclusion is corroborated by the results of a survey sponsored by the World Bank, reported in Lupşan (2001b, 16). Although the perception of corruption was quite general across public institutions and categories of respondents, the source of this perception was rarely direct contact with public officials. Only between 11 per cent of the households and 27 per cent of the firms interviewed based their perception of corruption on direct experience with public officials. On the other hand, some other kind of personal experience was quoted by between 40 per cent of households and 56 per cent of firms, while the mass media influenced 100 per cent of the households and 75 per cent of the firms.

Co-participation in the problem but selective attribution of blame can be found in other situations, as well. For instance during the campaign of the National Railway Company in May 2001 to crack down on the practice of travelling without tickets, more than a thousand passengers were found without tickets in one commuter train to Bucharest. The excuses offered vacillated between special pleading (poverty, inability to pay) and accusations about the poor quality of the service (Popa 2001). Thus, two attitudes, disinclination to assume responsibility and great expectations about the performance of others, were held concomitantly. A similar pattern was observed in the feedback to the World Bank's recent draft country assistance strategy for Romania. Realistic diagnosis of problems, such as distrust as the source of difficulty in creating alliances in politics and business, sat side by side with demands that the government should resolve the problems identified. Thus,

> Despite their readily acknowledged distrust of Government, participants [in the consultation over the country assistance strategy] consistently made it clear that they expect the Government to solve their problems. They typically did not recognise the ability that they might already have as private citizens or as private sector firms to mobilise and to act on their own behalf. The participants generally did not feel empowered to improve their situation and instead felt it was up to the Government, i.e. the same Government they distrust. (World Bank 2001a, chapter 8, 2)

This could be a part of a cluster of attitudes that reflect lack of self-confidence and reluctance to assume responsibility. In the November 2000 CURS poll, 74 per cent of respondents favoured the combination of job security and low pay over less job security and higher pay. At the same time, 67 per cent thought that only the one who risks wins (CURS 2000, 37). This split between the choice for a certain course of action and the concomitant disavowal of it mirrors the dilemmas created by living under the communist regime. There, informal practices of survival were embraced of necessity, and yet the public and the regime deemed them illegitimate.[11] In the post-communist period, it seems to be equally difficult to align declared value choices with practical choices of concrete action.

The debates around the privatisation of SOEs bore the stamp of these contradictions. Privatisation was always going to be a difficult operation. As will be shown in Chapter 3, the antagonism between parties complicated the decision-making process. It was not accepted, for instance, that certain trade-offs were inevitable. That privatisation could be rapid, but not deep, or it could be deep but not rapid. That it could favour workers and management, but this would affect the availability of resources for restructuring. That the participation of all Romanian citizens in the privatisation schemes across thousands of enterprises satisfied concerns for social justice and it involved the whole population in the new capitalist economy. At the same time, privatisation imposed costs in terms of time, as the institutions needed to implement the scheme were set up from scratch.

Public opinion surveys also reveal a diversity of reactions towards privatisation. Fears that it would lead to increased unemployment were paramount. More than 56 per cent of the working population was employed in the private sector in 1999 (of which about two-thirds were in agriculture), but the state sector still employed about 41 per cent of the labour force (CURS 1999, 11–13). The general perception (about 96 per cent of respondents in a survey conducted in 1999) was that there were no or very few job vacancies. About 53 per cent of respondents feared that they would lose their job in the near future (CURS 1999, 15). Among those who became unemployed in the six months prior to this survey, 52 per cent looked for a job without finding one, 32 per cent did not do anything, and only 9 per cent followed a training course and 4 per cent started a business in the informal economy (CURS 1999, 19). Of those who had a job at the time of the survey, many more expressed the intention to obtain a new qualification (39 per cent), look for another job (36 per cent), or start a new business (19 per cent). In addition 22 per cent of respondents said they would accept redundancy packages.

There was no straightforward solution to the difficult economic situation. There was broad agreement throughout the 1990s that economic reform was the main issue for the country and that a market economy was desirable (CURS 2001, 3–5). Also, loss-making SOEs were seen as the cause of economic difficulties. However, the support for their swift privatisation decreased from 76 per cent of the population in 1991 to 46 per cent in 1999 (CURS 2001, 5–6), largely due to fears about unemployment (CURS 2001, 18–9). More than 50 per cent of the respondents also thought that the state should continue to support these enterprises through direct payments (CURS 2001, 15). At the same time, the perception that the government was failing to deal with this issue augmented the general distrust in its capacity to provide leadership. The percentage of those who expressed distrust in the government grew from an already high 48 per cent in March 1997 to 60 per cent in March 1999 (CURS 1999, 18).

Also, there was suspicion that the privatisation deals were skewed in favour of politicians and foreigners. In June 1998, 66 per cent of the respondents believed that privatisation of the Romanian economy was most often dishonest, and only 10 per cent said the deals were honest more often than not (CURS 2001, 8). Foreign businessmen were considered to benefit most from privatisation by 26 per cent of the respondents, while 24 per cent thought that it was the local politicians, and 19 per cent the enterprise managers, who were favoured in the process. Only 9 per cent of the respondents expressed the view that privatisation benefited the whole Romanian population and even fewer, 2 per cent, saw the workers as the main beneficiaries (CURS 2001, 9). In spite of this, most people saw privatisation most of the time as proceeding too slowly, with the exception of the period in 1995–96 when the mass privatisation programme took place. About 67 per cent had this perception in September 1998 and 65 per cent in August 2000 (CURS 2001, 11).

This combination of views shows that privatisation was desired by virtue of its positive impact, i.e. increase in economic activity and the general standard of living. At the same time, its immediate negative consequences, such as the exit of certain enterprises, unemployment, etc. were feared.[12] The leadership role of the government was thus all the more important in creating the view and giving material reassurance that there would be a workable trade-off in the short-term between advantages and disadvantages. But this ability to reconcile opposing views was hampered by the oppositionist ethos of the political class and the post-communist culture.

This difficulty was also a feature of the press reports on privatisation. They tended to concentrate on corruption and the conflicting interests of those involved. The State Ownership Fund (FSP) in charge of privatisation and the government, individual civil servants or parliamentarians, came under close scrutiny, an exercise no doubt necessary in a fledgling democracy. However, the press also tended to represent their reports as though guilt was already established. Investigative journalism consisted of publication of confidential documents, usually taken as conclusive proof, or leaked information about police investigations that might or might not lead to prosecution.[13] The inclination to assume corruption everywhere reflects the old fear about the all-powerful, pervasive and coercive socialist state (Verdery 1996, 219). Thus, the 'evil eye' remained a more powerful metaphor than the 'hidden hand' (Jowitt 1998b, 100). Journalists did not take sufficiently seriously the difference between accusation and judicial sentence and the role of the courts in establishing the truth.

Accounts of conflicts of interest over the privatisation deals also reflected the difficulty of coming down consistently on one or the other side of the argument, or finding a way to take account of all views involved. For instance, worker unrest was generally approved of as expressing genuine grievances to which the government should find solutions. At the same time the government was blamed for lack of firmness in dealing with strikes and allowing some interests to prevail in the conduct of economic policy.[14]

On the other side of this fence, there was little attempt on the part of the government or the FPS to create a communications strategy on privatisation. Even the most basic information was either not assembled or it was not put across in a systematic manner. The FPS produced in 1993 and 1994 the annual reports to parliament, as required by law, but the reports were not publicised, and the practice was discontinued as the government took charge of the process in 1995–96 (Blaga 1994b; Earle and Telegdy 1998). The first annual report addressed to the public was produced in 2000 (FPS 2000b). In May 2001, the Authority for Privatisation, which replaced the FPS, started issuing twice-monthly bulletins, posted on their website.[15]

These difficulties reflect the enduring influence of the unrealistic model of action inherited from the communist culture that created both sporadic mobilisations on a grand scale and fear and a predilection to take on the familiar role of moral prosecutor. One path towards the removal of the sense of illegitimacy, self-doubt and lack of dignity that it generates would be the acceptance that this was not a useful or productive guide to action. Values such as respect for individual choice and the effort of dealing with very difficult circumstances of complex personal, professional, and social change would also have to be affirmed.

This would allow a contraction of the domain regulated by the excessive formal rules and expectations inherited from the communist culture, and would lead to a more consistent application of the rules that remain. It would also allow for a clearer definition of the role of the judiciary, and impose restraints on the assumptions of culpability with which the press and the public often operate. Time, a broader pool of experience on which to draw, the self-confidence that comes from success, accumulation of reflective and technical knowledge on the problems of the society will, barring some unpredictable catastrophe, gradually move society in this direction. Increased contact with other cultures is also an important resource in this process of creating a more balanced cultural model of action.

Technical knowledge and cultural change

Along with evidence of the persistence of the heroic model of action and inappropriate informality, accumulation of knowledge and expertise also took place. Side by side with articles in the dramatic style described above, there were others focusing on presenting information about new initiatives, projects, and events, which testified to a gradual process of professionalisation of at least parts of the press. In spite of this, the sense of a lack of grip on the overall picture was quite stubborn. Mihai Coman, a former Dean of the School for Journalism in Bucharest, described this by saying that the information disseminated by the press was not 'explained' (Striblea 2001, 9). Indeed, issues tended to be treated from one point of view at the time. Points of view could be juxtaposed (for instance Păis 1999), but as a rule, examples of articles that explored and integrated a variety of considerations were still rare (one example was Glăvan 1999).

The production of economic, political and cultural analyses increased significantly after 1990. This new social space had a number of features. The field was initially dominated by humanists, who had had some room for development under the communist regime. They were an important political force after the 1990s and had a gate-keeping role in creating a representation of the state of affairs in the country, both internally and in relation to foreign agencies and donors. Their position was similar to those of other local groups in the region which channelled foreign aid (Wedel 1998). Their lack of social science training encouraged a propensity towards sweeping, usually negative judgements about the state of the society and the economy, and a preference for metaphor at the expense of analysis.[16] It cultivated an uncompromising style based on essentialist and elitist ideas, of conservative and libertarian inspiration (Miroiu 2000a; Antohi 2001).[17]

In sociology, commercial opportunity stimulated the swift expansion of polling services. The development of a framework for the analysis of regional variations within Romania, originally funded by the European Community, later underpinned the regional policies of the state and other aid programmes. The few works on reform by Romanian sociologists did not break, initially, with the inclination in the wider culture to delegitimise the political sphere and the state. For instance, Pasti (1995, 220–233) analysed the parties at the periphery of the political spectrum by linking them to specific social interests. The major parties, however, were treated outside of that social context, as though they had self-willed themselves into existence, only to end up floating freely and ineffectually above the 'the real problems' and the 'power system' of the country. More recently, social science publications have become more research-led and less ideological.[18]

The contributions of economists to the setting up of new institutions and the formulation of policy were also significant. Although some of their works still had the character of exercises in taking stock of certain ideas and theories, there was a greater effort to understand the marketisation of the Romanian economy.[19] Romania did not have a powerful neo-liberal community of economists prior to the transition, on the scale of the Balcerowicz or Klaus teams in Poland and the Czech Republic. Even the most liberal economists, whose publication, *Oeconomica,* was endorsed by the Yale economist and student of the Romanian economy John Michael Montias,[20] were of neo-institutionalist persuasion. For instance, economic restructuring was seen as the main problem and priority for Romania and it was supposed to be state-led (Pilat 1995).

The impact of this group was not felt immediately after December 1989. The BNR, which had concentrated a number of these economists, began to play an active role in shaping both the banking system and the monetary policy after the launch of the reform programme in November 1990.[21] As shown in Chapter 5, BNR took a few years to gain and consolidate its independent status. According to Pilat (1993a), the idea of organising the commodities exchange was initiated at the end of 1991 by Daniel Dăianu, fresh from a stint of research at Harvard University, and was finalised a year later. Another member of this group, Ionel Blaga, was chairman of the parliamentary committee that promoted the privatisation law of 1991 and went on to head the Private Ownership Fund IV – Muntenia (Stoenescu 1994).

This section has illustrated the persistence of certain schemes of perception used to organise expectations and assessment of actions cemented during the communist rule. Storming, heroism, and unlicensed criticism co-existed with gradual consolidation of technical frameworks for the understanding of current social phenomena, such as those produced by the social sciences.

Conclusion

The heroic model of action on which the communist culture was based, backed by the ability of the Party to socialise this model through violence and control over society during more than four decades, had a lasting impact on society. In Romania, the modality of the transition, where the emblematic hero, the Party, failed to take responsibility for its actions and did not relinquish its formal claims, compounded the difficulties of leaving this model of action behind. It can be seen to be at work in the instability and the absolute character of the evaluations on political and economic reform, and in the fragility of many of the political alliances. Also, the inability to offer a vision of reform that can reconcile to a certain extent the conflicting interests of the state, the capital and labour is also a symptom of this.

However, this assessment has to be qualified by the recognition that over the last decade the freedom to experiment and reflect on these cultural norms led to a significant expansion of experience and vision. This has begun to erode the primacy of the heroic cultural model, as actors become more confident in their technical knowledge, and as some of the economic and political insecurities that characterised the beginning of the transition become at least partially resolved. While the values of liberal individualism that underpin Western market economies, such as self-confident actualisation but also fairness and co-operation are yet to gain a strong hold on Romanian culture, some significant steps have been taken.

Notes

1   In the broadest sense, culture is a collection of collectively held views, conscious or unconscious, that amount to a 'way of organising life, of thinking and of conceiving underlying assumptions about the family and the state, the economic system, and even of mankind' (Hall 1959, 23). It is not possible to enter here into an extensive discussion of how individuals and groups construct their reality. This analysis accepts the premise that experience and perceptions, as well as communications about one's environment, are already framed in a way that 'makes sense' socially (Goffman 1986); 'institutional facts' are created collectively (Searle 1995).

2   Hall (1959) suggests one way of understanding cultural change. He finds that different kinds of cultural beliefs – formal, informal and technical – acquire, through socialisation, different emotional overtones and tend to be lodged in different areas of consciousness; one kind of belief would tend to apply in a particular kind of situation, but the different cultural layers are independent of each other and satisfy different needs – for stability, for quiet, unobtrusive exploration of the possibilities in a situation, or for conscious, technical understanding. Changes in formal beliefs, otherwise the most stable and most deeply associated with interdiction and learning through powerful emotional sanctions, tend to appear sudden and radical because the social experimentation with new norms that goes on at the informal level has prepared the ground for the emergence of a new norm, that is then articulated and made explicit

through technical expertise. In the analysis of post-communist transformations, the concomitant removal of a great deal of formal norms, the coming to the fore of informal practices that used to be hidden and the expansion of expert knowledge occur at the same time and contribute to the impression of extraordinary effervescence and confusion. It would be impossible to trace a process as complex as change within all areas of the culture, so here the intention is to give the broadest contours of the process through reference to one that is especially relevant to politics: action in the public sphere. Thus, this analysis differs from others in that the emphasis is less on the particular beliefs that are said to constitute a 'totalitarian public consciousness' (Vainshtein 1994), or 'mental stereotypes' (Mihăilescu 1993) and more on the dynamics of change.

3 An additional example of political behaviour shaped by this formal model of action is given in Appendix 3.

4 Daniel Nelson (1988), an American scholar and writer on Romanian politics, observed during his visit to Bucharest in February 1998 that the use of the term 'political crisis' to describe the quarrels within the Ciorbea government was disproportionate to the real situation. As the democratic system was not in danger, the term 'crisis' was too strong. He went on to note the tendency of the media to use such notions loosely: the term crisis was applied to any negative occurrence, as though no gradations can be recognised between a catastrophe and more mundane difficulties (quoted in Patrichi 1998).

5 The reader will find additional examples presented in the next chapters: the sense of urgency in adopting the privatisation law of 1991, the long period of relative calm and apparent lack of activity in the subsequent years, the new mobilisation in 1995/6. Within the mass privatisation programme, most of the subscriptions of coupons against shares took place in the last month of the programme; the closure of Bancorex was decided in the last day allowed by the agreement with the IMF, etc. When the Democratic Convention gained power, the whole of the previous period was cast as one of non-reform, non-movement, and this was the justification for their radical programme.

6 Instances of this alarmist framing of issues are countless. See for instance Andarache (1996), Rădulescu (1997), Varvara (1998).

7 The significance of these results should not be overestimated, however. Surveys are very blunt instruments for exploring these issues because they cannot take account of the attributions that respondents make as to the meaning of the questions they are asked. However, they indicate that the observations about the press presented above might apply to the public as a whole.

8 In March 1995 the Soros Foundation for an Open Society in Romania launched a programme of public opinion research, which consisted of regular surveys using roughly the same set of questions but conducted by different polling agencies. In 1995 four, in 1996 and 1997 three such surveys were conducted. Since 1998 they have become biannual. Results of the newest poll are published together with comparative information from the previous years. Results were consistent across time. Unless otherwise specified, the results reported for 1997 can be assumed to be close to those from previous years.

9 The June 1997 poll was the last one available where the question on social class was asked.

10 The November 2000 poll showed a slight deterioration of this distribution. The poorest category, who cannot afford the minimum necessary represented 40 per cent, while 39 per cent said that they had enough to cover their minimum needs. Only 16

per cent thought they enjoyed a 'decent' standard of living, 4 per cent could buy some expensive goods occasionally, while 1 per cent could have anything they wanted (CURS 2000, 51).

11 The use of the survey information in support of this interpretation is only tentative. More sophisticated statistical procedures are needed to establish that both of these views were held by the same respondents. Based on this data, it is only possible to identify the minimum percentage of people that would have to hold both views, in order for the data to remain consistent with the fact that both series of answers were collected from the same people.

12 See for instance Bărbulescu (2001).

13 Examples are Mungiu and Pippidi (1994), Manoliu (1997), Teodorescu (1997), Davidică (1998), Halpert, Gălăteanu and Iacob (1998), Prahoveanu (1998), Ştefan (1998), Osman (1999), Paic (1999), Sădeanu (1999), Teleanu (1999), Antohe (2000), Nicolae and Diac (2000). They make frequent reference to 'mafias' and 'financial scheming' (*inginerii financiare*).

14 Here are a few recent articles in this vein: Antonescu (1997), Cercelescu (1998), Munteanu (1999), Veress (2001), *Capital* (1999c, 1999d, 1999e, 1999f, 1999g). Popescu (2001) is an exception; it applauds the firmness of the Năstase government, who refused get involved in a labour dispute in the private sector.

15 The internet address is www.autoritate-privatizare.ro.

16 See for instance early texts by Mungiu and Pippidi (1994). The mood of utter defeat and failure of the post-communist transformations and the country as a whole filtered through some works by sociologists as well, for instance Pasti, Miroiu and Codiţă(1997).

17 An example of this was Patapievici (1996). One of his arguments was that the Romanian people were not deserving of the right to vote and he advocated a return to an electoral system in which the right to vote was linked to property ownership and education. His arguments are analysed in Miroiu (1999, 126–133).

18 Examples are Zamfir, Bădescu and Zamfir (2000), Zamfir and Preda (2000), and Teşliuc, Pop and Teşliuc (2001).

19 Some of these works are cited in chapters 3 and 4.

20 His letter to SOREC (*Societatea Română de Economie* – Romanian Society for Economics) was published in *Oeconomica*, issue 3/1993. SOREC re-launched the journal after almost two years of interruption.

21 Among them were Mugur Isărescu, the governor of the Bank, and prime minister in 1999–2000, Daniel Dăianu, chief economist and minister of finance in 1997–98, Lucian Croitoru, member of the board, Eugen Rădulescu, head of the monetary policy division of the Bank and later Romania's representative to the IMF, and others.

3

Democratisation and the fragile political consensus

The recasting of the symbolic repertoire of politics, documented in the previous chapter, can be separated from the political struggles of the 1990s only for analytical reasons. In practice, the gradual shift towards new terms of evaluation occurred as political parties had to engage in the everyday business of constructing convincing identities and programmes, deciding on policies, contesting elections, building coalitions, learning how to handle the press and so on. The antagonism between the main political actors in Romania, FSN/PDSR on the one hand and the historical parties and the democratic opposition on the other, which lasted until the end of the 1990s, was reflected in and reinforced by the absolute expectations of the heroic model of politics. However, in the practical political activity during the decade the major political parties also forged a more realistic sense of politics and begin to confine themselves to conducting their debates within the tenor of 'normal politics'.

Romania was seen initially as a problematic candidate for democratic consolidation (Gilberg 1992; Linz and Stepan 1996). Its political parties and electoral process were declared a sham (Voicu 1996) with little actual power (Pasti 1995) or interest in providing leadership in the resolution of collective problems (Crăiuţu 1996). This chapter makes the argument that this evaluation reflects too rigid an application of neo-liberal norms of democracy. While it highlights the failings of the parties, it cannot account for their relative successes in mobilising the electorate and building a sense of their own identity.

The symbolic dimension of politics (Edelman 1964) is crucial to understanding how, in spite of the unpromising odds reviewed by Elster, Offe and Preuss (1998), political agency emerged in Romania in response to the needs of the public for leadership and reassurance. At the same time, as expected by Elster, Offe and Preuss (1998), the weakness of political agency was reflected in 'decree-ism' and hesitant delegation of authority to the subordinate levels.

Weber's (1994) analysis of the relationship between politics and ethics is also relevant for the empirical case of democratisation in post-communist Romania. The choice of holding ideas as ethical ends of political activity or subsuming ideals to an ethic of responsibility is a crucial determinant of the ability and willingness to negotiate differences with other groups. In Romania, the choice of the democratic opposition for an ethic of principled conviction led them to deny the right of their opponents to political existence.

Previous studies of post-communist Romanian politics, such as Gilberg (1992), Gallagher (1995), and Tismăneanu (1998), emphasised the negative side of symbolic politics by looking at the rise of nationalism and decrying the threat it posed to democracy. Indeed, liberal political theory contrasts the desirability of interest politics with the dangers of identity politics (Ost 1993; Offe 1997). In fact, the issue at stake is the degree of identification actors espouse in relation to ideas or interests, including ideas that are core to their identity claims, i.e. to their view of who they are. But in contrast to previous studies of democratisation in Romania, this analysis uses this Weberian insight to explain the structuring of the political system as a whole. The antagonistic relationship between the main political parties is considered the most important factor in the explanation of policies that others might see as nationalistic, neo-communist or anti-democratic.

The symbolic dimension of politics did not undermine democracy in Romania. Although this might have been impossible to anticipate at the beginning of the 1990s, by the end of this decade it can be argued that the democratic framework of rule had proved very robust. Successive elections and the experience of ruling tested the claims of the political parties and improved their political skills. The first section of this chapter documents this pattern of confrontation in the 1990s across a diversity of issue areas, while the second section focuses on privatisation.

Party politics in the 1990s: learning through participation in the democratic process

The initial structuring of Romanian politics presented in Chapter 1 continued to shape events during the 1990s. The grass roots mobilisation that was responsible for the Romanian revolution remained an important feature of the political landscape and materialised in frequent strikes and dramatic confrontations between state and labour. The ideological antagonism between parties became entrenched. Over time, however, as parties moved in and out of power, their claims were tested and this led to important adjustments in their alliances and their appeal to the electorate. The main features of these two trends are reviewed in this section: conflict and change within parties, in the relationship between successive governments, delays in parliamentary activity and the politicisation of state administration.

The prevalence of conflict over consensus can be traced in almost any area of political life in Romania in the 1990s (Stolojan 1999; Şerbănescu 1999). There was acute rivalry within parties, which led to frequent splits. For instance, the FSN split at the beginning of 1992, following the ousting of the Roman cabinet in September 1991. The parliamentary party sided with President Iliescu and was perceived as the conservative wing (Shafir 1992b; Ionescu 1992c; 1992e). Under the name of *Partidul Democraţiei Sociale din România* (Party of Social Democracy of Romania – PDSR) it won the elections of 1992 and formed a minority government. The FSN-Roman attracted some of the MPs and local organisations, but remained at the fringe of Romanian politics (Shafir 1993c). Under the name of *Partidul Democratic* (Democratic Party – PD), as part of the alliance *Uniunea Social Democrată* (Social Democratic Union – USD), it won about 13 per cent of the votes for both chambers in 1996 and entered a coalition government with the Democratic Convention during 1996–2000 (Popescu 1997, 181). In 2000, the PD obtained just over 7 per cent of the vote and decided to play the role of loyal opposition to the PDSR minority government.[1]

The opposition to the FSN/PDSR became organised in December 1991 in a broad coalition of 18 parties and civic organisation, under the name of *Convenţia Democrată din România* (Democratic Convention of Romania – CDR). Among their major internal debates were the nomination of a single candidate for the presidential elections in 1992 and 1996, electoral strategy, and the allocation of patronage (Shafir 1992e; 1992f). Its leading members were *Partidul Naţional Liberal* (National Liberal Party – PNL), *Partidul Naţional Ţărănesc, Creştin şi Democrat* (National Peasant Party Christian and Democratic – PNŢCD), and *Partidul Social Democrat din România* (Social Democratic Party of Romania – PSDR).

The Liberal Party experienced different splinters and factions, in and out of the Democratic Convention (Shafir 1992c). Differences arose around policy and electoral strategy between and within generations of politicians. The old guard (Radu Câmpeanu, Radu-Renée Policrat, Alexandru Paleologu, Mircea Ionescu Quintus) had been part of the Liberal Party prior to 1947. Younger liberals, mostly associated with business interests developed after 1990, found themselves in uneasy alliance with the old. After the 2000 elections, the latter consolidated their position, as some of the old leaders were blamed for the poor results. Prior to the elections, a recently established Commission for the Study of Securitate Archives revealed that some of the old leaders had been on the Securitate's payroll before 1989.

Similarly, the results in the elections of 2000 brought major changes to the PNŢCD and PSDR. After playing the leading role in the governing coalition in 1996–2000, the PNŢCD failed to obtain the required percentage of votes for entry into the parliament and is now in danger of disappearing from the political scene. After this defeat, a younger generation of politicians replaced the old guard of former political prisoners but an acrimonious leadership struggle developed between the main contenders: Victor Ciorbea, a former prime minister, and Andrei Marga, a former secretary for education (Ştefan-Scalat 2001).

PSDR participated in the 2000 elections on common lists with PDSR and the two parties merged in June 2001 to form the Social Democratic Party (PSD). PDSR was apparently seeking to shrug off its neo-communist image and bolster its social-democratic claims. The merger was seen as a way of reviving its 1993 application to the Socialist International, an organisation in which its junior partner was a member. The younger leaders of former PSDR supported the move, but old-guard leader Sergiu Cunescu saw it as a victory for 'communism' (Luca 2001)

Even *Uniunea Democrată a Magharilor din România* (Democratic Union of Hungarians in Romania – UDMR), which could count on a stable electoral base in the Hungarian minority, had their fair share of internal conflict between moderate and extremist nationalist and anti-communist factions (Shafir 1993a). This did not lead to a split, however. Their need to safeguard their culture, especially through education in Hungarian and rights to local autonomy for the Hungarian regions gained some recognition in the later part of the decade, when they co-operated in government with the Democratic Convention (Crăiuţu 1995). In the 2000–2004 parliament UDMR co-operated with the PSD government.

Romanian nationalist parties were *Partidul Unităţii Naţionale Române* (Party of Romanian National Unity – PUNR) and *Partidul România Mare* (Greater Romania Party – PRM). The main success of the PUNR was the election of its leader, Gheorghe Funar, as mayor of Cluj-Napoca, one of the major cities of Transylvania (Gallagher 1992a, 1992b, 1993, 1994). PUNR and PRM participated in government with the PDSR between 1992 and 1996, after the Democratic Convention refused the offer to create a coalition government with PDSR. In the November 2000 elections, PUNR did not earn any seats. PRM, however, was able to concentrate the nationalist vote and won an unexpected 20 per cent of the seats in both chambers. They capitalised on the dissatisfaction with the infighting within the ruling coalition and the poor economic performance in 1997–99, but were relatively isolated in the parliament.

Thus, at the end of the decade, after numerous splits and adjustments within individual parties, the party system appeared consolidated. PSD occupied the left-centre ground, while PNL and PD took up the centre-right positions. There were also two nationalistic parties, of which the moderate Hungarian party had an economic agenda close to PNL and PD. Given the affinities between the PD and PNL, a fusion should be possible, if personal ambitions can be reconciled (Miroiu 2000c).

Conflict was also a feature of the relationship between successive governments. Each government attempted to deny previous achievements and to present itself as the first to engage in serious reforms. Dissension within the

FSN, as mentioned above, came to the surface in September 1991, when President Iliescu accepted the resignation of Prime Minister Petre Roman and this led to a split in early 1992 (Shafir 1992a). After the victory of the conservative wing in the FSN, the PDSR, in the 1992 elections, the Văcăroiu Government seemed distrustful of the legislation and the international agreements passed earlier and proceeded to re-evaluate issues from scratch (Ionescu 1993a; World Bank 1996, 14–15).

The Democratic Convention on the other hand, refused to enter into an alliance with the Văcăroiu government. The choice of the CDR to bet on the failure of Văcăroiu and early elections was motivated less by differences in their reform agenda and more by the CDR's commitment to the ethic of principled conviction described above and the oppositionist stance it involved (Şerbănescu 1993). This left Văcăroiu with the costly option of having to rely on a coalition with the Romanian nationalist parties (Shafir 1992h; Fischer 1996, 204). The consequence was a great deal of delay and horse trading in ministerial positions (Shafir 1993d; Shafir and Ionescu 1993; 1994; Ionescu and Shafir 1994). Participation in government also gave nationalist parties a platform for the inflammation of nationalist sentiment and disputes (Shafir 1994b; 1994c). The economic reform programme was delayed as a consequence and the government lost credibility externally.

Similarly, after years of passionate opposition to what they saw as 'neo-communist' non-reformers, the CDR government vowed to finally give a strong start to reform when they came to power in 1996. Their critique of the PDSR had been that the reform was slow and that it had serious social costs. The Convention's electoral promise was both swift reform and social protection. But without a vision of how these two objectives could be reconciled (Mungiu 1996; Tismăneanu 1996b, 18–19), the alliance between CDR and PD came under pressure. During 1996–2000, changes in the top positions of government, prime ministers, secretaries of state and ministers, were the major outlets for these conflicts between reformers and those more mindful of public opinion, as the economic situation deteriorated sharply between 1997 and 1999.

The PSD government in power in 2000–4 avoided some of these problems by taking sole responsibility for forming the cabinet and seeking a principled agreement with the Democratic, Liberal and Hungarian Parties. One of their major proposals was a change in the constitution that would remove the duplication between chambers and differentiate their roles. Difficulties surfaced again, in May 2001, when the Liberal Party withdrew from the agreement, accusing PSD of disrespect for private property and for slowing down the reform in justice and privatisation (Gheorghiu 2001). Another issue that generated strain between the Romanian political parties was the initiative in July 2001 of the Hungarian government to give Hungarians who lived in the neighbouring countries selective access to the labour market, education and health services in Hungary. While the

Hungarian Party in Romania was favourable to the law, the other parties saw it as a cheap way to attract the loyalty of the Romanian Hungarians, without incurring the full responsibilities of giving them Hungarian citizenship.

These difficulties within the executive branch of the government in Romania during the 1990s were also reflected in the slow pace of parliamentary activity. This effect was compounded by the duplication of responsibilities between the two chambers, the Senate and the House of Deputies. Governments tried to get around the parliament by issuing executive orders. According to the Constitution, the cabinet could adopt a law without discussion in parliament, if it was prepared to take a confidence vote. Another procedure was to issue legislation that would be discussed by the parliament at a later date. In spite of initial advantages, in the long term, this added to the legislative confusion; laws issued by the executive were modified by parliament a few months after coming into effect. According to official data from the Legislative Council, reported in Drăgotescu (1999), between December 1989 and May 1999 the cabinet and the parliament passed about 5,700 pieces of legislation, of which 1,900 were rescinded and 900 were seriously amended. Of the legislation issued in 1998 alone, 61 laws and ordinances were modified in the same year, while in the first part of 1999, 19 acts had the same fate.

The excessive politicisation of the state administration was also an issue of concern. Distrust in the predecessors and the need for party patronage led to the practice of replacing civil servants, and bringing in 'their own people' with every change of government. For instance, between 1992 and 1994, the government-appointed prefects dismissed 133 elected mayors and another 264 resigned of their own accord (EECR 1995a, 22). This was remedied in 1996 when CDR imposed an amendment to the law on local public administration that forbade prefects to dismiss mayors (EECR 1996b, 20). After coming to power later in the year, however, CDR argued that selective dismissals were inevitable, due to the 'years of cronyism, patronage and partisan appointments, by means of which PDSR staffed all government agencies with loyal supporters' (EECR 1997a, 23). Similarly, in 1998, when Radu Vasile replaced Victor Ciorbea in the post of prime minister, partisan appointments followed for the top management of the FPS (EECR 1998c, 29).

It has become apparent that both conflict and a degree of reconciliation characterised Romanian politics in the 1990s. The clash between the uncompromising ideological position of the democratic opposition in relation to the culpability for the communist regime and the complexity of the practical problems left behind by this regime was acute. This choice can be explained through the preferences of the leading members of the historical parties, former political prisoners and archenemies of communism, but also through their need to differentiate their message in a very crowded political field. Their opponents, on the other hand, were susceptible to this radical criticism and failed to make the kind of conciliatory gestures that might have attenuated the opposition.

These interlocking identity choices by the main political parties were expressed in the design of central institutions: the electoral system, the parliament, the relationship between the executive branch and the state administration. Thus, the sources of institutional design are found in the power relations between the leading political parties. This complements the neo-institutionalist analysis that stops short of explaining how institutions come into being. At the same time, the institutional element of politics is given here due consideration. Once established, institutions have a structuring power of their own. Only a shift in the focus of politics, from conflict to co-operation and 'ordinary politics' (Jowitt 1998a) – as seems to have been the case after the 2000 elections – might modify the underlying political relations between parties and create the alliances necessary for a change in constitution and institutional design.

In the next section, these themes will be illustrated with reference to a crucial area of economic policy: privatisation. In addition, while so far politics has been discussed in separation from the economy, this section explores one of the links between the two spheres, the quality of the leadership on economic matters provided by the political system.

The politics of privatisation

This section shows how the choices made by parties in regards to privatisation legislation reflect less their distinctive outlook on the economy and more their relationship of antagonism and opposition.

The parameters of the privatisation process were drawn in 1990–91, during the Roman government. Subsequent governments, especially Văcăroiu in 1995 and CDR in 1997–99 made some changes to it, but the fundamentals remained the same. For this reason the bulk of this presentation will be dedicated to a detailed analysis of the arguments marshalled by parties during the parliamentary debates around the 1991 law. Later developments will be reviewed more briefly to show to what extent parties departed from their initial positions.

Setting the scene: the first privatisation law, 1991

The commitment to privatisation was a central element in the political programmes of all parties in Romania, after 1990. Privatisation was deemed crucial for the development of a market economy and for achieving prosperity. The first FSN government, soon after coming to power in June 1990, announced it as a core part of its mandate and a first step in this direction was taken in the same year. Law 15 regarding the re-organisation of state enterprises in commercial corporations and *regies autonomes*, i.e. fully state-owned public utilities, stipulated that only the former were to be privatised. Thirty per cent of their social capital was to be distributed for free to all Romanian citizens above the age of 18 (MOR 98/1990).

A year later, the privatisation law 58/1991 set out the framework for privatisation still in use today. This framework incorporated the decisions taken by the 15/1990 law and constructed the mechanisms through which the divestment of state-property was achieved (MOR 169/1991). The practical and political questions were numerous. What was going to be privatised and how? Who were going to be the beneficiaries? How was privatisation going to contribute to the creation of a market economy? How were funds to be obtained for the start-up of the process?

The core elements of the design of the privatisation process put down in the draft law, created by the government with the help of the consultancy firm Coopers and Lybrand, included in the privatisation mandate only industrial enterprises reorganised as commercial corporations, which at that time represented just over 50 per cent of the value of all state property. All of these companies had been requested by the 15/1990 law to express their equity as social capital and to issue shares against its value. Law 58/1991 defined the ownership rights over these enterprises as shareholder rights and transferred them to two kinds of institutions, to be created in the near future (articles 6 and 24). The FPS, representing the nominal owner, the state, would own 70 per cent of the shares in all of these enterprises (article 24); the remaining 30 per cent would be distributed equally among five *Fonduri ale Proprietăţii Private* (Private Property Funds – FPPs) (article 6). The FPPs were to represent the actual owners, all Romanians citizens above the age of 18, who were issued with property certificates (article 15). The certificates had no nominal value initially. Their value was expressed simply as the ratio between the total value of the capital to be transferred (unknown at the time) and the number of people entitled to receive the certificates (article 15). Property certificates could be traded, could be exchanged for shares in commercial companies, or could be converted into shares in FPPs (article 3). De facto, in the initial stages of the process, the certificates were shares in the FPPs, although the FPPs did not have to pay any dividends for the first five years of their existence.

Some of the features of the FPPs were intended to create a market ethos among enterprises and citizens. The FPPs were to be run on a commercial basis, and had to show that they were making a profit (articles 10, 11, 25, and 26). Also, each of the citizens benefiting from this law was to own one certificate in each of the five FPPs, to facilitate comparison between their results, and to create information for further investment decisions. The FPS had to privatise around 10 per cent of its portfolio each year, in order to ensure a speedy divestment of state property and stimulate the development of the private sector (article 28). It was also hoped that the free transfer of 30 per cent of the capital to the population would stimulate further privatisation. To link ownership to incentives for increased economic performance, managers and workers were offered discounts for the purchase of shares in their own enterprises (articles 48, 49), and this privilege also applied for workers buying physical assets (articles 59 and 60).

Finally, a pilot programme of privatisation, scheduled to take place before the Funds became functional, and organised by *Agenţia Naţională de Privatizare* (National Agency for Privatisation – ANP) was to provide the finances for the setting up of the Funds (articles 42–45). This exercise would also allow the privatisers to obtain some concrete experience with the process: the selection and evaluation of enterprises to be privatised; the evaluation of the reaction of potential buyers; and that of the labour force and management.

The subsequent debates over the law, in both the Chamber of Deputies and the Senate, in the last two weeks of July 1991, revealed the controversial nature of these choices and scrutinised the economic, political, and moral arguments behind them. Deputies speaking for the opposition parties had four core concerns: (i) the scope of privatisation; (ii) the role of the FPPs; (iii) the role of the FPS; and (iv) the pilot programme. As will be shown, all of these issues have a bearing on the understanding of the role of the state in the economy, the mechanisms of market economy, and the interplay between the state and the market.

(i) The scope of privatisation

The privatisation programme was considered too restricted by the democratic opposition in two ways. Firstly, of all the state properties, only about 53 per cent were to be privatised; the other 47 per cent was incorporated in *regies autonomes*. This was problematic from an ethical perspective. The promised 30 per cent for free distribution would amount to only 16–17 per cent of all state property. This represented too little compensation for the citizens who, under communist mobilisation, created them (MOR 180/1991, 5, 15). At the same time, from the point of view of encouraging the emergence of markets, it was too little to counterbalance the effects of the delays that could be expected due to the intricate institutional structures required for the implementation of the law (MOR 178/1991, 11). This restricted free transfer of state property would create few resources for the development of the private sector and further privatisation (MOR 177/1991, 21, 23).

To answer this, the government gave a different twist to the same concern for social justice. While the question of the great share of *regies autonomes* in the economy was sidelined by invoking concerns of national interest, the 30 per cent was defended because it was an approximation of the percentage of profitable enterprises in the economy. As the rest would represent more or less valueless properties, their transfer to the public would have been unfair (MOR 180/1991, 3, 11).[2] Also, the sale of 70 per cent of the value of commercial companies was necessary to raise funds for investment (MOR 179/1991, 8), even though the expected revenues were small.

Secondly, the opposition parties – PNL, PNŢCD, and UDMR – wanted this law to clarify the question of reprivatisation, i.e. the return of the properties confiscated during the 1947–48 nationalisations to their original owners (MOR 178/1991, 20). This would be a gesture of redress for former injustice (MOR 179/1991, 23) and, given that most of the properties included in such a reprivatisation would be small, reprivatisation would stimulate the development of small and medium enterprises in the private sector (MOR 179/1991, 24). Privatisation programmes in Czechoslovakia, Hungary, and Poland, which started off by legislating reprivatisation, were invoked in support of this view (MOR 181/1991, 7).

Although the FSN recognised the validity of the ethical concerns behind this position, a variety of practical issues were adduced as arguments for leaving the issue for subsequent legislation. The increase in complexity and the lack of records for the properties nationalised would make the implementation of present law unwieldy (MOR 179/1991, 23–25, 27–28). From an ethical perspective, since reprivatisation was not included in the 'Law for the Redistribution of Farm Land' its inclusion in this law would create inequalities between the pre-communist owners (MOR 179/1991, 23–24).

Interestingly, there was consensus around the fact that such a measure would not cover, in any case, the big properties, and that there would be a threshold of value for the properties considered for return or compensation (MOR 179/1991, 23). This can be interpreted as reluctance on both sides to encourage inequality of wealth in society. While this is consistent with the social-democratic credentials of the FSN, for the historical parties it seems to reflect some unease around the question of their association with the interests of the pre-war capitalist class. Such an association was attributed to them by the FSN, and it presented a real danger of undermining their appeal to a public long influenced by the communist propaganda of equality and opposition to capitalist exploitation.

(ii) The role of the FPPs

The idea of organising the FPPs was also hotly debated. The government argued for practicality and the need for financial intermediation, as well as protection of the interests of the population. Privatisation of such a large number of companies for the 16 million estimated beneficiaries could not be done through a physical transfer of assets. Instead, the value of the companies had to be translated into shares, and some mechanism of conversion had to be designed to enable the citizen-owners to use certificates to obtain shares (MOR 184/1991, 3–6). Since the issuance of shares by all commercial companies and the distribution of certificates would take time, to make privatisation an immediate reality in actual corporate governance, the 30 per cent dedicated to free transfer was to be entrusted to these five financial companies (MOR 181/1991, 12–13; MOR 186/1991, 4).

The government also argued that this was a way of protecting the certificate owners against the danger of losing their property (MOR 179/1991, 11; MOR 181/1991, 11). For the opposition, privatisation through FPPs was a way of impeding the individual owners in the exercise of their rights, and it anticipated that this method would create little capital for further privatisation (MOR 186/1991, 4–6). The members of the first councils of administration, the governing bodies of the funds, were nominated by the government and approved by parliament (article 8). The only way owners of property certificates could intervene in the actual governance of the funds was through introducing a motion provided that the motion was signed by 10,000 shareholders (article 21).

The opposition feared the monopolistic dangers created by FPPs (in MOR 181/1991, 9) and wanted a stronger link between owners and the management of the enterprises (MOR 181/1991, 8). Clear value should be given to property certificates and they should be used directly to acquire shares in commercial companies (MOR 184/1991, 2–3). This would make the FPPs redundant and would allow more scope for the free play of market forces (MOR 181/1991, 8).

(iii) The role of the FPS

The organisation of the FPS was for the FSN government a way of giving institutional form to the different roles of the state. The functions of the state as the owner of property were entrusted to the FPS, while the government acted as an independent and fair actor in the economy, representing all economic interests (MOR 181/1991, 5; MOR 190/1991, 16). Leftist FSN MPs argued for a mixed economy. In this scenario, the FPS would allow the state to continue to support the public sector, which was crucial for a state-led developmental strategy focusing on education and investment in advanced, information-based industries (MOR 190/1991, 13–14). Even members of the liberal wing of the FSN conceded that the FPS would have a role in the management of the commercial companies. FPS was to be responsible for the restructuring and technological overhaul of some of its companies before attempting to sell them (MOR 177/1991, 8; MOR 190/1991, 15).

For the opposition, the creation of the FPS was not a guarantee that a change would occur in the way in which the state exercised its role in the governance of enterprises (MOR 180/1991, 4–6, 7–8). The FPS would only reproduce the current pattern of centralisation and would undermine the autonomy of the commercial enterprises (MOR 180/1991, 11–12, 15, 17). Instead, the initiative for privatisation should be left to enterprises (MOR 177/1991, 16; MOR 179/1991, 13–14).

Secondly, FSN argued, the FPS was necessary because the state administration, the economic ministries in particular, was likely to hijack the privatisation process and apply the laws in accordance with their entrenched (i.e. bureaucratic *cum* communist) practices (MOR 180/1991, 24; MOR 181/1991, 4–5). Rarely defined clearly – but presumably to do with lack of transparency, shady dealings, and incompetence – such ways were nonetheless unanimously vilified by both government and opposition. In spite of this suspicion of the motivation and the ability of the ministries, the opposition was more willing to contemplate the use of existing state bodies, such as the ANP, for the co-ordination of privatisation (MOR 182/1991, 2; MOR 179/1991, 13–14).

To alleviate fears about the potential for government corruption and over-centralisation, the FPS was put under parliamentary control. Its annual report and plan for privatisation were to be approved by parliament, but there was no direct control over its everyday activities (article 28). The members of the FPS council of administration were nominated in equal numbers by the government, the parliament and the president (articles 30 and 31). The statute of the fund and its internal regulations had to be approved by the government (article 33). The fund was exempt from paying tax on its profits and it was forbidden to make any payments to the state or local government budgets (article 38). This diffuse control over the FPS satisfied the need of the parties for equal control over privatisation, but it also weakened the FPS. Dan Marţian, the President of the Chamber of Deputies, remarked upon the connection between the parties' distrust of each other and this type of institutional design. He noted that the decisions on the control of the FPS reflected the fact that 'the suspicions, the controversies, the passions, the accusations, and the acrimony around this law were so great' (MOR 190/1991, 22).

(iv) The pilot privatisation programme
Finally, the discussion over the pilot programme brought into focus again the concerns over the fact that it was left to the state bureaucracy, through ANP, to organise it. This was perceived as a case of 'total lack of control' (MOR 178/1991, 9). This time it was the opposition that argued for some form of control of outcomes, to stop the most likely potential buyers, former nomenklatura, barons of the black economy, or foreign capital, from taking advantage of this opportunity (MOR 180/1991, 8; MOR 178/1991, 15). Another fear was that this programme would lead to the sale of the most attractive enterprises and this would deprive the rightful beneficiaries, the citizen-owners, of their entitlements (MOR 178/1991, 19, 22). As a consequence, this programme was reduced to 0.5 per cent of the total number of commercial companies (article 42).

Strikingly, although both contenders, the FSN government and the democractic opposition, claimed to promote privatisation as a means for systemic change and the development of a market economy, neither of them sided consistently with the market. The positions they supported were not inspired by a consistent view of what the role of the state and the market should be. When it argued for a restriction of the free transfer or the establishment of

FPPs, FSN promoted a view of the responsibility of the state that came close to controlling the outcomes of privatisation. The opposition was similarly inspired when it argued for scrapping the pilot programme.

Thus, the state was asked to provide excessive safeguards for the market-players. At the same time, its administration could not be trusted to implement the privatisation law. FSN seemed guided by a paternalistic sense of its duties towards its citizens, while the opposition had strong concerns about the ideology of the new economic winners. Both feared that foreign capital might acquire undue dominance over domestic interests. In this, the opposition contradicted its willingness to entrust the current state institutions with the management of the privatisation shown in the discussion over the FPS. The FSN's criticism of the state bureaucracy might have been an attempt to distance itself from accusations that it wanted to protect the incumbent, supposedly neo-communist, bureaucracy. The urgency of privatisation could have been an opportunity to push through the reform of public administration, but the two issues were de-linked by entrusting an alternative bureaucratic apparatus with the management of privatisation. This decision and the lack of progress with public administration reform had a significant impact on the implementation of the privatisation law, an issue that will be explored further in Chapters 4 and 5.

In relation to the market, the positions were equally ambivalent. Both FSN and the opposition agreed that the market was desirable as a mechanism for generating efficiency and wealth and both had some misgivings. They wanted to see the state intervene not only to provide safeguards in the form of rules, but also, at different junctures, to guarantee certain outcomes. None of the parties came out in defence of the survival of the fittest or the profit motive. However, the opposition was more consistently on the side of the market. This was the case when it argued for a broader scope for privatisation and less managed intermediation. At the same time, by rejecting the role of the intermediaries, it did not see the need for market forms that could accommodate sophisticated agent and principal relations inevitable in a complex economic system.

Does all this mean that the FSN was indeed anti-reformist, as the opposition claimed? And that, in spite of their formal commitment to change, the FSN acted to undermine it? The evidence is mixed. Government ministers certainly used the rhetoric of the market to argue for different points in the law and the mechanisms contained in the law, could, in principle, attain their declared objective. A number of practical conditions had to be met, however. Commercial enterprises had to be registered as corporations and a whole institutional framework, such as a stock exchange, was needed to facilitate the creation of markets for property certificates and shares. Even the counterproposals of the opposition, who wanted a stronger role for the ANP, the removal of the funds, and more free play for citizen-owners, depended on these conditions.

None of these conditions was in place at the time. The corporatisation of commercial enterprises was mandated by law 15/1990 and it should have been completed by the middle of 1991. However, this was not achieved due to practical difficulties. The 58/1991 law had to rescind the deadline set a year earlier. There was as yet no law for the establishment of a stock exchange. This law was enacted two years later and the Bucharest Stock Exchange opened in 1995.

To wait until the fulfilment of these conditions and postpone the legislation on privatisation would have created significant political risks for the FSN. By the middle of 1991 the pressure to deliver on their promise to reform the economy was very great indeed. Other CEE countries had achieved significant successes on this path. The comparison between Romania and these countries made by the international financial institutions (IFIs), the European Community and the Council of Europe was crucial for the recognition of Romania as a bona-fide member of the international community (MOR 188/1991, 4). The MPs clearly showed that they had internalised the norms promoted by these organisations – such as democracy, as well as principles of economic management, including privatisation. In fact, the perceived need to pass the law was intensified by past failings to conform. Up to that point the record for democracy and economic reform had been mixed, especially due to the gradual liberalisation of prices and foreign exchange and the perception that FSN was responsible for the vigilante actions of the miners in June 1990.

Thus, there was a clear sense in the speeches delivered by the members of both sides that passing this law was crucial for establishing the legitimacy of the government as bona-fide democrats and reformers (MOR 177/1991, 9; 178/1991, 11; MOR 179/1991, 12–13). The end of the parliamentary session was approaching and the time allowed by the law 15/1990 for creating a framework for privatisation was running out.

This pressure to pass the law was resisted by the opposition and the ensuing confrontation between the government and opposition tested the resilience of parliamentary rules. In the preliminary negotiations about the agenda for the last days of the parliamentary session, the opposition asked that the debate over the privatisation law be postponed (MOR 160/1991). When the law finally got on the agenda, the opposition parties, after presenting their criticism of the law, asked that the law be returned to a special parliamentary commission for further discussion, under the threat of not participating in the debates at all (MOR 177/1991, 1–4). After a few days of negotiations in the plenum of the parliament and behind the scenes, with mediation from President Iliescu, members of some of the parties (PNŢCD and PNL in particular) refused the compromise of allowing the commission a few more days for discussion. They did not participate in the debates (MOR 186/1991, 1–7) but returned for their conclusion to make scathing declarations over the law and the process (MOR 195/1991, 4–5). There were different

degrees of non-participation and discontent. Some deputies did not participate in the debates at all. Others participated in the debates but declined to
vote. These two groups numbered 130 deputies, out of 396. Others (10) voted
against the law, or abstained (9) (MOR 195/1991, 6).

Dissenting deputies and senators who declined to participate in the
discussion or the vote on the law did so, they claimed, because of substantive
disagreements with the law. They also objected to what they saw as the heavy-
handed approach of the government, whose majority guaranteed that it could
pass any law it wanted. It can only be surmised that, just as passing the law
was seen as a political necessity by the ruling party, the opposition used this
occasion for their own political ends. In this case, shock tactics, such as
leaving the chambers when the law was debated and non-participation in the
vote were attempts to portray the majority enjoyed by FSN as the privilege of
a bully and to undermine the effort of the FSN to establish their democratic
credentials. Leaders of the two chambers, the government advocates and
President Iliescu appreciated the importance of this point and would have
liked to obtain a compromise. But such a middle way was simply not good
enough politically for the historical parties, who were prepared to undermine
the credibility of parliamentary activities in order to affirm their uncompromising attitude towards their opponents.

At the end of two weeks of debate, the UDMR and the ecological group
which were part of the more moderate sections of the opposition secured the
approval of a few amendments to the law. Politically, this was an indication
of the willingness of the government to compromise and to try to induce the
opposition to express a view on the law and vote, even against it. Concretely,
pensioners became entitled to discounts for buying physical assets and the
right of first choice, if their offer was equal to the best offer (MOR 192/1991,
3–4). Members of the management were excluded from buying assets in order
to avoid conflicts of interests (MOR 192/1991, 14–16) and public officials
involved in privatisation had to declare their wealth at the beginning and the
end of their mandate (article 69). Requests that any buyer in the pilot
programme putting up a great sum of money should have to justify its source
were defeated (MOR 192/1991, 19).

Thus, the tensions inherent in the law reflected the economic, institutional and political constraints – or structural conditions – present in
Romania at the time. Privatisation involved a number of funds because of
the concentration of property in big enterprises and the lack of institutional
prerequisites for markets: the corporatisation of enterprises and the stock
exchange. Choices by actors also played a role. A parallel bureaucracy was
the preferred solution due to lack of trust in the existing state bureaucracy.
Most importantly, the law had to be passed as soon as possible, in spite of
practical difficulties and the stern rejection by the opposition, to buttress
the democratic claims of the FSN government and the international standing of the country. According to the political wisdom imparted by John

Redwood and quoted by the FSN, this was a case where 'any law was better than no law'.[3]

Appropriating privatisation: subsequent attempts to shape the process, 1995–99

Two months after the privatisation law was passed, the Roman cabinet was dismissed. The dismissal was caused by demonstrations by miners from Valea Jiului who came to Bucharest in September 1991 to protest against price increases and request better pay and working conditions. For a year, the caretaker government of Theodor Stolojan prepared the pilot privatisation programme. Given the weak institutional basis – further explored in Chapter 5 – and the political instability, this programme was not completed until late 1992. These conditions continued to prevail until the second year of Văcăroiu's mandate. In 1995, the legislative process resumed through the discussion of law 55/1995, which spelled out the mass privatisation component of the 1991 law and added some incentives for buyers outside this scheme (MOR 122/1995).

The influence of the Văcăroiu government on the privatisation process during this period was mixed. Increased dynamism went hand in hand with some reversals. After the issuance and the distribution of property certificates, in 1991–92, a market on these certificates developed very slowly, in spite of assistance from banks. Part of the reason was the lack of clarity about how certificates could be used to buy shares and what sort of profit they would provide. The only obvious outlet for them was the management-employees buyouts (MEBOs), the main method of privatisation at the time. The associations of workers and management could use certificates as part payment for the 30 per cent of shares owned by the FPPs.

A relative setback to these market-based beginnings was the decision of the government to re-value enterprises, in accordance with inflation, in 1994. This increased the book value of enterprises and made their sale more difficult. Another reversal was the decision to invalidate the spontaneous activity of concentration of certificates through buying and selling (Dochia 1994; Munteanu 1994b). The law for the acceleration of privatisation, law 55/1995, valued the certificates at 25,000 Romanian lei, a few times below their market value at the time (in the MEBO sales certificates had been valued at about 130,000 lei). In order to cancel what the government saw as the undeserved losses of those who had sold their certificates, supposedly out of ignorance, all the citizens who had not participated in MEBO transactions received new coupons worth 975,000 lei (articles 1 and 3).

Also, five more cohorts of Romanians, those who became 18 between December 1990 and December 1995, became entitled to receive coupons (article 2). A person could use his or her coupon for buying shares in only one company from the government's list. S/he could remain a shareholder in one FPP (soon to become *Societăţi de Investiţii Financiare*, Societies for Financial

Investment – SIF) (articles 2, 4, 6), or buy shares in the companies included in the programme (article 5). Shares in companies that were under-subscribed could be valued below the nominal price (article 2); up to 60 per cent of shares in a company could be exchanged against coupons (article 3).

The new law gave impetus to the programme, and by the end of the 1996 the free component of the privatisation programme was almost complete. The law also created incentives for buyers of shares offered in the privatisation process outside the mass privatisation scheme. The FPS was mandated to sell its shares as soon as possible. In order to facilitate this, up to 60 per cent of the proceeds of a sale could be returned to the buyer to extinguish any outstanding debts or to make investments in new technology (article 8). The scope of privatisation was extended to service providers for agriculture. Agricultural producers who had long-term commercial relations with these companies had the right of first-buy for up to 35 per cent of shares. A similar right, for first-buy for up to 20 per cent of shares in food processing plants, was accorded to agricultural producers who had long-term relationships with them (article 22).

The new law reflected the political predicament created for the PDSR by the fact that, having been shunned by the Democratic Convention, it ruled in coalition with the nationalist PUNR and PRM and the minor left-wing *Partidul Socialist al Muncii* (Socialist Labour Party – PSM). The competing pressures of realising privatisation and attaining wider social and ethical objectives were even more difficult to reconcile. For instance, a member of the PUNR led the Senate's Commission on privatisation and economic reform. When the Commission received the draft privatisation law, the chair of the commission ignored it and instead focused the debate on a draft law proposed by the PUNR, which was later defeated in the plenum of the Senate (Ştefoi-Sava 1995, 80). To buy off the opposition within its own coalition and pass the privatisation law, Văcăroiu reshuffled his cabinet for the fourth time. He gave the Socialist Labour Party two posts in the cabinet (culture and trade), PUNR members received posts of prefects and managers in the FPPs, and the PRM gained some ministerial posts (culture and tourism departments) (EECR 1995b, 21).

Like Văcăroiu, the CDR governments (1997–2000) attempted to put their own stamp on the process, and to this end made some changes that did not affect substantially its overall shape. The Ciorbea government aimed to increase the number of privatised companies. The first two pieces of legislation in the area of privatisation were passed under the governmental responsibility clause in May 1997 (EECR 1997b, 28–29).[4] The first, Ordinance 15/1997 (MOR 88/1997), put FPS under direct governmental control and spelt out again the methods of privatisation, conditions for sale, the responsibility of the different institutions involved and the destination of proceeds from privatisation. The local authorities could for the first time act as agents for privatisation, 20 per cent of sale receipts were to go to the budget (article

1) and the use of privatisation funds for restructuring was forbidden (article 9). The FPS was to complete its activities by 31 December 1998. The second major privatisation law passed in May 1997 was dedicated to the privatisation of banks (MOR 98/1997). In this case, the agents for privatisation were specially appointed commissions, who could use the services of the FPS and other agencies as technical consultants.

In December 1997, another urgent ordinance restated much of the same content. The main difference was that all proceeds from sales were to go to the state budget; the 60 per cent remittance to the buyer, to pay off debts and invest in new technology, was cancelled (article 9) (MOR 381/1997). The FPS was subordinated to a new Ministry for Privatisation (article 4), which lasted only one year, until December 1998, when its functions were again demoted to the rank of governmental agency (MOR 515/1998). As well as lending more authority to FPS, the responsibilities of its employees as persons were distinguished from those of FPS and judicial action against FPS was put under the authority of the regular courts (article 10). The FPS regional offices were put in charge of the privatisation of small and medium enterprises (article 8). In addition, the FPS could contract out some of its operations and could sell its shares without having to keep to a minimum price. The market price could be the sale price (article 13).

The emergency ordinance 88 was passed by the parliament under article 113 of the Constitution in December 1997. The debates within the coalition around this decision brought to the fore tensions that had accumulated during the year. Firstly, it was becoming clear that the liberalisation measures introduced in early 1997 had led to a deterioration of the economic situation, with inflation reaching 151 per cent and GDP falling by almost 7 per cent. Second, Ciorbea had backed down in the summer of 1997 when the announced closure of over twenty loss-making enterprises brought their workers into the streets. This setback undermined the image of the government as a determined reformer. The Democratic Party was trying to lay to blame for these events on Ciorbea's lack of decisiveness and his union connections. When faced with the decision to present the ordinance 88 on governmental responsibility, the Democratic Party had to choose between opposing the government and maintaining their pro-reform image. Although they went with the government on that occasion, resentment towards the manner in which the law was enacted fuelled a cabinet crisis (EECR 1998a, 29) that was resolved in April 1998 when Radu Vasile was appointed prime minister. In a moment of weakness, in March 1998, before accepting that he had to resign, Ciorbea had tried to summon parliamentary support from the erstwhile enemy, the PDSR, by offering concessions in regards to privatisation (EECR 1998b, 23–4).

Finally, the last major piece of legislation on privatisation, law 99/1999, was adopted in May that year under the same procedure of 'governmental responsibility'. The opposition filed a motion of no confidence – its nineteenth in just two and a half years – but it was defeated by 286 votes to 147 (EECR 1999b, 2). The content of this law simplified earlier legislation but did not introduce new elements, confirming the inclination of the Romanian governments to resort to legislation as a remedy for implementation difficulties, and the symptom of decree-ism identified by Elster, Offe and Preuss (1998). The Vasile government passed 220 emergency decrees in 1998 and 300 in the first eight months of 1999 (EECR 1999c, 1).

This review of the politics of privatisation in Romania in the 1990s shows that in spite of their claims to the contrary, all political parties had mixed views about the role of the state and the market in the new economy. The use by CDR of democracy and the market as ultimate ends obscured the similarities between parties and led to unnecessary confrontation between them. This ideological commitment of the CDR led to their blanket opposition to FSN/PDSR, while their practical policy decisions, while in opposition and in government, were contradictory. The rivalry between the PDSR and the CDR, and the alliance of the former with the nationalistic parties created difficulties for the reform programme of the Văcăroiu government between 1992 and 1996. In the second part of the decade, the failure of the allies within the Democratic Convention to reconcile the social-democratic and neo-liberal elements of their agenda put a serious strain on their ability to govern. In spite of this predominance of conflict over co-operation, all of these governments made significant progress towards the privatisation of state assets, as will be shown in the next chapter.

These findings support the point that an autonomous political factor, the antagonistic relationship between the political parties, explains why the leadership provided to economic reform was uneven.

Conclusion

This review of political events in Romania in the 1990s substantiates the empirical arguments about the structuring of the post-communist political system and its impact on economic reform. The sudden breakdown of the communist regime, grass roots mobilisation, the rejection of communism, and the void of power at the centre created a political agenda characterised by contradictory needs, for stability and for a radical break with the past. The political parties that emerged after the revolution politicised these needs in the form of an apparently irreconcilable conflict. Those who wanted a process of moral purification and the exclusion from political life of the former communists (the historical parties) could not reconcile their differences with those who were willing to compromise with the former establishment to buy social peace and pursue marketisation more slowly (the FSN). This antagonism between parties was reflected in the institutional design of the electoral and parliamentary systems (and privatisation), and coloured the alliances between parties and the debates around economic and foreign policy.

However, the democratic system proved robust during this decade. Parties went in and out of power and this tested their claims and led to a restructuring of the party system. The most dramatic events were the failure of PNŢCD to gain seats in the 2000–2004 parliament, the consolidation of the nationalistic left in the PRM, and the fusion between the PDSR and PSDR to form a stronger and possibly more legitimate social-democratic party, PSD. PNL and PD are now the main centre-right parties.

The review of privatisation policies illustrated the conceptions over the role of state and market of the parties. For both sides, it was found that inconsistencies existed in the way different aspects of the role of the state and market were evaluated. The democratic opposition was pleading more consistently for individual freedoms, but wanted to eliminate the possibility that a free market system might favour the former communist nomenklatura. The FSN was more concerned with ensuring equality of outcomes for citizens entitled to free shares. At the same time, they did not want to increase the overall share of state property that was to be distributed freely. Beyond this confrontation of ideas, the antagonism between parties surfaced in the shock tactics of stalling the passing of the law and attempts at de-legitimatising the parliamentary procedures.

Thus, on the one hand, the antagonism between parties was reflected in their rhetoric and their inability to create consensus around certain policies. It might have been expected that this antagonism would be justified by very different ideological positions, but this was not the case. Similarly, their record in office showed that both sides had to negotiate conflicting societal pressures. Domestically, there was the resistance of organised labour to reform (this will be explored further in Chapter 4) and the hostility of the political opponents. Internationally, the need to abide by the norms of democracy and market economy and to negotiate entry to NATO and EU was recognised by both, as will be discussed in Chapter 6.

The reason why these similarities led to conflict rather than co-operation is that the democratic opposition could not move out of its position of principled conviction. Their need to be the morally pure survivors of communism and the moral prosecutors of their adversaries who were deemed tainted by their association with that regime could not be satisfied through compromise. Ultimately, this position proved self-destructive. Absolute commitment to this view of who they were led them to take decisions contradictory to the values they espoused, simply because those decisions reaffirmed their fundamental opposition to the FSN/PDSR. This tension at the core of their identity could not survive the next test. When in office, the inability to govern effectively undermined their claim that moral purity is the most important qualification for effective political leadership.

Paradoxically, it was the robustness of the democratic system itself that allowed this evaluation to take place and offered a correction to the politics of absolute identity. In this sense, the liberal cautionary tale that identity politics is intrinsically dangerous does not hold. More generally, identities can be understood as definitions of self, whose meaning is continuously tested and renegotiated as new events pose new challenges, opportunities or threats (Wendt 1995; Castells 1997). Under these circumstances, resilient actors would be characterised by self-definitions that do not depend on a radical exclusion of others but are able to negotiate difference without losing one's voice or distinctiveness.

Notes

1   For the results of the 1990, 1992, 1996, and 2000 elections see Appendix 1.
2   There is a gap in the argument here, between saying that only 30 per cent of the enterprises are profitable and claiming that a transfer of their value would be approximated by giving away 30 per cent of the social capital of all commercial enterprises. This gap was not noted in the debates.
3   John Redwood, the UK Minister for Corporations in the Department of Trade and Industry, visited Romania in July 1991 while the privatisation law was being debated. He confirmed in a communication to the author that his view on the law and the debates around it was that 'the best was the enemy of the good'.
4   Under Article 113 of the constitution it was possible for the government to pass legislation by risking a no confidence motion. The parliament had three days to lodge a no confidence motion. If the motion was not introduced or did not carry, the legislation was considered passed.

4

From plan to market: reforming the socialist economy

The constitution of the economy as a sphere relatively autonomous from politics has been understood differently by different theories about post-communist transformations. Each of these theories offers prescriptions for the redefinition of the role of the state in the economy and the creation of new mechanisms for macro-economic intervention to supplant direct intervention through the plan. The dominant theory in early 1990s, neo-liberal economics, suggested that swift, radical changes in the economic environment would induce firms to adapt or disappear, and would create markets. Restructuring would occur both as a consequence of firms adjusting to competition and because markets would re-allocate resources from the declining to the competitive sectors. The overall effect would be enhanced economic performance. To create this new economic environment, the state was to introduce a number of policies: the liberalisation of all prices (including the price of money – credit and foreign exchange), stabilisation and the control of inflation, low budget deficits, and balance of payments equilibrium (Blanchard et al. 1991, 1993; Sachs 1993; Williamson 1994). Their prescription for change was 'shock therapy' – the introduction of all these measures at once to force the desired adaptive reaction on the part of enterprises and the economy.

Evolutionary economists also believed that markets were desirable mechanisms for allocating resources and encouraging innovation, but appreciated that firms rely on entrenched routines to co-ordinate the activities of their members. Change in these routines is costly: it takes time and it disrupts the production flow (Clague 1992; Murrell 1992). Systemic change, as in the case of the economies in CEE after 1990, creates a great deal of uncertainty and this complicates the firms' task to adapt. For this reason, the maintenance of state control over some enterprises and some mechanisms of direct control over the economy could offer a semblance of macro-economic stability

(Carlin and Mayer 1994). Definition of the new rules of the game, property rights and the rule of law, as well as the swift development of the new private sector should be the focus for reform, as well as liberalisation, competition, hard budget constraints and stabilisation (Rausser and Simon 1992; Olson 1992).

Economic sociologists take the insights of evolutionary economics further. The embeddedness of economic activity means that decisions are taken within relationships and networks (Granovetter 1985). In the post-communist context, Stark (1990, 1992), and Stark and Bruszt (1998) argue that enterprises will adapt to their new circumstances by using the relational assets they have in their networks. Good economic policy should encourage the use of these resources to enhance production and restructuring. At the level of the economy as a whole, Polanyi (1992) observed that the mechanism of economic integration is associated with a certain social structure and distribution of power in society. The implication of this is that systemic change, the change of the integration mechanism, in this case from plan to market, takes place together with a re-alignment in social structure.

In this chapter, it is argued that while the assessment of the neo-liberal economists – that the marketisation of the Romanian economy occurred only slowly – is valid, this theory does not explain why this is so. They simply blame politicians for not implementing a vigorous enough programme of reform (IMF 1996, 1997, 2000, 2001). In contrast, by using insights from evolutionary economics and economic sociology it can be established that structural imbalances in the Romanian economy at the end of 1989 were a major factor in explaining the pace of marketisation after the fall of communism.

Although the commitment to reform and to market principles of the political leaders was a factor, their room for manoeuvre, both in the political field, as shown in Chapter 3, and given the inherited economic conditions, was limited. This was the case even after 1996, when the Democratic convention governments adopted a neo-liberal reform agenda. For this reason, it can be argued that given these structural constraints within the economy, the size of the transformations required for the divestment of the state sector, restructuring and creation of macro-economic instruments of governance, the record of the Romanian post-communist governments is defensible.

The economic situation at the end of 1989 was presented in Chapter 1. In the following, I discuss the succession of economic policies during the 1990s in two policy areas, stabilisation and liberalisation, that provided the context for structural reform and privatisation. The second section then provides a detailed account of the privatisation process. The role of the international financial institutions in pushing through some of the economic policies in Romania is investigated in more detail in Chapter 6.

The context for structural reform: stop-and-go stabilisation and liberalisation[1]

The loss of power by the Romanian communist party in December 1989 was associated with wide-scale grass roots mobilisation in enterprises and an explosion of pent-up consumption demand (Pasti 1995, 102–104; Dăianu 1996a, 232). In the first few months of the 1990s, the provisional government scrambled to ensure some continuity of economic activity against this eruption of popular mobilisation (Iliescu 1990). Reliable knowledge about the particulars of different sectors and enterprises was scarce and the direct mechanisms for economic management came under increased pressure (Ionete 1993).

In this period of break with the old regime, of uncertainty at the top as to the new framework for governance and mobilisation from below, the direct controls of the ministries over enterprises were temporarily suspended. But the transformation of state owned enterprises (SOEs) from links in pre-planned chains of production into self-assertive and self-promoting enterprises guided by the market ethos of their managers and workers proved very difficult. The SOEs blamed the government for creating chaos in the economy and fell back upon the old links with the ministries to secure inputs and markets, a development consistent with the expectations of evolutionary economics and economic sociology.

Within firms the breakdown of the PCR was followed by the organisation of independent unions. These re-elected managers and asked for the reimbursement of the 'social contributions' extracted by Ceauşescu's regime in the 1980s, wage increases and the reduction of the working week to five days, even though the production and productivity levels were in decline. Little prepared to resist such pressures, the FSN provisional government granted these changes (Teodorescu 1991, 78–79). Labour mobilisation was a constant feature of the 1990s, especially in the heavy industries and the public utilities.[2] The antagonism between parties, documented in Chapter 3, made impossible a bi-partisan agreement on how to deal with this issue. On the contrary, political parties tried to use labour unrest to their advantage (Ronnas 1992; Shafir 1992a; Ionescu 1992b, 1993e; EECR 1999a).

Thus, in the struggle over property rights, the state failed to assert its role as the sole custodian of what had been the property of 'the entire people'. The unions pressed the legitimacy of their concerns in a climate favourable to their demands. The rejection of the communist regime was determined by its failure to live up to its own ideals; these ideals were re-affirmed when the grass roots mobilisation of the Romanian revolution imposed some elements of direct democracy.[3] In any case, all subsequent governments were unable to stand firmly by their policies in the face of protests and strikes. The economic consequence was that a vicious cycle between inflation and wage increases became established in the early 1990s and this made the tasks of restructuring harder (Blaga 1994a, 70; Drăgulin and Rădulescu 1999). At the time of writing, in the autumn of 2004, inflation is yet to be brought into single digit figures.

Lack of preparation for reforms prior to 1989 and the frequent strikes and political challenges to the central authority in the aftermath of the revolution led the FSN governments to choose a gradualist programme of market reform (Ronnas 1992). The Roman government launched this programme in November 1990 with a partial liberalisation of prices.[4] This was the first in a series of steps to reduce the number of administrated prices (the next took place in April and June 1991, May and September 1992, May and June 1993 and March 1994). Prices of certain foods, such as sugar, bread, and meat, were not liberalised until 1994 for reasons of social protection. Intermediary steps included a 30 per cent cap on the margins for wholesalers and retailers, and the obligation for enterprises that did not have at least two domestic competitors to notify the ministries and seek approval for their prices (Munteanu 1995, 23). Prices for energy, petrol and gas remained controlled and in agreements with the World Bank and the IMF the Romanian governments undertook to raise them in line with world prices (World Bank 1994a, 6; 1995b, 3, 12).

Related measures included a tight control of money and credit supply, a small budget deficit, and the partial indexation of wages. Due to the low level of foreign currency reserves, and the lack of a stabilisation fund similar to that put together by foreign donors for Poland in January 1990, worth $1 billion, the exchange rate was not used as a nominal anchor for inflation. The leu was devalued in November 1990, however, and kept constant for much of the next year (OECD 1993, 53). Interest rates remained negative thus depriving the government of one important lever for containing the inflation created by the liberalisation of prices. According to Rădulescu and Drăgulin (1995, 75), Romania was the only country where the IMF agreed to this basic lack of co-ordination between economic policies.

The gradual liberalisation of prices reflected the concern to protect the interests of consumers (the prices of basic foodstuffs were liberalised last) and the heavy industries, who also benefited most from low energy prices. The management of the exchange rate between 1990 and 1996 had similar objectives.[5] The exchange rate fluctuated to respond to competing pressures: the need to control inflation and balance of payments problems. Having decided in November 1990 that the convertibility of the leu was not possible, the exchange rate was used initially as a suppresser for inflation. By allowing the leu to appreciate, the costs of imports were lower and, it was hoped, they would not feed the inflation.

Given the high proportion of energy products in imports, this measure was also a form of subsidy for the energy-intensive industries. But the effect on the economy was that the opportunity costs of imports were low and imports grew faster than exports, putting pressure on the balance of payments

(Dăianu 1996a). Alternative resources, such as FDI and external borrowing, were also difficult to mobilise, which led to periodic depreciation of the currency. This happened for instance at the end of 1992 when a delay in the transfer of $800 million promised by the Group of 24 countries (G24) led to a shortage of foreign currency reserves.

Another pressure on the exchange rate was the slow introduction of real positive interest rates, which did not become effective until 1993. With levels of annual inflation in the hundreds in 1991–93 and interest rates of about 70–80 per cent, the effects of money illusion initially protected the run from lei in 1991 and 1992. The lack of historical experience with inflation explains why the initial increase in nominal incomes obscured the erosion of real incomes. However, from late 1992 the demand for foreign currency and goods, as more reliable stores of value, expanded. This in turn intensified the pressure on the exchange rate and led to an increase in the velocity of money, another source of inflation. Thus, in seemingly seeking to control inflation by controlling the exchange rate, the government created a pattern of currency appreciation and sudden depreciation that ended up fuelling inflation (Rădulescu 1993; Rădulescu and Drăgulin 1995).

These measures can be easily criticised by neo-liberals for not respecting some basic economic mechanisms: the signalling role of prices was distorted by the gradual liberalisation of prices; the failure to use interest rates to control inflation and the delay in the liberalisation of the exchange rate created confusion in the economy with damaging long-term effects. These conditions amounted to a failure to create hard budget constraints and the tendency of the enterprises to perpetuate non-competitive behaviour, such as reliance on arrears and soft loans became entrenched. Indeed, arrears were a persistent phenomenon in the post-communist Romanian economy (Dăianu 1993a; Croitoru 1994a; 1994b).

Thus, 'losses made at the enterprise level in that particular set-up inherited from socialism' were the link between macro-economic instability and the structure of the economy (Ruhl 1999, 7–9). These losses were absorbed in the economy through four channels: (i) arrears (inter-enterprise, to the budget, to the utilities); (ii) the banking system (bad loans, loans at subsidised interest rates); (iii) domestic debt; and (iv) foreign debt (Ruhl 1999, 7–9). While this might be an accurate observation at the macro-economic level, the evidence on the behaviour of firms is mixed. Recourse to non-monetary transactions, such as barter, delayed payments and arrears, did not necessarily mean that firms were doing poorly and did not restructure. For instance, a survey of firms from twenty countries at different stages in their transition, including Romania, showed that barter and other non-monetary transactions between firms were not significantly related to their performance or restructuring, except for Russia (Carlin et al. 2000). In other words, networks of enterprises can be resources for adaptation and growth, as argued by Stark and Bruszt (1998).

Empirically, it is not possible to establish whether shock therapy would have determined the restructuring of the economy, as the neo-liberal economists argued. The neo-liberal prediction of successful restructuring was based on the belief that structural interests could be displaced by the market forces. The experience of the first seven years of reform in Romania showed that the government could not resist being swayed by the pressure of economic interests. This was reflected in hesitations and reversals in liberalisation, which led to some unwanted consequences such as the entrenchment of inflation expectations and counterproductive adaptive behaviours. Moreover, actors often used to their advantage the new economic environment created by government policy. For instance, exporters used the instability of monetary policy to obtain the right to full retention of their foreign currency earnings, thus restricting the access of BNR to hard currency. Exporters also became able to take advantage of currency fluctuations on the domestic markets (OECD 1998, 80). Equally, the control of prices and direct credits to favoured industries shifted some of the economic pressure from heavy industries to agriculture and the banking sector.

Direct attempts by the government to tackle the cycle of price increases, inflation and arrears (by the end of 1991 the latter had reached 80 per cent of GDP) also met with mixed results. In December 1991, the BNR was instructed to facilitate credits worth 1.8 trillion lei to enable enterprises to compensate their arrears. After compensation, the net amount of new credit extended by the BNR was 400 billion lei. This led initially to a reduction of arrears, but by the end of 1992 they reached again 30 per cent of GDP (OECD 1993, 45).

For the sake of providing a semblance of macro-economic stability, certain institutional arrangements were changed only slowly. A new accounting system was introduced in 1994, but before that the calculation of profits and taxes inherited from the plan contributed to the relative equilibrium of the state budget. For instance, costs were included in calculation of tax only for products sold and cashed, and not for stocks. Similarly, the depreciation costs were calculated historically, ignoring the 1,000 per cent plus inflation since their valuation in April 1990. Both procedures made firms look better financially and increased their taxes (OECD 1993, 67; Antohi 1995). This was recognised in 1994 when SOE re-valued their assets to take account of inflation and recovered some of the de-capitalisation of the previous years.

It seems that the liberalisation of prices exposed but did not resolve the structural difficulties in the economy. A pro-market measure – the liberalisation of prices – interacted with the economic structure and led to a number of perverse results: inflation, the accumulation of arrears and the de-capitalisation of enterprises. These effects show that, as Polanyi (1992, 50) observed, price systems reflect 'an institutional history of their own in terms of the types of equivalencies that entered into their making' and that economic actors will modulate their reaction to changes introduced by the government by using this status quo.

The impact of the gradual liberalisation policies on economic growth and restructuring was also mixed. The output declined between 1990 and 1992 by nearly 25 per cent; inflation reached 200 per cent in 1992, while real wages kept much of their value. After this initial period of recession, in 1993 growth resumed, exports grew faster than imports, and in 1994 inflation became stable.[6] The policy of the government to cushion the impact of term of trade shocks to the heavy industries allowed them to recover. Unfortunately, this opportunity to restructure during a period of economic growth was lost in 1995 and 1996. Having reached their potential for growth based on export demand in 1993–94, the growth of industrial production relied on subsidised domestic demand in 1995–96. To maintain the momentum for growth, the Văcăroiu government reversed some of the liberalisation measures, especially in the foreign exchange market (BNR 1997b, 83–86; Hunya 1998, 244–247).

The response of the enterprise sector to the new economic circumstances was certainly less drastic than in other CEE countries in transition. In Poland for instance a reduction in industrial production of 24.2 per cent in 1990 and almost 12 per cent in 1991 led to a decrease by 11 per cent and 8 per cent of the industrial labour force in the two years. In Romania, a much greater decrease in industrial production, of 23.7 per cent in 1990 and 22.8 per cent in 1991 led to a shrinking of the labour force of only 5.3 per cent. In 1993–95, as industrial production recovered, the shedding of labour continued, but it did not lead to the levels of unemployment of 16–18 per cent known in Poland. Unemployment in Romania hovered at around 10 per cent during the 1990s (BNR 1997a, 232). The greater decline in industrial production in Romania reflects the disorganisation of production after the revolution and the severity of the trade shocks. At the same time, the recalcitrance of labour in Romania – unlike in Poland, where the Solidarity Union was backing the reform – explains why the costs of the recession could not be easily shifted towards the industrial workers. Other sectors, such as education and health, took the brunt of the budget cuts.

Direct attempts by the government to restructure loss-making enterprises also reflect the ability of the SOEs to use pressure from above to their advantage. The isolation programme run between 1992 and 1997 included 147 enterprises (of which about half were state farms). They were put under special supervision and asked to design financial recovery plans, with the help of a restructuring agency, foreign technical assistance and funds for severance payments to workers from the FPS. Intense lobbying on the part of some of the SOEs ensured that only 4 of the 10 largest loss-makers, 46 of the largest 100, and 82 of the largest 300 were actually included. Once in the programme, contrary to expectation, these enterprises were actually able to receive more subsidies and greater write-offs of their debts, as the restructuring agency pressured their creditors to show leniency.

The performance of these SOEs deteriorated in comparison with similar enterprises that faced the pressure to adjust on their own. In the event, only four firms graduated from the programme (two were privatised and two were liquidated), and only seven top managers were fired (Djankov 1999, 7–9). Another author claims that by the middle of 1997, the number of enterprises from this programme, either privatised, liquidated or turned profitable was much higher – 31, 33 and 10 respectively, with the agricultural farms representing the worst failures (Negulescu 1999, 11).

A degree of adjustment did take place but to a lesser extent than in other CEE countries (Commander, Dutz and Stern 1999). Thus, 6,023 SOEs, out of a total of about 7,500 SOEs and *regies autonomes* analysed by Negulescu (1999, 4), shed 22.3 per cent of their labour force between 1994 and 1997. Among these, some of the worst offenders in terms of operational losses, about one third of the total sample, reduced their employment figures by as much as 60 per cent. Many of these enterprises remained in a tenuous financial position. Only about two-thirds of the enterprises surveyed had a positive net cash flow from operations (Negulescu 1999, 4–5).

In the new private sector, a survey conducted in the second part of 1997 found that Romanian new firms compared well from the point of view of job growth, security of property and market development with firms in Poland (Johnson, MacMillan and Woodruff 1999). For the whole of the economy, however, although there were promising beginnings for the new private sector, the loss of employment in industry was not absorbed completely by trade and services. In 1989, industry (mining and manufacturing) represented 35.6 per cent of employment, and this shrank to 25 per cent of the labour force in 1997. Trade employment grew from 5.9 per cent to 10.3 per cent between 1989 and 1997, and there were some positive developments in finance services (a growth in employment from 0.3 per cent to 0.8 per cent), but other services, such as community services (education, health, administration, social services) declined from 15.3 per cent to 13.7 per cent.

The most significant transfer of labour was to agriculture. Romania was the only country in the region where the proportion of agriculture in total employment increased during this period from an already high 27.9 per cent to 37.5 per cent (Păuna and Păuna 1999, 12–14). The land reform of 1991 gave land to more than 50 per cent of the population (CURS 1997, 52) and the exemption from taxes still in force at the end of 2000 made agriculture an employer of last resort.

The attempt of the FSN/PDSR governments to pursue economic growth through expansionary policies favourable to the heavy industries did encourage a degree of restructuring, but by the end of their term in office, macro-economic imbalances resurfaced. Inflation was on the rise, balance of payments problems were becoming acute and the budget deficit reached 4.9 per cent of the GDP. The sovereign foreign debt of the country increased to almost $10 billion in 1997 (nearly 30 per cent of the GDP) (EBRD 2000, 200–201). Peaks in government spending, at the end of 1991, of 1992 and 1996 coincided with peaks in the evolution of money supply, which suggests that social peace was bought by 'printing money' (Dăianu 1996c).[7] After 1997, The Ciorbea government attempted to put a stop to this use of government funds and to tackle the delay in the marketisation of the economy by pushing through a programme of complete liberalisation of prices, control of money supply, real positive interest rates and subsidy cuts.

The result was a jump in inflation to 154.8 per cent in 1997, and three years of recession (GDP growth was –6.9 per cent in 1997, –5.4 per cent in 1998 and –3.2 per cent in 1999). This macro-stabilisation programme did curb inflation (it was down to 45 per cent in 1999 and 2000) and restored a degree of health in the public finances (the budget deficits were less than 3 per cent of GDP in 1998 and 1999) (BNR 1999a, 28–29). It also increased the transparency of the financial situation of the state; not only budget deficits, first reported in 1994, but also subsidies were made public.

However, the attempts after 1997 to impose hard budget constraints for firms did not lead to the disappearance of arrears. The economic recession shrank the taxing base of the state, who then raised taxes. The CDR governments, like their predecessors, proved unable to keep a tight rein on the wage bills of the state sector, especially the *regies autonomes*. The result was a shift of some firms from the formal to the informal economy (Croitoru and Tărhoacă 1999). For the private sector that remained in the formal economy the recourse to arrears became an important phenomenon. In 1999, the arrears of the private sector represented 19.52 per cent of GDP, while the state sector was owing slightly less, 18.24 per cent of GDP (the total for the national economy was 42.22 per cent of GDP) (IMF 2001, 183).

The liberalisation of energy prices allowed the public utilities to use their monopolistic position to transfer their inefficiencies to the rest of the economy and undermine the competitiveness of other sectors, such as the small and medium private enterprises that had sprung up after 1990. This situation did not ameliorate until 2000, when the effects of organisational changes in the utilities began to make themselves felt. In any case, the state could not avoid taking responsibility for some of the costs of liberalisation and recession. It paid for the re-capitalisation of the state-owned banks in 1997 and 1999 and accepted lower BNR profit transfers to the budget (IMF 2001, 43). This pressure on the budget was compensated for through higher-than-targeted inflation (IMF 2001, 44).

The fact that the stabilisation programmes attempted during the 1990s could not eliminate inflation completely was linked to the lack of progress with privatisation and restructuring (Dăianu 1996c, 1999). But the expectation that privatisation, as the main means for restructuring proposed by neo-liberals (Sachs 1993), could resolve the question of discipline in the state sector was probably unrealistic (Brada 1996). Enterprises had to cope with a fluid economic environment, where the form of property may not have been the determining factor in their performance in any case. This is an interpretation that, again, shifts the focus from faith in the efficacy of neo-liberal prescriptions, to an appreciation of practical difficulties highlighted by evolutionary economics.

The instability of the economic conditions had a few deleterious effects on privatisation. The decline in GDP reduced the resources that might have been available for the purchase of SOEs (Wojtyna 1994). Private domestic borrowing was unattractive due to inflation and persistent high interest rates (Borc 1999). Similarly, foreign investors, although tempted by some of the privatisation offers in 1997–2000, came in smaller numbers than elsewhere in the region, although their number increased after 1997. Romania attracted only $4.9 billion between 1995 and 1999, while Poland, the Czech Republic and Hungary received investments worth $18.2 billion, $12.6 billion, and $11.6 billion respectively during the same period (BNR 1999a, 29). Indeed, this influx of funds, a more competitive industrial structure, and the proximity with the Western markets might account in greater measure for the economic success of these countries than the virtues of their economic reforms (Kochanowicz 1998, 143–4).

At the firm level, complete and definitive data on the performance of privatised firms are difficult to find. In Romania, the FPS began in 1996 a vast exercise of assessing the economic performance of the privatised firms. Unfortunately published results include only a list of successful cases, which tend to score higher than the average for the whole population of privatised firms. Only 11 such cases are listed in a report from October 2000 (FPS 2000a, 2). In the 'White Book of Privatisation' produced by FPS at the end of 2000, a couple of examples are given for each county, about 90 in total, which represent, of course, a very small percentage of the whole (FPS 2000b, 33–44). Perhaps an indication of the overall success of these privatisations is that at the end of August 2000, of the 12,327 contracts signed by FPS for the sale of shares in 6,489 enterprises, only 1,155 had been cancelled, representing about 9.37 per cent of the total (FPS 2000b, 22).

A survey of privatised firms conducted in 1994 in Hungary, Poland, and the Czech Republic showed that although all firms were affected by the contraction of the GDP, the privatised firms were able to withstand better this downward pressure. This was more evident in those cases where privatisation led to a relatively concentrated structure of ownership. But this survey excluded large SOEs, whose privatisation posed serious problems everywhere in the region. However, the positive results found in the performance and investment behaviour of privatised firms could be an indication that in these countries the negative impact of the large SOEs on the emerging private sector was more effectively contained than in Romania (Frydman et al. 1997).

In another survey conducted in June–September 1998, the privatised Romanian firms were found not to have any excess labour, which suggested that they had completed the first phase of their adjustment to market competition. At the same time, unlike the Polish privatised firms, they were still reluctant to engage in new investment and research and development activities (Carlin, Estrin and Schaffer 1999, 8).

To conclude, this section has shown that in the absence of prior experimentation with reform, lacking mechanisms for indirect economic control, and faced with widespread labour mobilisation the governments of 1990–96 chose a gradualist approach to reform. This obtained some initial positive results in terms of growth and restructuring but it also led to increased budget deficits and balance of payments problems. On the other hand, the liberalisation and stabilisation programmes introduced by the Ciorbea government induced a three year recession, which was not reversed until 2000, when increased competition, the restructuring programmes of the public utilities and the re-capitalisation of banks took effect.

The fact that both types of approaches to post-communist marketisation were tried in Romania and both had mixed results illustrates that the constraints created by the structure of the economy and the social interests it reflected could not be changed quickly. In this sense, the economy always had a degree of autonomy in relation to the political sphere. Also, the links between the economic structure and politics were stronger than mere voting patterns along class lines. Direct labour action occurred with intensity at major junctures of the political process, in September 1991 and the election years of 1992 and 1996. The fact that it could be avoided in 2000 reflects, perhaps, both resolution on the part of the government and significant success in the restructuring of the economy.

The antagonism between the political parties weakened the autonomy of the political sphere and the ability of the political system to impose unpopular economic policies. The ideological investment in neo-liberal norms, so central to the identity claims of the democratic opposition, also put the focus of debate on liberalisation and stabilisation at the expense of encouraging the new private sector. The positive results obtained through the gradualist strategy in this direction before 1996 were temporarily undermined after 1997.

Realising privatisation: 1990–2001

The results of the privatisation process are impressive in terms of enterprises sold. The initial portfolio of 5,937 commercial companies (worth 45,212 billion lei in social capital) transferred to the *Fondul Proprietăţii de Stat* (State Ownership Fund – FPS) increased over the years to 9,137 (worth 53,455 billion lei social capital). Of these, 720 were later given to the Ministry of Agriculture and the Ministry of Finance. At the end of September 2000, only 1,600 companies (31,261 billion lei social capital) remained in the FPS portfolio, of which 1,286 were to be sold and 314 liquidated. But while nearly 85 per cent of the commercial companies were privatised, this represented only 45 per cent in terms of social capital. The remaining enterprises in the FPS portfolio represented only 15 per cent in number but over half of the total social capital (FPS 2000b, 9–10).

Another limiting factor is that from the start, privatisation was going to affect only about 50 per cent of state industrial property; the rest belonged to the *regies autonomes* and remained under state control. Thus, of the total state industrial property, at the end of September 2000, only 27.51 per cent had been privatised (including the mass privatisation programme). About 16 per cent were owned by the FPS, but four other agencies also exercised ownership rights on behalf of the state. The Ministry of Finance and the Ministry of Agriculture controlled 4.14 per cent of state property; the state electricity industry represented 9.5 per cent; the National Society of the Romanian Railways 3 per cent, while the remaining *regies autonomes* accounted for a staggering 39.40 per cent of the state property (FPS 2000b, 9). However, the significance of this fact has to be assessed against another measure of privatisation: in 1999, the share of the private sector in the GDP was 62 per cent (IMF 2000, 41). This means that although the state still owns a great deal of industrial property, its importance in the GDP has declined. The new private sector has displaced the state from certain economic sectors.

This section shows how this outcome came about, both in its successes and limitations. The constraints encountered in the privatisation process are linked to the political and economic conditions presented in the previous chapters.

A certain amount of privatisation occurred even before the organisation of the FPS and *Fondurile Proprietăţii de Stat* (Private Property Funds – FPPs), during 1990–93. Similar to developments in other CEE countries, some managers used the loopholes between old and new regulations for personal benefit during this period of 'spontaneous privatisation' (Hankiss 1990; Staniszkis 1991). Anecdotal evidence suggests that sometimes associates of the manager of a state firm established private firms in order to serve as the main sub-contractors. This arrangement was used to siphon out through discretionary prices the profits or other assets of the state firm (Brucan 1996, 103–104; Dochia 1999, 13–16).

Another formula was the setting-up of joint ventures between new companies and state firms, in which the assets of the latter were undervalued. Between 1990 and 1993, 721 such joint ventures were registered, but their number decreased in subsequent years due to FPS's reluctance to approve them (only 76 were created in 1995, 86 in 1996, 17 in 1997 and 16 in 1998) (Negrescu 1999, 26). This was the dominant method of privatisation for the import–export companies that had cheap physical assets and former employees could take the lucrative contracts and clients with them (Brucan 1996, 108–13).[8]

Another form of privatisation was the sale of assets and the concession of activities, organised by the *Agenţia Naţională de Privatizare* (National Agency for Privatisation – ANP). From March 1990, as part of the implementation of Decree 54 which regulated the start-up of new private firms, SOEs were allowed to identify and sell self-sufficient units of production (MOR 33/34 1990). As well as the pilot privatisation programme, which is discussed below, the sale of assets became part of the conditions for the structural adjustment loan (SAL), approved by the World Bank in June 1992. Only about 3,000 small assets of this kind were privatised by the end of 1993, even though the offer was twice as much (ANP 1994, 9; World Bank 1995a, 16). The book value of these assets was just over 33 billion lei; the auction started at about 53.5 billion lei and the final price was over 62 billion. Most of these assets were in trade (1,741), tourism and restaurants (782) (ANP 1994, 9).

As mentioned in Chapter 3, the privatisation law 58/1991 stipulated the sale of up to 0.5 per cent of the total number of commercial companies under a pilot privatisation scheme organised by the ANP. The aim of the exercise was to provide the funds for the setting up of the FPS and FPPs, to explore the strategies feasible for privatisation, and to formulate methodologies and regulations for future privatisation. This activity started in 1992 and by the end of the year most of the contracts for the twenty-two firms privatised under this scheme were signed.

ANP started with an initial list of sixty enterprises for this programme. The main criteria for participation were good financial situation, stable markets and attractiveness for investors, either Romanian or foreign (MOR 200/1991). All of these enterprises were relatively small. Gradually, enterprises were dropped off the list due to lack of clarity about the ownership rights over land, disappointing show of interest from investors and last minute opposition from managers and employees (ANP 1993b, 1–11).

Of the twenty-two enterprises, fifteen were sold through management-employee buyouts (MEBO) and four were sold to foreign investors. These enterprises were evaluated through a combination of methods, by Romanian or foreign consultancy firms; their services were paid for by the companies in question or, when foreign investors were involved, through Phare assistance.[9] The sales were negotiated. It was concluded that in the two cases of public offering of shares the procedure was costly and comparatively ineffective. The conditions of sale also included investments and keeping on the current number of employees for at least two years (ANP 1993a, 3–13; 1993b, 1–2).

In a survey of firms privatised in the pilot programme conducted a few months after the completion of the sale, ANP found that the most difficult problem they encountered was discrimination in relation to both private start-ups and public companies. Compared to the former, the privatised firms did not benefit from tax breaks, and in relation to the latter, their access to credit and raw materials was restricted. Banks and other public companies preferred to deal with customers backed by the state ministries. Also, privatised companies were subjected to repeated controls from state agencies and to biased public scrutiny by the press (ANP 1993c, 6–11). In spite of these circumstances, however, most of the privatised companies kept to their investment programmes and regular payments of their debts to ANP (1993d,

1–5). As expected, particularly successful were sales to foreign investors, especially where these built on existing trade relations (Bauer 1994).

During the remaining years of the Văcăroiu government (1993–96), FPS and FPPs engaged in case-by-case privatisation and began the organisation of the mass privatisation programme. As well as organising the pilot privatisation, ANP began implementing other requirements of the privatisation law 58/1991. By 31 December 1992, it had issued and distributed the property certificates (MOR 318/1992). During 1992, ANP prepared the secondary legislation for the starting up of the funds (MOR 121/1992; MOR 208/1992a; MOR 208/1992b; MOR 262/1992). The most important was the 'Shareholders Agreement' (MOR 208/1992a). As will be recalled from the discussion in Chapter 3, the privatisation law 58/1991 had transformed the conditions for governance in the commercial companies owned by the state. The shares of each of these companies were split between the FPS (70 per cent) and an FPP (30 per cent). Each of the 17.5 million Romanian citizens entitled to property certificates had one in each of the FPPs.

The fraction of shares owned by FPPs was in principle already private, but co-operation between FPS and FPPs was necessary in the day-to-day running of enterprises. The FPS and one FPP, at any one time, were sharing responsibility for the governance of each firm. An individual who participated in a MEBO sale could use her five certificates from the five FPPs to buy shares owned only by one FPP. Thus, the rules for exchanging shares and certificates from the different FPPs and FPS were worked out. Additionally, according to the Shareholders' agreement, the FPPs were required to promote the privatisation of enterprises in which they were shareholders (MOR 208/1992a, articles 2e and 8.1g).

The FPS and the FPPs agreed that small enterprises should be privatised according to a standard procedure to be elaborated by ANP. For enterprises in this category the right to exchange certificates for shares was abolished, except for the case when all the shares were bought through MEBO: there, certificates from all the FPPs could be used (MOR 208/1992a article 1.1 annex 2, article 1.2c annex 3).

The FPS was responsible for the privatisation of big SOEs and for the co-ordination with the industrial policies of the government. When an offer was made for the purchase of 100 per cent of shares, however, the FPP implicated became the agent for privatisation and the sale had to be approved by ANP (MOR 208/1992a, article 1.2 annex 2). Finally, for medium-sized SOEs, the FPP was the agent for privatisation (MOR 208/1992a, article 1.3 annex 2). Perhaps to respect the fact that FPPs remained private entities, all the costs of restructuring and the preparation for privatisation of all SOEs were the responsibility of the FPS (MOR 208/1992a, articles 1.7 and 1.8 annex 2).

ANP duly prepared the 'standard strategy' for the privatisation of small enterprises, which was approved by the government at the end of December 1992 (MOR 12/1993). This strategy was to become in the next few years the main focus of the privatisation activities. It favoured two methods of privatisation: MEBO, and, as a fall back option, the sale through auction (offers were to be presented in a closed envelope and opened at the same time in the presence of the bidders). The main criteria for awarding the sale, in descending order of importance, were the amount of money offered, the size of the upfront payment (payments could be scheduled over a maximum of six years), investment committed, and the commitment to retain the workforce (MOR 12/1993).

A commission would be set up for the privatisation of each small enterprise, made up of three members, one each from ANP, FPS, and FPP. The preoccupation for finding buyers was evident in the fact that this regulation even contained as 'suggestions' forms for the setting up and the statute of the Association *Programul Acţiunilor Salariaţilor* (Employees Shares Programme – PAS). This was the organisation the privatisation commission would recognise as a partner for a MEBO sale (MOR 12/1993 annex 3). MEBO sales increased in importance during 1993–94 and received a firm backing in August 1994 when a special law defined even more precisely the status and attributions of PAS (MOR 209/1994).

It was under this 'standard methodology' drawn up by ANP that most of the privatisation activities took place in 1993 and 1994. Of the FPS portfolio of 5,934 SOEs at that time, 2,600 were small, their social capital of about 400 billion lei representing barely 3.4 per cent of the total social capital (MOR 81/1994a chapter 4.2). In addition to their relative importance in number, a few factors tipped the balance on focusing the privatisation strategy on small enterprises, a strategy common to other privatisation programmes in the region (Fischer S., 1992).

One conclusion from the experimental pilot programme was that the most likely buyers would be the associations of workers and managers. The economic recession between 1989 and 1992, the steep inflation in 1991–93, and the relative lack of interest from foreign investors also suggested that available funds for buying shares would be quite small (MOR 81/1994a, chapter 3.2; Blaga 1994b, 61). Apart from speed, this form of privatisation was likely to contribute to the creation of a constituency for privatisation, an important objective for the government (Winiecki 1992; Przeworski 1993). As a downside, MEBO sales also led to a diffuse ownership structure and the new owners were unlikely to be able to bring large scale new investment and know-how (Commander, Dutz, and Stern 1999, 15).

Focus on the small and medium enterprises also postponed tackling big enterprises. FPS felt that the privatisation of big enterprises had to be coordinated with the industrial policy of the government and the sectoral policies of the line ministries. All of these were in the process of being elaborated. Also, the FPS was severely understaffed (it had 148 personnel in March 1994) and essential steps in establishing its governance role in the enterprises were still to be completed. For instance, not all of the SOEs were even formally transferred to the FPS by the end of 1993, and it was unclear how many SOEs were to be transferred to FPS. The nomination of the FPS representatives in the new general assembly of the shareholders was also in flux, as will be shown in more detail in Chapter 5 (MOR 81/1994a, Chapters 1.2, 1.3, and 1.4).

In 1993, of the 669 SOEs prepared for privatisation by the FPS, 561 were small and only 134 of them were sold by the end of September that year. The book value of the SOEs sold was 13 billion lei, and the price obtained for them was 23.3 billion lei (MOR 81/1994a, chapter 4.2). Of the 109 medium-size enterprises offered, 5 were sold and another 8 were under negotiation (MOR 81/1994a, chapter 4.3). By the end of December 1993, the figures were a bit higher with 265 enterprises sold (238 small, 24 medium and only 2 big enterprises) (World Bank 1999a; FPS 2000b, 20).

Although the sale price looks quite competitive, other conditions of sale can modify this perception. Thus, only about 15–30 per cent of the price was paid up front, 30 per cent was bought against certificates and the rest was transformed into a six to ten year credit to FPS with an annual interest of 24.5–26 per cent, well below the market rate (MOR 81/1994a, chapter 4.2). These conditions of sale became even more flexible after November 1994, when the annual interest rate charged on the FPS credit was between 5 and 10 per cent and certain SOEs providing agricultural services could obtain credit for up to twelve years (MOR 21/1995, articles 11 and 13). A pressure in the opposite direction – of higher sale prices – was the sharp increase in the book value of all enterprises following new regulations on their evaluation in 1994. These new rules led to a slowing down of privatisation in the second part of 1994 (Negrescu 1999, 32). The softening of the credit regime was perhaps a necessary correction to this effect and sales picked up again in December.

In 1994, the SOF put up for sale 1,930 small, 403 medium and 35 big enterprises, with a total social capital of 1,165,000 million lei, representing about 10 per cent of the total social capital in the portfolio (MOR 81/1994b, chapter 3.2). By the end of the year less than a third (595) were sold. Most enterprises sold were small (472), and only 110 were medium and 12 big. The performance for 1995 is slightly higher with the number of sales going up to 623; the number of medium-sized enterprises was much higher, at 268, coming closer to the 322 figure for small enterprises. Also, 30 big SOEs were privatised in 1995 (World Bank 1999a; FPS 2000b, 20).

During 1993–94, the FPPs began to play a more active role in the privatisation process. The property certificates issued as shares in FPPs were used in many privatisation transactions through MEBO and FPPs had the responsibility of providing the institutional infrastructure for the transactions. The activities of the FPPs were beset by similar difficulties to that of the FPS: slow recruitment and training of personnel, nomination of their boards of administration, and transfer of the SOEs in their portfolio (ANP 1993a, 13–14; ANP 1993b, 9–15; ANP 1993d, 6–8).

The allocation of firms to the FPPs was made in August 1993 and followed a combination of territorial and industrial criteria. Thus, in strategic sectors, such as the chemical industry, finance and banks, insurance, machine building and ferrous metallurgy, each FPP received an equal percentage of shares. In other sectors, all the firms were allocated to one fund, presumably to enable the Funds to implement an 'integrated' privatisation strategy (MOR 77/1993). For instance, the firms belonging to the textile industry were allocated to FPP II Moldova. The paper industry and non-ferrous metallurgy went to FPP I Banat-Crişana, FPP III Transilvania took tourism, food and fish industries, FPP IV Muntenia received the glass, cosmetics, pharmaceuticals and building materials sectors, and FPP V Oltenia acquired the electronics and fur industries (Popescu 1992, 8).

Very little was achieved, however, in facilitating the exchange of property certificates for shares either in FPPs or in SOEs outside of the framework for MEBO sales (ANP 1994, 1, 3–5). To give new impetus to this process, law 55 for the acceleration of privatisation was passed in June 1995. The political debates around this law and the controversy around its main decisions were presented in Chapter 3. Its main innovations were the issuance of duplicates to the property certificates, in the form of coupons for privatisation, and the extension of the pool of individuals entitled to coupons to five more cohorts of young people, those who became 18 between December 1990 and December 1995.

Interestingly, the cabinet assumed a hands-on role in the process and drafted much of the secondary legislation for the implementation of this law. A special secretariat was created with regional branches at the county level. Representatives of the FPS, FPPs, and ANP were included, but the leading role was assigned to the prefects (MOR 138/1995). To achieve the targets for the issuance and distribution of the coupons by the end of September 1995, schools, local administration, *regies autonome* and other organisations were asked to provide personnel and organise centres for the dissemination of information and the subscription of shares (MOR 158/1995, EECR 1996a, 20). The list of the enterprises included in this offer was drafted by the cabinet as well (MOR 190/1995).

Until 31 March 1996 owners of coupons and certificates could subscribe for shares in SOEs and had until the end of April to opt for shares in FPPs. Their subscriptions were centralised by a department in the Ministry of Finance (MOR 50/1996 articles 3 and 7.1). The property certificates issued in 1991 were valued at 25,000 lei each, and the coupons at 975,000 lei. The number of shares available in each SOE was the total value of the social capital on offer divided by 25,000, the standard value of one share. If the number of shares requested by the public was equal or lower than that on offer, the value of each share was 25,000 and a coupon could buy 39 shares. If the demand was higher, all requests were to be satisfied proportional to the value of the certificates and coupons subscribed. The social capital available would be divided by the total number of offers, thus resulting in fewer shares for each subscriber than in the previous two cases (MOR 223/1995, article 26).

The outcome of this flurry of activity was that, on average, 18.7 per cent of all shares in nearly 5,000 SOEs were transferred to the public, creating a dispersed ownership structure. As its critics remarked, this was an unusually complex exercise that included a significant number of small companies, which were incorporated inappropriately (Earle and Teledgy 1998, 313, 329). Mass privatisation programmes in other CEE countries included much fewer enterprises and more investment funds (Lieberman 1995). The Czech Republic pioneered this method in 1991 and by 1994, 1,600 firms had been privatised completely. There, citizens could use coupons to buy shares in a national auction in any firm included in the programme or could invest their coupons in an investment fund. About 70 per cent of shares were invested in 550 funds. In Poland, 512 firms were put in the care of 15 investment funds, usually under foreign management, each of them having a controlling stake of 33 per cent in some of the firms. Citizens received certificates that gave them ownership rights in all 15 funds (Pohl et al. 1997, 12).

In any case, in 1996 the number of enterprises privatised in Romania doubled compared to the previous year, from 620 in 1995 to 1,245 (FPS 2000b, 20), and there was a significant increase in the contribution of the private sector to GDP from 42.6 per cent in 1995 to 54.1 per cent in 1996. The mass privatisation programme also left behind a great deal of administrative issues to be resolved by the FPPs and the FPS. The offer for FPP shares had attracted about 15 per cent of the participants in the mass privatisation programme, just over two million people, compared to the thirteen million who acquired shares in SOEs (Earle and Telegdy 1998, 323). FPPs thus owed dividends to people who had not used their property certificates prior to 1995. They also had to settle by negotiations among themselves the values given to dividends and to certificates that had been used by individuals in the mass privatisation.

Some of these issues were regulated at the end of 1996 when the FPPs were transformed into *Societăţi de Investiţii Financiare* (Societies for Financial Investment – SIF) just as the Văcăroiu government was preparing to face the November elections (MOR 273/1996). This matter was also among the priorities of the Ciorbea government, which issued swiftly the secondary legislation for the implementation of the law (MOR 21/1997). The process of 'regularisation' between the investment funds and the FPS lasted until March 1999. It tied up significant resources and complicated the decisions of the FPS about the shares it could sell (as opposed to those that were the object of negotiations with the SIFs). There were also doubts about the transparency of the dealings of the investment funds (Negrescu 1999, 36). Shares in the SIFs traded at Bucharest stock exchange from 1999.

After these difficult beginnings the change in political leadership, after the elections of November 1996, led to the speeding up of the privatisation sales. Although busy completing the mass privatisation programme, the FPS began to sell its shares more quickly. Compared to 2,725 SOEs sold between 1992 and 1996, between 1997 and the end of September 2000, the FPS sales almost doubled to 5,364. The total value of the social capital sold in the latter period was 18,053 billion lei (compared to 3,570 billion in 1992–96) (FPS 2000b, 19–21), but it is unclear whether these figures have been weighed to take account of inflation.

The privatisation process deepened as well. The privatisation of banks began with the law 83/1997 for the privatisation of banking commercial companies, which had been waiting for parliamentary time for two years (MOR 98/1997). This law stipulated that each bank was to be privatised by a commission, that domestic banks could not provide credits for the purchase of shares in other banks and that these shares could not be used as collateral for borrowing. Consultancy firms were to be hired to elaborate the privatisation strategy. Any buyer that purchased more than 5 per cent of shares had to be assessed by the BNR as to their credibility and no buyer could acquire more than 20 per cent of the shares offered.

In order to prepare the banks for privatisation, the shares that were initially allocated to FPPs were returned to the FPS, in exchange for shares in other enterprises. Two banks were privatised in 1998. Société Générale Group was the main investor in the sale of the Romanian Bank for Development; Bank Post was sold for $92 million to, among others, General Electric Capital and Banco Portugues de Investimento (FPS 1999a, 4; BNR 1999a, 42). During the same year, the Ministry of Finance, seemingly preparing them for privatisation, was still trying to rescue the two banks that had accumulated most of the bad debts in the sector, the Bank for Agriculture and the Romanian Bank for Foreign Trade (BANCOREX). The cost of this rescue package – an increase in the budget deficit – paid off only partially (BNR 1999a, 41). In the next two years BANCOREX was closed; its liabilities were transferred to a governmental agency and the healthy part of the business to the Romanian Commercial Bank. The Bank for Agriculture was sold to a German investor in 2001 and the Romanian Commercial Bank has also been privatised.

At the end of 1998 some sectors, for instance the cement industry, were privatised completely, while in other sectors, such as textiles, and plastic and construction materials, 85–95 per cent of capacity was privatised. Between 70 and 80 per cent of the ceramics industry, glass and porcelain and some of the food industries (cooking oil, pastries, and soft drinks) have been transferred into private hands. At the other end of the spectrum were the big SOEs in metallurgy, chemicals and heavy machinery, whose privatisation was complicated by their debts to the state budget, banks, and suppliers (BNR 1999a, 42).

However, some progress was made in tackling these big enterprises in 1999. A number of liquidation procedures were started by FPS for companies that accounted for 12 per cent of its losses, while the losses of six mining companies decreased by 37 per cent (BNR 2000, 40). Under the Private Sector Adjustment Loan (PSAL) agreed with the World Bank in June 1999, sixty-four of these firms were offered for privatisation, and a number of reputable privatisation agents were hired to handle the evaluation, advertising and sale of these enterprises. Well-established consultancy firms such as Barents Group, Raiffensen Investment AG, Société Générale Conseil Pays Emergents Paris (in association with their local office BRD-Group Societe Generale Romania), Paribas, France, and Roland Berger Partner GmbH won the contracts and started the preparations for privatisation.

Much of the momentum was lost in 2000, however, when the privatisation of these enterprises stopped short of public offerings, although the preparation was completed. The new government elected at the end of the year vowed to pursue this matter vigorously. As of the end of February 2001, seventeen of these enterprises were about to be put on sale. For the rest, Prime Minister Năstase asked his prefects to get involved with their evaluation and make sure that relevant strategic information was included in the process. Of special concern was the fact that some of them produced armaments and had a monopolistic position in the economy. The objective to privatise quickly had to be weighted against the danger of simply transferring a monopoly from state to private ownership (Năstase 2001, 1–2).

This review of evidence allows us to assess the relative merits of the policies introduced by the various governments. The acceleration of privatisation after 1997 took place against a background of economic recession. It would seem that the contraction of the economy did not impact negatively on the demand for shares in the SOEs, unless it could be established that the price at which the shares were sold was correspondingly reduced. There are some indications that this might have been the case, as the new administration made the choice to rank the promise for future investment higher than the offer on share prices on the list of criteria for closing deals. A definitive evaluation of this issue is encumbered, however, by its intense politicisation.

A certain cause for the expansion of demand for FPS shares was the increased interest of foreign investors. While between 1992 and 1996 the FPS had signed only 11 contracts with foreign partners, between 1997 and September 2000 their number increased 23.45 times, to 258 (FPS 2000b, 20). Also, investment commitments denominated in American dollars – by far the main hard currency used in these transactions – amounted to only 212 million during 1992–96, but increased 15 times between 1997–2000 to 3,231 million (FPS 2000b, 27).

A comparison between the sums committed and the sums actually invested or in the process of being invested reveals a wholly different picture. The results of FPS post-privatisation surveillance published at the end of 2000 showed great disparities between investments committed and realised. As an analyst for the specialist weekly *Adevărul Economic* pointed out, for the period 1993–2000, only 6.5 per cent of the investments in lei, 5.1 per cent of the investments in US$, and 29.7 per cent of the investments in German marks were actually realised (Ion 2000, 3). If the figures for investment in process are added, these percentages go up to 18.40 per cent for investments in lei, 9.34 per cent investments in US$, and 30.25 per cent for those in German marks.[10]

Interestingly, although the investment commitments were much lower for the period 1992–96, they were either fully realised or were in the process of being realised. The huge discrepancies began after 1997. For instance, while for 1997 the situation seems in relative balance (143,10 billion lei committed, 124,32 realised, and $31.53 million of which $9.85 was realised), in 1998 of 567,69 billion lei and $125.7 million committed, only 177,87 billion lei and $31.1 million were actually spent. For 1999, the gaps are even greater: only 127,58 billion lei and $54.52 million of investments were realised, against 1300,65 billion lei and $804.76 million committed (FPS 2000b, 28).

It is impossible to determine to what extent these discrepancies are due to inevitable delays as the new owners needed to assess, plan and execute the respective investments. Their communication with the FPS and provision of the necessary documentation could be another reason why the recorded data might not necessarily reflect the whole reality of the situation (FPS 2000b, 27–28). It is also conceivable that FPS might arrive at some acceptable rescheduling of payments. Unfortunately, it was such data that made it difficult for the outgoing government to defend their record in privatisation. What might have been a necessary trade-off between speed and depth of the privatisation deals was instead portrayed by the media as a case of 'selling the state property to those who told the most beautiful lies' (Ion 2000, 3).

After winning the 2000 elections, the PDSR government evaluated negatively the activities of the FPS between 1997 and 2000. The PDSR policy statement claims that during 'the pre-electoral period, illegal and damaging activities to the national interest by the FPS became even more serious; these illegal activities amounted to a true plundering of the economy' (GR 2001, 10). The document alleged that the FPS asking prices were lower than the market value, and that FPS selected the buyers from the clientele of the governing coalition. The FPS also supposedly avoided or falsified auctions, it did not exercise any serious post-privatisation control, and the specialised institutions of the state were not allowed to control the activities of the FPS (GR 2001, 9–10).

For their part, the Democratic Convention governments after 1996 promoted the statistics that confirmed their 'true' commitment to privatisation (the much intensified pace of closing the sales; the increased involvement of foreign partners). At the same time they disparaged the former government for their slowness and for the amount of subsidies channelled to enterprises under the name of privatisation (FPS 2000b). At the end of 2000, the Party for

Social Democracy tried to gain the upper hand by denigrating their adversaries. This verbal competition can be considered the usual fare of the political game, but the fact that the PSD is repeating the mistake of not giving credit where it is due could perpetuate the antagonism between parties.

The privatisation process is a contested one in any society, all the more so in a society whose economy and politics are undergoing systemic transformation (Rausser and Simon 1992). A more balanced assessment of the course of the privatisation process in Romania in the 1990s amends both sets of claims. As in other countries in the region, the beginning of the privatisation process was quite slow (Kiss 1994). Some of this was due to economic conditions – the decline in GDP and inflation in particular – some was due to policy (Munteanu 1994a). The choice of an extensive mass privatisation scheme, which determined the design of the institutions put in charge of the process, was, in retrospect, an important reason for the delay of privatisation. It was based on the assumption that all companies would be incorporated and their shares would be traded immediately. The expectation that privatisation could be concluded in seven years was unrealistic, as was the choice of including small companies in the mass privatisation scheme. Even in economies with developed capital markets only a small percentage of all firms are incorporated and have their shares floated on the stock exchange.

At the same time, ANP, FPS and the FPPs started from scratch and created the procedures for corporate governance and privatisation. This was all the more commendable given the climate of uncertainty in which they operated. After 1997, the quicker pace of privatisation was due to the change in priorities of the government, from deep to swift privatisation. But this switch was made possible by the fact that an institutional structure – implementing agencies and procedures – was already in place.[11]

This review of evidence on privatisation has focused on the decisions that shaped the privatisation process as a rational-bureaucratic process. Some of these choices could be interpreted as attempts by political parties to pick winners, and they reflect certain ideological preferences. During 1990–96, privatisation consisted mostly of MEBO sales at discounted rates. The buyers – managers and employees in small enterprises – can be considered the winners, but the value of their purchase depends on future market conditions. Similarly, the beneficiaries of the mass privatisation programme, the entire population, received shares whose value depends on the evolution of the economy as a whole and the capitalisation of the stock market on which the shares can be traded. Thus, it can be argued that privatisation was an effective exercise in creating at least the appearance of 'popular capitalism' by giving everyone a stake in the economy. At the same time, the restructuring of the backbone of the economy – heavy industries and public utilities – was put outside the remit of privatisation.

After 1997, the process of marketisation in Romania received new impetus. Privatisation was extended to banking and some public utilities, following their restructuring. The sales to foreign investors and the use of the stock markets to sell FPS shares increased. Encouragingly, workers' associations continued to be the main buyers for shares in the small and medium enterprises still owned by the FPS, a sign of trust in the future of their companies.

This is evidence that the marketisation of the economy did occur, as Polanyi (1992) would have expected, together with a change in social structure. In this case, the mode of insertion of the citizens in the economy evolved from compulsory labour in the planned economy to ownership of shares in industrial sectors, as well as participation in other markets, such as those for labour and land.

Conclusion

The explanation of the slow pace of marketisation exclusively through reference to the ideological orientation of the different governments does not stand up to closer scrutiny. The structural conditions in the economy also exerted significant constraints on the formulation and implementation of policy.

Available economic theories, neo-liberal and evolutionary economics and economic sociology shed different light on various aspects of the economic reform in Romania. Neo-liberal theories inform the prevalent judgement on progress here as being slower than in other CEE countries. While the expectation behind the neo-liberal assessment, that structural changes in the economy could be executed through a change of environmental conditions, is unrealistic, it is important to accept the emphasis of neo-liberal economics on the need for restructuring. In the post-communist economies, the shift of resources from the industrial sector to trade and services is necessary, if these economies are to enhance their capacity to compete in world markets.

At the same time, it has been argued that the difficulties of the reform can be better understood by using the framework of evolutionary economics. This theory recognises the real-time dimension of changes, the need to maintain a degree of stability in the economy while changes are taking place and the relationship between the size of enterprises and sectors and their willingness or ability to change. In addition, insights from economic sociology illuminate the mechanisms for the resistance to change exhibited by certain sectors, as they use the relational assets within their networks to respond to state policy. This review of privatisation in post-communist Romania also shows that the change in the mechanism of economic co-ordination, from plan to market, was accompanied, and perhaps facilitated, by the change in the social structure and the modalities of insertion of the citizens in the economy. These citizens moved from being employees in the command economy to being shareholders and players in other markets, such as the labour, land and housing markets.

The change of economic strategy in 1997 from gradualism to shock therapy makes it impossible to establish a simple relationship between developments in the first and second period. Gradualism had achieved a return to growth by 1993, macro-stabilisation by 1994, and the setting up of some indirect mechanisms for the management of the economy. It also encouraged a degree of spontaneous restructuring of enterprises. The shock therapy of 1997 on the other hand led to a steep three-year recession. It is unclear whether the resumption of growth in 2000 and the successes with privatisation in 1997–2000 were the result of shock therapy. It is likely that the active restructuring of public utilities and the financial sector as well the effective institutional structure built in the previous years contributed to these positive developments. Both of these could have taken place in the absence of shock therapy measures.

The consistency over time of the orientation towards market reform – although in doubt at particular moments in time – shows that all parties had to respond to the same structural constraints: the dominance of the neo-liberal ideology internationally and the power of certain domestic groups domestically. But the leeway of actors was also apparent in the different ways in which these pressures were played out in policy. In the case of the social-democratic governments of 1990–96, this balancing act consisted of more reform than they might have desired on their own. For the right-of-centre governments of the Democratic Convention, their initial disregard for domestic constraints led to a severe downturn in economic activity and later a change of tack in their policy, from stabilisation and liberalisation to direct restructuring of certain public utilities.

The next chapter discusses the role of institutional dynamics both in facilitating and slowing down post-communist reforms.

Notes

1   Appendix 2 presents the main indicators of macro-economic performance in Romania, 1989–2000.

2   See also reports in the *Financial Times:* 'Romania slides towards anarchy amid coup claim' (27 September 1991); 'Romania's steel workers join strike' (19 May 1993); 'Romania acts on pit strike' (7 August 1993); 'Romania gives rail strikers ultimatum' (18 August 1993); 'Romania faces general strike' (15 February 1994); 'Survey of Romania 4: Slow reforms threatened – The unions' (3 May 1994); 'A fascinating but unfulfilled outpost: Tourism potential is being squandered and heavy industry refuses to accept its fate' (25 June 1997); and 'Police attack Romanian miners' march' (19 January 1999).

3   For instance, some saw the worker organisations as the only authentic political force that had emerged out of the revolution and that could have given the reform a clear

direction (Pasti 1995, 102–104). Pasti decried the Roman government's decision to distance itself from them in February 1990.

4   The price liberalisation programme was introduced by a governmental ordinance, rather than a law; this avoidance of debate in parliament was taken as evidence that the measure was non-democratic and ill-prepared (Vosganian 1994a, 36–37).

5   Finally, in 1998 Romania signed up to Article VIII of the IMF Articles of Agreement and introduced the current account convertibility of the leu.

6   The fact that inflation was stabilised after growth resumed was unique to Romania and Bulgaria. In other CEE economies analysed by Fischer, Sahay and Vegh (1996) stabilisation preceded growth.

7   These were, of course, times of intense political struggle. Protests by miners brought down the Roman government in 1991, and the end of 1992 and 1996 were dominated by parliamentary and presidential elections. In a break from this pattern, monetary policy did not slacken during the 2000 election year.

8   The ensuing disorganisation and the temporary lack of capacity for handling complex foreign trade contracts were then blamed for the decline in exports and imports in the early 1990s. The Romanian Ministry of Finance justified the delay in disbursing the Structural Adjustment Loan from the World Bank in this way (World Bank 1995a: 6 appendix B).

9   The European Community launched in 1989 the Phare (Polish-Hungarian Aid for Economic Restructuring) Programme to support the economic reform in Poland and Hungary. Subsequently, the programme was extended to the other CEE countries.

10   These are the author's calculations based on data in FPS (2000b, 28).

11   The role of institutional factors in the privatisation process in Romania will be addressed more fully in Chapter 5.

5

Institutionalising the separation of state and economy

However crucial the new mechanisms for macro-economic policy are for redefining the role of the state in the economy, the separation between these two spheres is not complete without the construction of a whole host of market institutions. Institutional analysis in the broadest sense is indispensable to any account of politics or economic development. Institutional dynamics account for the time constraints to change, the inertia embedded in organisational arrangements, and the accumulation of effects of economic policy over time, in spite of the claims to discontinuity by the different governments. Equally, it is at the institutional level that we can document the mechanisms through which the economic and political spheres can become, and remain, autonomous. In each of them, their specific institutions have a degree of autonomy which means that their processes can be put under pressure but cannot be swayed completely by interventions from the other sphere.

During the 1990s in Romania, when the boundaries between the economy and politics were still in the process of being drawn, we would expect to find evidence of how, as Searle (1995), and Elster, Offe and Preuss (1998) would argue, institutions are established through an act of political delegation. Elster, Offe and Preuss (1998) also anticipated that weak political authority would lead to weak delegation, decree-ism and reversals. This hypothesis is confirmed by the study of change in state and market institutions in post-communist Romania.

The distinction between institutions – as ways of doing things, ideas that have already acquired or are acquiring the capacity to structure interactions between actors – and organisations (North 1990) is also relevant here. Organisations act within the rules of the game to the extent that they have assimilated these rules. And in any case their behaviour carries norms and values and thus reflects the uneasy co-existence of old and new institutions. Organisations also seek to promote their own interests by negotiating the rules. Piecemeal institutional change is usually the result. In post-communist transformations, the change in institutions was concomitant with changes in the organisations that had a role in creating and enforcing new rules (Frydman, Murphy and Rapaczynski 1998), for instance the state administration, *Fondul Proprietăţii de Stat* (State Ownership Fund – FPS), banks, and other regulatory bodies.

In the analysis presented in this chapter, these organisations are investigated to establish to what extent changes in their behaviour reflect institutional changes. The general trend has been towards reform of the public administration, re-definition of the role of the state in the economy and entrenchment of the institutions that support the market. At the same time, during the first decade after the fall of communism, old and new institutions co-existed. Also, attempts by the relevant organisations to change themselves and to impose changes in their environments took effect gradually, and temporary reversals were common.

Neo-institutionalist analysts also appreciate that changes in formal institutions, which can be realised by fiat and legislation, become effective when informal institutions ensure their smooth, taken for granted functioning (Berg 1994; Rapaczynski 1996). From this perspective, the significance of weak political agency (Elster, Offe and Preuss 1998) has to be evaluated against a view of the limits of what political will can achieve in this domain. The change in informal institutions is a broader social phenomenon, for which the dominant political organisations can provide a model, but which retains a high degree of autonomy.

This chapter builds on the discussion in Chapter 1 about the starting points of institutional change, from plan-related institutions to market institutions. It was argued there that there are institutions common to the plan and the market: money, prices, trade. The role of these institutions was redefined though the broad macro-economic policies already described – liberalisation of prices and trade in particular. Equally, new market institutions, such as private ownership, shares, an autonomous banking and accounting system, stock exchanges, and rules for entry and exit for firms in the economy were set up. My contention has been that this institutional differentiation is supported by the relevant legislation, but the character of these legislative measures and the extent to which they are implemented also reflect the pace at which incumbents in the inherited state administration redefine their roles and construct strategies of conversion of their positions – as managers of now (or soon to be) privatised enterprises or personnel in the new market institutions.

This is evident, for instance, in the process by which the transfer of property rights to enterprises and the redefinition of the rules of corporate governance took place. The vast task of privatisation and post-privatisation surveillance created professional opportunities for people who were already part of the system. The role of international organisations, such as the IMF,

World Bank, and EU in supporting institutional development in Romania is analysed in the next chapter.

State capability, banks and capital markets: changing the context for corporate governance

As shown in Chapter 3, the leadership provided by political parties in Romania for the transformation of the planned economy into a market economy was relatively weak. The weakness of the political parties was reflected in the fact that their democratic pact, a convergence towards democratic norms in politics, had to be mediated by overly complex legislative institutions. Thus, even though the political reform was swift, the general climate of uncertainty and lack of legitimacy undermined the leadership potential of the political elites. Another manifestation of this weakness was the fact that political parties did not perceive that it was in their collective interest to strengthen the state administrative apparatus. Additionally, politicians were frequently checked in their efforts to assert the role of the executive by the inertia of the bureaucracy. One adaptive response to this was to turn several upper levels in the bureaucracy into political appointments. But since this was in itself seen as a rather blatant attempt to create economic opportunities for political acolytes, the practical result of this competition between political and bureaucratic strategies of adaptation to system change was to slow down the process of differentiation of the economic and political spheres.

The breakdown of the communist regime in Romania represented an opportunity for swift institutional change, in the sense that the old rules according to which the parliament, the presidency and the cabinet worked were removed at one stroke and had to be created from scratch. The role of the cabinet in generating policies was strengthened. But below this level, the reform of the central administration, with the aim of eliminating obsolete entities, creating new mechanisms to carry out new functions and linking the new organisational units in a workable system of co-ordination and communication, was quite slow (Nunberg 1999, 56–59).

The civil service was fragmented. As late as 1998, the pay of civil servants was linked to the scale of pay within the sectors they administered; it was not unified across the civil service. As a percentage of October 1990 salary levels, in January 1998, the average salary in the economy was 63.27 per cent, but in the public administration it was only 42.72 per cent. Within the public administration major discrepancies existed between the salaries in the *regies autonomes* for instance, which were 75.71 per cent of their 1990 levels, and the health sector, where the level was only 46.63 per cent. The rise to 53.53 per cent in February 1998, although important, was only a small step in covering this gap. In education, the 1998 salary levels were 67 per cent of their value in

1990 (World Bank 1998b, vol. I, 17). Thus, line ministries had stronger ties with the sectoral interests they were meant to supervise than with the political centre.

There was no central authority for the management of the civil service and there was very little co-ordination between ministries in the elaboration of policies (OECD 1998, 23). This impacted on the ability of the cabinet to articulate and deliver policies. For instance, President Constantinescu (1997, 5) explained in a press interview that the cabinet meetings were excessively long because ministers spend a lot of time smoothing over differences that should have been ironed out at a previous stage. The effects of this fragmentation were obvious in the elaboration and implementation of the state budget. The Ministry of Finance did not establish a department of economic forecasts, on which to base budget calculations, until 1998.[1] This was one reason for frequent adjustments in the state budget, at least two or three times every year. Conveniently, it also allowed a great deal of discretion to individual ministries in the management of the funds allocated to them.

A World Bank mission in Romania found in 1998 that budget adjustments during the budget-year were the result of indiscipline on the part of line ministries and of sudden changes of policy, tax cuts and wage increases (1998b, vol. I, 1–4, 13). The budget decisions were not treated as binding, and there was a great deal of ad hoc decision-making and lack of control. According to OECD (1998, 48), 'the budget appears to be more an act of political signalling than a tool of management and guidance for the steps that follow'. Simple instruments, such as regular meetings between the BNR and the Ministry of Finance to review the cash flow of the treasury, or an integrated computer system, were still missing in 1998 (World Bank 1998b, vol. I, 11, 15).

This situation testifies to the absence of a concerted effort on the part of the government to set new standards for the state bureaucracy. Also, as shown in Chapter 3, party loyalties were important for the advancement of civil servants (Wiatr 1995). Thus, the ability of the civil servants to uphold an independent point of view was undermined at both ends. There were few incentives or practical means for the bureaucrats to resist pressure from sectoral interests. The fragmentation of the administration system meant that responsibilities for policy outcomes were unclear. The advantage of interest groups with practical knowledge and ability to apply pressure at crucial points in the decision-making process was enhanced by that fact that such undue influence was difficult to trace.

As the course of reforms described in Chapter 4 ascertained, certain groups or sectors, such as the energy-intensive industries, were able for a time to delay restructuring and to shift the costs of their inefficiencies onto the economy as a whole. The perpetuation of this state of affairs seems to have had an important demonstration effect for the private sector, as shown by the numerous tax exemptions accorded to private firms in the last few years

(Dochia 1999, 15–21; IMF 2001, 45–46).[2] The segmented bureaucracy facilitated rather than impeded such a development. Indeed, the inclusion of Romania among the states in danger of being captured by particular interests, in a recent survey (Hellman, Jones and Kaufmann 2000) lends credence to this view of the state administration.

Along with the state administration, banks can play a crucial role in promoting the rules of the market and the restructuring of the SOEs (Perotti, 1994; van Wijnbergen 1998). After the fall of communism, as in other economic sectors, the agenda for change was complex. The immediate concerns were to enable banks to turn inherited systemic bad debts into good debts, to introduce new systems of non-cash payments, and reliable mechanisms for avoiding bank failure. Questions about the ownership of banks and their role in the economy as creators of credit and equity owners were also important. In addition, all inter-bank markets in the region tended to be dominated by one or two big savings banks (Rostowski 1995).

In Romania, the reform of the banking system started after the liberalisation of prices, which led to a replication of the experience of Poland, Yugoslavia and Russia, where inflation was allowed to rise because the interest rates remained highly negative (Rădulescu 1993). One positive effect was that all bad debts were wiped out by inflation. But in the absence of strong measures to discipline enterprises, bad debts accumulated again very quickly (Croitoru 1994b). After the spinning off of all commercial activities of the monobank of the socialist era, in December 1990, the BNR began to play a role in the formation of monetary policy, and acted as a strong promoter of reform (Dăianu 1995).

For instance in 1993 the BNR won the argument with the government, in parliament, about the need for a stabilisation programme (BNR 1997a, 102–105). From 1993, the bank was also able to formalise its duties in the administration of the consolidated treasury accounts, so as to avoid inflationary financing of deficits. Along with these successes, the BNR occasionally gave in to pressure from the government (Isărescu 1994; Cerna 1996, 51). In 1996, the monetary policy was overburdened with quasi-fiscal functions: covering the budget deficit; preferential refinancing for agriculture and the energy-intensive sectors (Perotti and Cărare 1996). The Government also forced the BNR to take on its balance sheet the debts incurred by Romania to the IMF (BNR 1997b, 73–86, 121–123).

The BNR created the framework for the licensing of banks and their prudential supervision, established norms for liquidity, set the reserve requirements and generally built the regulatory framework for the banking system. This was a process punctuated by crises, as loopholes in the existing legislation were exposed through the intended or unintended predatory behaviour of various economic agents. Disciplining the propensity of the state to use the banking sector to subsidise failing industries and to cover for macro-economic imbalances was only one aspect of the BNR's struggle to assert its independence. The first major crisis in the Romanian banking sector emerged in 1995, when in-site inspections by the BNR revealed gross mis-reporting and misconduct on the part of two private banks, Dacia Felix and Credit Bank. Their financial position became unsustainable, and they had to close for new business. The BNR continued to finance these banks until the middle of 1996, in order to prevent panic in the financial system and allow these banks to repay their savers as they held about 14 per cent of total house-hold savings. In the absence of a credit insurance scheme, the BNR acted as a lender of last resort (BNR 1997a, 291–294). These banks put pressure on the BNR to continue to refinance their losses and tried to shift the blame for their bankruptcy onto the National Bank, because it had initiated the bankruptcy proceedings. Significant delays in handling this crisis were due to the courts and the rules on sanctions which allowed only gradual intervention by the BNR (BNR 1997b, 104–108).

The refinancing by the BNR of these two banks added to the inflationary pressures in 1995 and 1996, when the control of inflation achieved in the previous years was lost. The incident provided, however, an opportunity for driving home the need for greater market and regulatory discipline, and the BNR regulations were subsequently tightened. An insurance scheme for banks was introduced.

These measures were introduced too late to obviate another crisis in 1998–99, when *Banca Agricolă* (Bank for Agriculture) and Bancorex were discovered to hold a concentration of bad loans, many of them extended under political pressure during 1995–96 to the agriculture and energy sectors. These bad debts amounted in December 1998 to 253.6 per cent of the capital in the banking system. Under pressure from and with active technical support from the IMF and the World Bank, Bancorex was closed, and its bad debts transferred to an assets recovering agency. The Agriculture Bank was restruc-tured. As a result, by the end of 1999 the proportion of bad loans fell to 31.2 per cent of own capital, and decreased to 4.5 per cent in November 2000 (Isărescu 2001).

In spite of these bank crises, common in one form or another to all CEE transition countries, the skill base of the sector increased (Oeconomica 1993) and the regulatory framework improved. Entry by private, domestic and foreign banks, as well as privatisation in the second part of the decade, changed dramatically the structure of the banking sector in Romania. By the end of 2000, of the forty banks in existence, the state owned majority shares in four. Of the twenty-nine private banks, in twenty-one the majority stake belonged to foreigners and there were seven additional branches of foreign banks. State-owned banks still represented 43.89 per cent of the social capital in the system and 47.40 per cent of the total balance sheet, while the banks in which foreigners have majority stakes represented 47.47 per cent of the social capital and 49.55 per cent of the balance sheet. The domestic private capital had 8.64 per cent of the social capital and 3.05 per cent of the total balance sheet of the banking system (Isărescu 2001).

The ability of the banking system to allocate capital resources efficiently to the enterprise sector was constrained by systemic conditions and state intervention, especially in 1995–96. The increasing share of the state debt in the domestic credit, the protracted crisis of the Bank for Agriculture and Bancorex were the cause of persistently high interest rates at levels well above inflation (Borc 1999). Banks also used big spreads between deposit and credit interest rates. They depended on rents to survive (Boot and Wijnbergen 1995, 45–50). Expensive credit and the availability of almost interest-free alternatives in the form of arrears, explain why the average ratio of credit to the enterprise sector in the GDP was only 11 per cent in Romania, during 1991–97. The same ratio was much higher in the Czech Republic (59 per cent) and Hungary (25 per cent) in the same period, while for Poland and Bulgaria the rates were closer to those in Romania, 14 per cent and 16 per cent respectively. In Russia and Ukraine, the average ratio of credit to the private sector to GDP was somewhat lower, at 9 per cent and 2 per cent respectively (Doltu 1999, 4).

Alternative institutions able to raise capital, such as investment funds and stock markets began to play a role relatively early in the transition. Mutual funds emerged spontaneously, as neo-liberals expected. To attract deposits, they used projections of their value in the future as a measure of their present success. But when, in 1996, the newly established state agency *Comisia Naţională a Valorilor Mobiliare* (National Commission for Securities – CNVM) published its rules for the calculation of the net assets of the mutual funds, their value was slashed to about half of their previous estimates. This provoked a run on the funds and the bankruptcy of some. Those who survived adopted a conservative attitude and invested predominantly in treasury bills (BNR 1997b, 92–94).

Bursa de Valori Bucureşti (Bucharest Stock Exchange – BVB) started to operate in November 1995 and the RASDAQ, the over-the-counter market, modelled on NASDAQ and set up with help from USAID, opened a year later. At the end of 2000, BVB listed 114 companies, the majority of which were on a second, less restrictive, tier (92). The five *Societăţi de Investiţii Financiare* (Societies for Financial Investment – SIFs), the former *Fonduri ale Proprietăţi Private* (Private Property Funds – FPPs), were listed in the first tier. The capitalisation of BVB was over $365 million in 2000, almost half of its peak value in 1997 (CNVM 2001). The rules for quotation are similar to those in other exchanges in the world, and require disclosure of information and regular audit by independent auditors. All the companies privatised in the mass privatisation programme are quoted on the RASDAQ; the total number of companies whose shares were tradable on that market was over 5,200 in 1996 (BNR 1997b, 94).[3]

As explained in Chapter 4, the privatisation programme in Romania envisaged that shares in all companies should be tradable and that public offering should be one of the methods for privatisation. From the start, the activities of the Bucharest Stock Exchange and the RASDAQ were influenced by privatisation. The mass privatisation programme led to a diffuse shareholder structure for the traded companies. A flourishing market for brokerage services developed as a consequence. But the main problem yet to be addressed is the weak regulatory regime for the protection of minority shareholders (Pogonaru and Apostol 1999, 4–5). These markets promoted new rules of the game by creating an arena for transparent trading, by imposing disclosure requirements on companies and by exposing distortions in the accounting system (Pogonaru and Apostol 1999, 10).

This section has reviewed changes in three areas of activity decisive to the marketisation of the economy: the reform of the public administration, of the banking sector and capital markets. The broad conclusion here is that in all of these areas, and in spite of setbacks and delays, new institutions and new rules of the game are reflected in new objectives for these organisations and that they are developing appropriate routines and procedures for carrying them out.

Privatisation and corporate governance

The organisations entrusted to manage the privatisation process had a crucial role in the creation of secure property rights and rules for corporate governance (Dăianu 1994a). The creation of the FPS and the FPPs was core to the conflict between the FSN government and the democratic opposition, as shown in Chapter 3. The government argued that since privatisation had to be managed, it was better placed in the hands of a new set of organisations. Adrian Severin, the minister for relations with parliament, put the argument for FPS and FPPs to his fellow deputies in the speech recommending the privatisation law in July 1991. He argued that the only alternative to these institutions was the state administration, which would not be 'the best alternative' because it was, 'inevitably ... [the] ... most bureaucratic and stagnant of structures' (MO 177/1991, 9). He saw the new institutions as a victory over the old ones:

> To give up on these funds is tantamount to abandoning the role of doing the privatisation in Romania to precisely those institutions that are more predisposed to bureaucracy, that are more pre-disposed to stagnation, and more vulnerable to corruption. This seems to me completely inadequate. (MO 180/1991, 24)

The opposition, on the other hand, warned that these new organisations would repeat the problems of the old, due to their size: FPS had control over all commercial companies and even the five FPPs had portfolios of over 1,000 enterprises. They were expected to fall prey to the dangers inherent in bureaucratic organisation: the tendency to expand and to prolong their life unnecessarily.

This section assesses the actual role of the FPS and FPPs in corporate governance and the consequences of the decision to entrust the privatisation programme to them. The decision *for* the funds was presented as a decision *against* the existing state bureaucracy. In spite of problems with their independence from the state in the first few years, the FPPs gradually assumed the role of representing the rights of private owners. The relationship between the FPS and the state, however, in spite of the initial desire to give the FPS independent status, remained complicated. Although it owned 70 per cent of the shares of the enterprises in its portfolio, the FPS remained an agent for the state. The transfer of state property rights to the FPS was not a complete transfer, because, ultimately, the state was understood to remain the owner. Had the ministries on behalf of the state retained these rights, the consistency of the process would have been preserved since both the FPS and the line ministries were representing the final owner.

As it was, the huge transfer of responsibilities and information from a number of line ministries to the FPS was supposed to take place even before the FPS was sufficiently prepared to exercise its role in corporate governance. The privatisation plan overburdened the FPS and compromised its ability to carry out fully its twin functions: corporate governance and privatisation. By and large, the privatisation process was slow, and the effects of the FPS to introduce effective governance principles, such as hard budget constraints, had mixed results. As was shown in Chapter 4, lack of discipline at the microeconomic level was reflected in inflation, large amounts of inter-enterprise, bank and budget payment arrears.

Disruptions in the continuity of the regime for corporate governance, and the information costs of transferring the corporate governance responsibilities from the ministries to the FPS were huge. The FPS had to produce records for over 6,300 companies, before even contemplating the task of nominating its representatives in the *Adunarea Generală a Acţionarilor* (General Meeting of Shareholders – AGA) for each of the enterprises in its portfolio. There were also costs associated with the friction between ministries, which in some cases resisted the move, and the FPS. Finally, the slow build-up of capacity in the FPS compounded the overall impression of delay, confusion and ultimately lack of credibility and transparency (Blaga 1994b). In the following, these aspects will be explained in turn.

Corporate governance was thrown into disarray initially by the spontaneous revolution in enterprises. In the days immediately after the fall of Ceauşescu, grass roots mobilisation led to the constitution of new trade unions, which affiliated themselves to the National Salvation Front (FSN). The Unions elected new managers and played a role in the decision-making of the enterprises. In February 1990, the FSN required these organisations to close (Pasti 1995, 102–103). Responsibility for corporate governance returned to ministries, whose role was confirmed by Law 15 on the organisation of SOEs as commercial companies and *regies autonomes*, in August 1990 (MOR 98/1990).

A small council of delegates nominated by ministries was asked to supervise the performance of managers. At this time, SOEs had to perform in a climate of uncertainty, beset by contradictions. Prices were partially liberalised and SOEs were encouraged to operate according to new rules – to seek new partners and markets, to put relationships with their clients and suppliers on a contractual basis. At the same time, they were also required to abide by the allocations of inputs still drawn up by the Ministry of Resources and Industry, 'until such time as all prices will be liberalised' (MOR 98/1990, article 52).

A year later, the privatisation law required that the council of delegates should continue their activities until the FPS organised the AGAs as the new governing bodies in enterprises (MOR 169/1991, article 39). In effect, the ministerial councils operated for almost four years, until 1994, when the FPS became fully operational. Difficulties in the transfer from the ministry to FPS authority were signalled by official documents issued by the ANP and the FPS. In March 1994, the FPS was stating in its report to parliament that it was unsure about the total size of its portfolio. For 5,934 SOEs the legal operations for their conversion into commercial companies and *regies autonomes*, and the transfer of their social capital, had been completed. But about 2,300 SOEs had not been entered into the Registry of Commerce, and it was unclear how many more enterprises had yet to be processed. This was because, according to the FPS, it was unclear who held responsibility for these operations, and what were the agreed procedures and deadlines (MOR 81/1994a, annex 1, article 1.3).

The change of government at the end of 1996 did not lead immediately to changes in this framework for corporate governance: AGA remained the most important forum for decision making and it was its responsibility to nominate the Board of Administration. In 1999, a 'sole administrator of the enterprise' replaced the Board. The decision was introduced by a government ordinance, which was later invalidated by parliament. It can be surmised that on the whole these frequent changes in the management of enterprises could not have led to the desired improvement in performance. In the FPS's view, this was also due to the fact that managers were not offered the right incentives, and the pool of qualified managers in Romania at the time was very restricted (FPS 2000b, 19–20).

These choices about corporate governance opened avenues for what might be considered a type of political capitalism. The nomination of FPS representatives in the AGAs started in September 1993, and by March of the next year, it was completed in thirty-five out of forty-two counties. The FPS had 148 personnel at the time, so it is not surprising that it relied on appointees from ministries and other state organisations to fill all the posts. This was not a position of strength for the FPS and if the legislators had hoped that the FPS would be able to impose a different 'spirit' in the management of enterprises, its dependency on the resources of the central administration soon put paid to such aspirations (MOR 81/1994a, annex 1, articles 1.2 and 1.3). The relations between managers (appointed by the government under contract from 1993) and the representatives of the FPS in the AGAs became 'subjective' very quickly and the criteria of performance negotiated between the two parties reflected rather slack expectations about performance and financial discipline (FPS 2000b, 19).

The great number of new positions, as representatives of the FPS in the AGAs, provided opportunities for employees in ministries and parliamentarians. The payment for their services consisted of a flat fee and bonuses linked to the performance of enterprises. The potential for conflicts of interests did not go unnoticed, but efforts to eliminate it had mixed results. President Iliescu pleaded in February and March 1995, when the law on the status of parliamentarians was debated, that deputies and senators should be proscribed from acting as members of AGAs. But this position was not supported by the major political parties. The National Council of the ruling party, the PDSR, for instance, avoided taking a position on this matter (Brucan 1996, 124–128).

In some of the more lucrative cases, the monthly payments to the FPS representatives in the AGAs were in the millions (that is, thousands of dollars at an average exchange rate of 2,000 lei to the American dollar in 1995). Some deputies argued that the services they rendered, obtaining credits and other contracts for the enterprises, entitled them to such reward. In the view of at least one analyst this was an example of the 'symbiosis between power and capital' in Romania at the time (Brucan 1996, 124). The Romanian media was quick to play up accusations of corruption and shady dealings, which undermined the credibility of the political class as a whole. Ultimately this affected the authority and the ability of the FPS to shape the behaviour of managers in its enterprises.

Another form of co-operation between the FPS and employees in the economic ministries was the establishment of 'firms for strategy'. These were consultancy firms which had the role of identifying and catering for the restructuring and privatisation needs of a cluster of related commercial companies. A hybrid between the FPS and the ministries, these 'strategy firms' were established to allow for an 'efficient utilisation of the restricted pool of (market-orientated) specialists, combined with the decentralisation and the acceleration of the [privatisation] process' (FPS, in MOR 81/1994a, article 1.4). Strategy firms elaborated the restructuring plans and after approval by the Board of the FPS, became responsible for their implementation. They could also act as the representatives of the FPS in the AGAs (MOR 81/1994a, article 4.5).

Beyond this co-optation of individuals from ministries and the parliament to exercise the governance role of the FPS, some line ministries also raised the cost of their co-operation with the FPS in the privatisation process. Early signs that this relationship was not going to be straightforward emerged during the transfer of roles in corporate governance, as mentioned above. After the FPS began the privatisation of its portfolio, some ministries obtained the right to participate in the decision over the privatisation of certain enterprises. For instance, the Ministry for Research and Technology convinced the FPS that its research institutes were of 'strategic importance' and that their privatisation had to be approved by the ministry (MOR 102/1996, article 4). Similarly, in the defence sector, the cabinet elaborated the strategy for privatisation, and the receipts from sales were earmarked for the military (MOR 88/1997, article 51).

The Ministry of Food and Agriculture also preserved its role in privatisation and obtained special status for the SOEs specialising in services for agriculture. These SOEs were included in the mass privatisation programme under a separate set of prescriptions. They were to be evaluated by district commissions comprising representatives of the MFA and FPS and had permission to take account fully of the depreciation of the machinery. Customers of these SOEs had a pre-emptive right to buy up to 35 per cent of shares (MOR 122/1995, article 22). According to the secondary legislation on the implementation of the law, these special commissions were in charge with all the privatisation decisions (MOR 251/1995). Also, the Agriculture Ministry lobbied to receive 80 per cent of the receipts from privatisation in its sector similar to a concession secured by the Ministry for Tourism (Negrescu 1999, 19–20).

Unstable legislative conditions have beset the work of the FPS and the privatisation process from the onset, as already indicated in Chapter 3. Interference from above in the activities of the FPS also occurred during the implementation process. Thus, the cabinet took over the implementation of the mass privatisation programme in 1995 with massive help from the local administration, the *regies autonomes*, and the Ministry of Finance. Only after the subscription of coupons and certificates was completed with the help of these organisations, did the FPS and the FPPs have a role in finalising the process by making a record of the changes in the ownership structure. The ANP played a role in the supervision and publication of the results (MOR 21/1997, MOR 51/1997). Although the mass privatisation programme was realised, delays in the completion of these recording operations, which dragged on until 1999, were due to this awkward shift of responsibilities between agencies (Negrescu 1999, 14).

After the change in government in November 1996, the leadership role of the FPS in the privatisation process was redefined again. The decision on the privatisation of the local commercial companies was entrusted to the local authorities (MOR 88/1997, article 1c). Line ministries and local authorities, as well as the FPS, exercised the property rights on behalf of the state over the companies resulting from the reorganisation of the *regies autonomes*. Equally, all three organisations were responsible for their privatisation (MOR 125/1997).

At the end of 1997, the Emergency Ordinance 88/1997 redrew the boundaries of the FPS's authority again to include all of the commercial companies resulting from the re-organisation of the *regies autonomes* (MOR 381/1997, article 8.1). In May 1999, Law 99 reversed the situation yet again. The line ministries were given the task of representing the ownership rights of the state in these commercial companies, both in terms of governance and the preparation for privatisation (MOR 236/1999, article 6.4^3).

These examples of interference with the governance and privatisation tasks of the FPS show that the initial hope that the FPS would be able to shape the process according to a 'new spirit' did not materialise. Moreover, the duality of its roles exposed the FPS to requests from the government to get involved in the restructuring of enterprises. Especially before November 1996, the FPS was used for channelling subsidies to SOEs. In 1993 alone, the FPS committed 17.5 billion lei (it earned 23.8 billion that year) for the restructuring of state animal farms as a way of preparing them for privatisation (MOR 81/1994a, chapter 4). Overall, during 1992–96 the FPS spent 2,000 billion lei, a little more than it earned from privatisation (1,902 billion) on restructuring failing enterprises. The major beneficiaries were the machine building, petrochemical and metallurgy industries (Ionete 1996, 38). Unfortunately, this effort did not lead to significant improvement in the productivity or the financial situation of the recipients, many of whom were scheduled for liquidation after 1997. The procedure thus amounted to a financial transfer from profitable enterprises to loss-making ones (FPS 2000b, 21).

The Democratic Convention government forbade in May 1997 payments by the FPS to SOEs, and restructuring took the form of initiating bankruptcy proceedings. In 1997, twenty-six animal farms were closed, twenty-one were privatised, and another thirty-four were slated for privatisation. In addition, more than 61 per cent of the firms for agricultural services were privatised that year, while the distribution network remained state property (BNR 1998, 53).

Loss-making enterprises in other sectors were also closed in larger numbers after 1997. In the mining sector, where production subsidies amounted to $2.8 billion between 1990 and 1996, 160 mines were closed by March 1999. The World Bank (1999c, 4) estimated that of the remaining 118 mines only thirty-five were economically viable and the sector required further restructuring. In 1999 alone the FPS closed or nominated the agents in charge of liquidation of SOEs accounting for 12 per cent of its losses. Many of these were in the energy-intensive sectors such as petrochemicals and metallurgy (BNR 2000, 40). Thus losses by SOEs were reduced from 2.39 per cent of the GDP in 1997 to 1.3 per cent in 2000 (FPS 2000b, 22).

Another way in which the FPS served broader governmental policies was by extending credit to the buyers of its enterprises. The FPS official publications disclose the price for which shares were sold, but they do not give the sums actually received by the FPS. The difference is significant because only up to 30 per cent of the total sale price was paid up front; the rest of the payments were spread over a number of years (initially 3–5, then 10 years, and after 1997 the period was reduced again to 3–5 years). The interest rates for these FPS credits varied, but they were much lower than inflation. Of all the buyers, the most lenient terms were extended to associations of workers and managers in the MEBO sales. Other subsidies for buyers were introduced by the decision in Law 55/1995, in effect until the end of 1997, that 60 per cent of the price obtained from the sale of shares in an enterprise was to return to that enterprise. The money was to be used for extinguishing debts (towards the state budget, the energy suppliers, the banks and other creditors) and for investment. After 1997, the introduction of debt-equity swaps fulfilled a similar role.

The FPS was the focus of a diversity of pressure groups and interests and this was reflected in the debates about the control over its activities. Initially, it was put in the care of the parliament, to ensure 'democratic control', and to give the opposition a chance to take part. This was a weak form of control and in order to strengthen the role of the executive in privatisation and reform, in December 1997, the ANP was re-organised as a ministry for privatisation and the FPS was subordinated to it. The ministry was an additional bureaucratic layer that gave opportunity for friction between the FPS staff, which by this stage had accumulated considerable expertise in privatisation, and the relatively less experienced ANP which had languished in a peripheral role in the previous years. Also, the rivalry between the minister for privatisation and the executive manager and the president of the FPS board was another source of problems (Negrescu 1999, 15).

This arrangement was reversed in May 1999, when the ministry for privatisation was replaced by the *Agenţia de Restructurare* (Agency for Restructuring) as the link between the Government, the office of the prime minister in particular, and the FPS (MOR 236/1999). The Năstase government changed this again: the FPS was renamed the *Autoritatea pentru Privatizare şi Administrarea Participaţiilor Statului* (Authority for Privatisation and the Administration of State Shares – APAPS) and received ministerial rank. A council of between nine and eleven members representing line ministries shadowed the board of administration, and it was envisaged that some of the privatisation and post-privatisation responsibilities of the new Authority would be transferred to these ministries.[4] This was in preparation for winding down the APAPS after the completion of privatisation.

Accountability for the privatisation deals has been another source of concern for the employees of the FPS in particular. Early regulations were vague about the personal responsibility of these employees. In practice, *Curtea de Conturi* (Court of Accounts), which oversaw the formation, management and use of government funds, took an active role, especially through ex-post inquiries in privatisation deals. As the Court had both audit and judicial functions, its verdicts could not be contested in the regular courts. The standard procedure was to apply to civil servants the personal liability clauses used for private citizens in civil law cases (Nunberg 1999, 62–65). Not surprisingly, the agents for privatisation were sometimes reticent in closing deals, for fear of having their judgement invalidated later.[5]

The Ciorbea Government clarified the boundaries between personal and corporate responsibility for privatisation in the 1997 legislation mentioned above, but this was questioned again in December 2000. Before relieving the former FPS management of their role, the new government had their activities checked by the Court of Accounts. Fears about its politicisation were fuelled by the assessment of the PDSR that the FPS had 'plundered' the economy during 1997–2000.

To conclude, this section has demonstrated that the FPS had to work within the constraints of limited resources and also tense relations with other state agencies. It could not, by itself, impose a new market ethos through its role in privatisation and corporate governance. In spite of being the formal 'owner' of the SOEs, the FPS never ceased to represent the state. However, the achievements of the FPS in accumulating valuable experience over the years and realising a fair degree of privatisation should not be underestimated. At the same time, politically, the fiction of its independence from the state was extremely useful. The presence of the FPS, nominally in charge of privatisation, blurred the lines of accountability over the conduct of the privatisation policy. Conflicts of interest and media attention were focused on the FPS and to an extent away from the government and away from the more insidious influences over policy of the vested interests from the heavy industries.

As argued in Chapters 3 and 4, the ideological antagonism of the Romanian political parties was reflected in frequent changes of regulations as each new government avoided giving credit to their predecessors and wanted to start things from scratch. Privatisation by the FPS was a process of gradual attrition of its portfolio and these discontinuities slowed down the process. In the case of its corporate governance role, the effect of these discontinuities was more damaging. It created unnecessary uncertainty and increased the costs for SOEs of adaptation to change.

Conclusion

This chapter has shown that taking into account institutional factors in post-communist transformation can add a significant dimension to the evaluation of the reform efforts. The recasting of institutions such as money, trade, firm management and bank management from their incarnations under the plan to new definitions consistent to the market is a complex process of learning for individuals and for organisations. This dis-embedding and re-embedding became possible because of the shift in the basis for political power and the decision to change the structuring principle of the economy, described in Chapters 3 and 4.

At the level of institutions, the change involved redefinition in theory, in the sense of finding the words and the rationale. But also, the test for institutional development is the ability of ideas to structure to a certain extent the activities of the actors. This efficacy assumes that their assumptions and requirements are already internalised by these actors. Behind this efficacy is the effective deployment of authority – in the examples presented here, the authority of the state administration, the BNR and the FPS.

The ability of the state administration to model and impose changes in the rules of the economic game for enterprises – from reliance on the state to self-reliance and competition in the open markets – was relatively weak. The reform of the state administration and the development of new mechanisms and relationships between the bureaucracy and economic and political actors were not a priority for the political elites. Greater changes were visible in the development of the banking sector, where, over time, the BNR increased its capacity to act as the regulatory authority in the system. This process also contained phases of retreat on the part of the Bank, under the pressure of the government or the failing banks. This evolution was similar in the stock markets.

The governance role of the FPS was also weakened by the delay in the reform of the public administration. The FPS relied on information and personnel from the line ministries, and it could not impose by itself a new market ethos. On the contrary, the signs are that its attempts to introduce new regulatory procedures for enterprises – contracts and performance indicators for managers, for instance – were undermined by collusion between its representatives and managers. It is clear that the new administrative tasks created by the transformation process provided an outlet for administrative personnel made redundant by the downsizing of the role of the state in the economy. Political actors also found lucrative economic niches for themselves, through the politicisation of the upper echelons of the state administration and the posts in the AGAs.

Certain economic structures, although in the process of being displaced, also put a great deal of pressure on the state to cushion the impact of changed economic conditions of competition in the world markets and to allow them to delay restructuring. In spite of the slowing down effect of all of these factors, privatisation has advanced significantly and by the end of the decade the balance between the private and the state sector in the GDP was tipped in favour of the former.

Notes

1 According to one witness, this unit was not fully functional in October 1999.
2 Professor Adrian Miroiu also made this point in an interview in February 2001. The Senate's unwillingness to pass a cabinet ordinance that was extending tax cuts to certain media companies was met with negative coverage of the parliamentary institutions by those media companies.
3 Other Stock Exchanges in CEE were also affected by the flight of investors from emerging markets and considered merging operations (Green 2001).
4 Emergency Ordinance 296 from 30 December 2000, at www.sof.ro/fps/oug296.htm.
5 This was one of the major causes for delays in privatisation identified by employees of the FPS and ANP in interviews conducted by the author in Bucharest in April 1998.

6

International factors in Romania's post-communist transformations

International actors have played a role in all of the processes analysed so far, in the reconstitution of politics as democratic politics, in the gradual institutional differentiation of the political and economic spheres and in economic reform. The following sections discuss some of the avenues through which important international actors, especially the international financial institutions, the International Monetary Fund and the World Bank, and the European Union, have come to exert this influence.

The gradual recasting of political discourse has been facilitated by the contrast with different frameworks of understanding proposed by external actors. In the second section of this chapter I show how the need to articulate credible political programmes and identities has led all political parties to seek to display an affinity with the mainstream western European or atlanticist political orientations. In spite of their antagonisms, different factions of the Romanian political elite have recognised the pragmatic interests of the country and tried to obtain recognition and validation of its transformational goals from authoritative organisations such as the IFIs and the EU. The third section analyses the involvement of these organisations in steering the transformation of the economy at the level of macro-economic policy-making, while the fourth section investigates their role in the construction of the institutional underpinnings of the market economy.

Cross-cultural communication: neo-liberalism meets post-communism

The reactions of foreign diplomats, business people and the media are an important mirror to Romanian reality and they can open new opportunities for learning and co-operation. After the revolution of 1989 and the opening up of the country, a degree of globalisation has occurred. Networks of communication, forms of organisation, production processes, markets, and patterns of social consciousness have become increasingly autonomous of the territorial boundaries of the state (Scholte 1998).

The most important cultural referent in this process has been, as already indicated, the West. In Romania, as in other countries in CEE (Prizel 1998), there was a great desire to assimilate the knowledge and experience of governance from the West and to raise the standards of domestic economic, social, and political life accordingly. Inevitably, this situation had its difficulties. In this unequal relationship, admiration for the West stimulated efforts to emulate it and led to some progress. At the same time, the perceived failure of the country to achieve these objectives quickly was also a source of resentment. Assignment of blame for this failure was a constant element of the domestic political process. In this way, western standards were sometimes instruments for a critique of domestic affairs that was undermining rather than constructive.

For instance, IMF pronouncements were often taken as the reference point for the evaluation of economic policy and the quality of government. The Democratic Convention governments used the IMF's approval of their policies as a source of legitimation, and they enjoyed the approval of the IFIs at the beginning of their term in office. For the first time in post-communist Romania the IMF chief negotiator for Romania, Paul Thomsen, broke the reserve of official announcements and gave two interviews, in August and December 1997, to *Adevărul* (Thomsen 1997a, 1997b). On both occasions he explained both the position of his organisation and that of the Romanian government, and made predictions about the evolution of unemployment, the development of the private sector, increased FDI, taxation, and bank restructuring.

As his visit to Bucharest in December 1997 coincided with a cabinet reshuffle, the reporter asked him which of the new members of the cabinet the IMF had imposed. He was clearly under pressure to restate the politically correct view on the advisory role of the IMF and the independence of the Romanian government, but without being able to eschew entirely the ambiguity of his position as a spokesperson for both:

> Let's be honest. We, at the IMF, are not stupid. Cabinet reshuffling is not our business. If we started picking people and they failed, who would assume responsibility? We support policies, not people. This is the truth. We will discuss with anybody who represents the Romanian government. (Thomsen 1997b)

But this close association between the IFIs and the Ciorbea government became something of a disadvantage later. During 1998–99, the structural reform – the privatisation and restructuring of some of the loss-makers in the economy – slowed down, and the IMF reviewed negatively Romania's performance. This offered their opponents vast opportunities for vicious attacks in the media and, unfortunately, in the heroic pattern of evaluation of success and failure, this critique tended to vacillate between contradictory value positions. It went beyond the confines of normal political competition, and reinforced the impression held by foreign partners that Romanian political elites were unable to offer constructive, effective leadership for economic reform.

One line of criticism was that the government lacked direction and it was unable to generate a reform programme of its own (Pasti 1998a, 1998e; Mărgărit 1999; Stolojan 1999). Another often noted failure was that of not using the funds borrowed from abroad (Capital 1999b). The IMF itself was portrayed as an authoritarian force, leaving the Romanian governments with little choice. Sometimes, this was seen as a positive situation, as the failing Romanian governments would thus be forced to shape up and resolve their problems. The IMF and the opportunities they represented were 'the last chance', the 'only way for Romania to go out into the world' (Capital, 1999a).

The IMF was also seen to have overwhelming power. It was a 'vice' and a 'god' from whose dominance the country should try to free itself (David 1999a, 1999b). Its position was likened to the feudal bond between the Otoman Empire and the Romanian principalities in the seventeenth and eighteenth centuries (Lupşan 2001a). The dogmatic aspect of the policy prescriptions and the fact that they relied on unrealistic expectations about what could be achieved in a short span of time were also criticised. This passionate revolt was also a measure of how great the influence of the IMF was perceived to be. The politically correct definition of the relationship between the IMF and Romania as a sovereign state seemed to offer little succour. At other times, however, the Romanian negotiators used the sovereignty argument to obtain concessions. In the case of the 1999 stand-by agreement, the IMF backed down from their requirement that Romania should meet its debt servicing obligations by getting the creditors to roll on the debt (GR 1999a, 1999b).

Beyond this battle of metaphors, the representatives of foreign organisations in Romania, businessmen, and journalists also provided important opportunities for interaction and learning that could, in time, lead to the development of a more balanced or cautious view of internal affairs and the relationship with the outside world. For instance, François Ettori (1998), the chief of the World Bank resident delegation in Romania in the mid 1990s, gave a lucid inventory of some of the cultural biases he encountered during his time there. Among them was the reluctance to impose obligations in economic transactions, and to accept that the failure of some enterprises was part of the normal functioning of the market economy. Also, he believed that Romania was ambivalent about allowing foreigners to have economic power in the country, while at the same time foreign direct investment was sometimes regarded as the 'miracle' that would provide the necessary impetus to the economy. Most importantly, Ettori's (1998) assessment of reform in Romania was also balanced, focusing on the importance of institutional change and recognising the fact that this was a long-term project.

Among the many examples of such public statements by foreign visitors were also Michnik (1997) and Serdar Oghan (1999). Adam Michnik (1997), a Polish dissident to the communist regime, avoided simplistic assessments of contested issues such as the lustration of former communists, the closure of the big loss-making enterprises, the role of the IFIs and corruption. Oghan (1999), the president of the Bucharest office of the United Garanti Bank International, a Dutch bank with Turkish capital, offered an alternative viewpoint about the health of the banking system and the business opportunities in Romania to that of the international credit rating agencies. According to Oghan, when foreign banks attempted to penetrate emerging markets, they tended to do so by promoting the idea that local banks lacked professionalism. Similarly, rating assessments by remote agencies that had relied on second hand information could be considered 'extremely subjective'.

Thus, when they enter the cultural environment of post-communist Romania, IFIs and the EU can become drawn into the logic of representation presented earlier, that of the heroic model. This logic is based on extreme definitions of good and evil. As tools for making sense of a complex and often contradictory reality, their application led to endless fragmentation of explanations and visions (Pop 1998), dissolution of authority and multiplication of criteria (Barbu 1997, 15). As actors attempted to fit the contradictory and complex considerations of post-communist transformations into the certainties of the moral schemes inherited from the past, reality inevitably fell short of such expectations. This background of perpetual failure justified and induced a tendency to fall back upon informal networks in which it was acceptable not to conform to rules and to forge ad hoc alliances and decisions that might undermine the formal institutions (Vlăsceanu 2000, 19–20). This clashed with the ethos of technocratic rationality of the IFIs and their frustration was reflected in their pronouncements about the lack of reform in Romania.

At the same time, the IFIs represented a relatively stable alternative to the cultural patterns still prevalent in Romania. They were both a challenge and an opportunity. As has been shown, in those areas of the Romanian institutions where the technocratic ethos was stronger, such as the BNR, this led to swifter progress with reform. Where the incumbents were not or could not be persuaded to embrace this value system, the process of implementation of the agreements was uneven.

Thus, it would be naïve to expect the IFI's prescriptions to take root very quickly. Such a scenario assumes that the cultural and institutional environments already share the assumptions of these prescriptions and there are no obvious conflicts of interests or bureaucratic politics at stake. However, in interaction with the local realities, these organisations have contributed interpretations and rationalisations of events that restored a sense of continuity of the reform efforts during the 1990s. In this sense the claim that these organisations contributed to the continuity of reform efforts in Romania is valid. In the longer term, it can be hoped that these models might be assimilated at a cultural level, if the gap between the respective sets of assumptions could be identified correctly and bridged through specific arguments about agency and action, expectations of success and the basis for political consensus.

Romanian political elites and the West

Influence from the international environment can also be traced within and through the dynamics of the domestic political process. To establish a distinct identity, all political parties used representations about what they saw as their international partners. These were international organisations or foreign states or values and institutions. Consistent with the line of argument followed so far, it will be shown that all the political parties in Romania strove to find affinities between themselves and their vision of prestigious European traditions. Their domestic rivalries extended to the issue of 'ownership' of these values, especially democracy and market economy.

'The West' was a constant reference point for the Romanian political elites and for the state during the 1990s, as was the case with other CEE states (Prizel 1998). Whether it takes the shape of the European Union, the IMF, the World Bank, NATO, or individual states, 'the West' was invoked as witness, arbiter, supporter, or rescuer. It was the bearer of great wealth and superior civilisation (Pleşu 1997). The comparison between this imagined West and economic and political developments in Romania is a frequent exercise, permeating all domestic issues. Feelings range from awe and admiration, through to despair at the impossibility of bridging the gap between the two standards (Mungiu and Pippidi 1994). By its very unattainable superiority, the West also represents a screen on which fears of inadequacy and helplessness are easily projected. In this scenario, the West becomes the potential cultural invader and destroyer of national identity (PRM 2000).

Each of the political parties sought to define the West and its particular relationship with it and for all of them the reference to the West is in a relation of relative consistency with the claims to identity exercised on the domestic scene and the motivation to promote certain economic policies. There are four political stances in the attitude towards the West which occur with greater frequency across the Romanian political spectrum: ambivalence, aggressive imitation, constructive engagement, and parasitism.

Ambivalence towards the western institutions characterised the PDSR. The international recognition afforded the Romanian state was very important for them, perhaps out of nostalgia for the times when, under Ceauşescu, Romania had played a greater international role than its size or importance warranted. In this sense, of asserting national sovereignty and making a contribution to international affairs, the PDSR fought for recognition of its democratic credentials and the progress with economic reform of the country. The democratic image of Romania, and that of the FSN in particular, suffered a major setback in June 1990 when the ruling party was seen to make recourse to the vigilante activities of the miners from Valea Jiului in order to silence the opposition. After enduring the ostracism of the international community for almost three years, in 1993, the PDSR obtained Romania's inclusion in the Council of Europe, associate partner status to the EU and membership in the Partnership for Peace with NATO (Ionescu 1993b; 1993f; 1994b). It also concluded important treaties with Russia in 1991 and Hungary towards the end of its term in office in 1996.

For the PDSR, the reading of international relations as relations between states was more important than conformity with the ideology represented by the so-called Washington Consensus. This inclination was recognised by the IMF and informed their cautious attitude towards the PDSR governments. Before the 1994 stand-by agreement was considered by the IMF Board of Directors, the PDSR government was asked to provide further proof of its commitment to the stabilisation programme agreed with the IMF by having the Romanian parliament endorse the memorandum. Interestingly, the PDSR and their nationalist allies prioritised according to national interest and voted for the memorandum. The democratic opposition did not want to partake in the responsibility for a measure initiated by their opponents and voted against it, although the memorandum was in agreement with their own programme (Ionescu 1994c, 22–23). This decision was consistent with the pattern indicated by the democratic opposition's attitude towards the privatisation law of 1991 and the decision not to participate in government with the PDSR in 1992.

This shows that domestic actors have some leeway in relation to international pressure and that domestic actors can turn this pressure on its head in order to pursue power and influence domestically. The dynamics of the international/domestic divide can cut across domestic structures with unexpected consequences. At the same time, it is clear that the identities of parties, the images of what they stand for, can sustain, at least temporarily, a degree of incoherence and even contradiction. However, the cost for this is a dent in their credibility that, depending on other decisions by the parties, could accumulate and lead to dramatic results, such as the defeat in the elections of the PNŢCD, the leading member of the CDR, in 2000.

Thus, the co-operation of the PDSR with the IFIs stemmed from considerations of national interest, rather than perfect coincidence of value commitments. The PDSR economic policies tended to reflect the interests of domestic industry and the notion that the state had a role to play in encouraging it. Although unable to fully articulate or carry out a consistent industrial policy, they do favour such an approach. This is evidenced by their record and pronouncements in the governing strategy of the Năstase Cabinet (GOR 2001). However, the PDSR, far from being rigidly neo-communist in outlook, was willing to adjust its policies pragmatically in order to make this relationship with the IFIs work and thus obtain international recognition for their government and Romania's achievements in reforms.

Aggressive imitation is the attitude based on a willingness to adopt political values, policy recommendations, and advice generated in the West unquestioningly and with little local input. Although it is local agents who translate such measures into local parlance and implement them, the internal point of view as an alternative focus of power is generally absent or subdued. In a sense, the wholesale abandonment of the communist system, without an analysis of what had been achieved and what exactly needed to change is an example of this and justifies the interpretation that the fall of communism came about because of the perceived superiority of the West (Verdery 1996). Similarly, the swift adoption of generic values such as democracy and market economy without prior consideration and consensus building as to what these might entail also carried and still carries such connotations (Pasti 1995, 9–26).

Among the political parties, the Democratic Party, the Democratic Convention and the UDMR displayed an inclination towards aggressive imitation. The PD, and its earlier incarnation as FSN-Roman, seemed to base its identity almost solely on this political position. In the first year of democratic government, the Roman government was responsible for re-establishing links with the IMF and the World Bank, and it hired the foreign consultancy Coopers and Lybrand to advise on privatisation (Shafir 1992a). As shown above, the determination of the government to push through this plan alienated some in the party and antagonised the opposition. The argument that foreign experts and politicians, such as John Redwood, the British Minister for Corporations in the DTI, found the plan adequate was marshalled by the FSN in support of the privatisation law in 1991 (MOR 177/1991, 9). For others in the party, the argument was seen as another example of Romania subordinating its policies to foreign influence (MOR 178/1991, 9). The experience of the 1950s when Russian advisers staffed every Romanian ministry was used as a comparative, uncomplimentary, reference point and resentment was expressed for the fact that issues were decided before they could be properly considered by the parliament (MOR 181/ 1991, 5–6).

The Democratic Convention and the historical parties have consistently sought to portray themselves as the true democrats and to this end professed unquestionable commitment to western values, including principles of economic management according to the 'Washington Consensus', such as liberalisation, privatisation, and stabilisation. However, as shown above, they prioritised not around the promotion of policies consistent with such values but around acting against the proposals of their 'neo-communist' opponents, even when the policies were consistent with their political programme. The Ciorbea government in particular was accused of replacing domestic economic policy with IMF recommendations and of failing to generate complementary domestic policies, especially in the first part of 1997 (Pasti 1998e, 3–4). Having linked his hopes of political success to international recognition, Ciorbea's government had to go when the stabilisation programme plunged the economy into a severe recession (Pasti 1998a). The CDR governments were left to fend for themselves after failing to implement all the components of the stand-by agreement of 1997. The disbursement of the IMF loan was suspended at the beginning of 1998. A new agreement was signed in the second part of 1999, after the Romanian government passed the privatisation law, and restructured Bancorex, the bank that concentrated most of the bad loans in the sector (GR 1999a, annex A, 1).

Interestingly, the hesitation of the Ciorbea government in the summer of 1997 to carry out the closure of over twenty enterprises among the greatest loss-makers in the economy, while it disappointed the IMF, was actually designed to achieve another foreign policy objective of equal importance. By giving in to protesters, and thus ensuring social peace, the Ciorbea government was hoping to strengthen Romania's case as a factor of political stability in the region and bolster its chances for entry into the North Atlantic Treaty Organisation (NATO) (Secăreş 1998). Although this objective was not achieved, the CDR governments continued their support of the alliance, especially during the bombing of Kosovo, when NATO used some airports and the national air space to reach their targets. It was not lost on observers in Romania that this show of solidarity with the priorities of NATO in the former Yugoslavia in 1999 might have been a stronger argument for IMF extending a new stand-by agreement to Romania that year than the country's compliance with their economic criteria (David 1999b). It might have played a role in the surprise decision by the Blair government to support Romania's application to start accession negotiations with the EU, in 1999.

In general, the Democratic Convention enjoyed greater trust and recognition on the part of their foreign counterparts and this can be attributed to the lack of ambiguity in their pro-western rhetoric, if not in their actions, especially during their years in government. Gestures such as the visit of the then President of the USA, Bill Clinton, to Bucharest in the summer of 1997, after Romania's application to join NATO was postponed, and the invitation to start negotiations for accession to the European Union, in December 1999, reflect this. At the same time, their performance in government also revealed the discrepancy between rhetorical and substantive commitment, as demonstrated by their inability to push through the required policies. By the end of 2000, the World Bank's evaluation on Romania seemed to have overcome the polarisation of the 1990s, and moved towards appreciating the limitations of the CDR and some of the merits of the PDSR (World Bank 2001a).

The UDMR, which represents the interests of the Hungarian minority in Romania, received a sympathetic ear from the Council of Europe and other organisations that promote human rights and democracy (Andreescu 1998). This created the perception of a natural affinity between the UDMR and

European values, a perception that has endured in spite of internal divisions within the Union and the temporary ascendancy at one point or another of their more conservative or nationalistic factions (Mungiu-Pippidi 1999, 173–186). This orientation facilitated the coalition between the UDMR and the CDR after 1996. As shown by their persistence in the negotiation of the privatisation law, the UDMR was also pragmatic on economic matters, and this, together with a positive change in the credibility of the PSD, facilitated their co-operation in the post-2000 governments.

The third major stance towards the West, constructive engagement, stems from a genuine commitment to social-liberal values, and it is the attitude of some of the prominent technocrats. Amongst the economists and social scientists employed in research institutes or in government under the communist regime, there emerged a group of people interested in and conversant with western social science and who had a clearer notion about the global economy and tasks involved in running a modern open economy. They display the characteristics found by Eyal, Szélenyi and Townsley (1998) in their study of post-communist elites in other CEE countries. Under the previous regime they accumulated expertise in their respective fields and also switched to a substantive attachment to democratic values and rational administration that were avowed by the communist regime but undermined in practice. At the same time, members of this group, unlike the exponents of aggressive imitation, were more interested in balancing the received wisdom of the west with the priorities created by the situation in Romania. They were attentive to the embeddedness of the economy and the importance of institutions in the working of the economy.

The local technocrats were present in the government with varying levels of responsibility during the 1990s. Some of them were close to the FSN/PDSR, for instance Mişu Negriţoiu (1996a, 1996b), Mircea Coşea (1993), Eugen Dijmărescu (1993a, 1993b, 1994); others, to the CDR: Daniel Dăianu (1996b, 1999), Adrian Miroiu (2000a; 2000b; 2000c), Mihaela Miroiu (1999), Ilie Şerbănescu (1993, 1994, 1999), Lazăr Vlăsceanu (2000). Still others worked for the National Bank – Eugen Rădulescu (1993, Rădulescu and Drăgulin 1995) and Mugur Isărescu (2001) or animated non-governmental organisations such as the Foundation 'A Future for Romania' – Vladimir Pasti (1995, 1998d), Vasile Secăreş (1998) – which provided advice for President Iliescu. Although this position is one of the most promising and productive intellectually, it has not yet found a unified and effective political vehicle. Often, their contributions to policy formulation and implementation were overshadowed by inconsistencies in the programmes of the political parties they supported. Entering into alliance with political parties from an independent platform, they were usually sacrificed in the interest of keeping party alliances together, as in the case of Ministers Şerbănescu and Dăianu. In 1998 Dăianu, who was the Minister of Finance, had to resign because he refused to sign the contract with Bell Helicopters, an American company who tied their purchase of a

Romanian factory for about $150 million to the purchase by the Romanian government of army helicopters worth more than $1 billion. The IMF also objected to this privatisation deal, in spite of arguments that the purchase would have increased Romania's chances to join NATO, and supported Dăianu's resistance.

Nationalism of different shades was a feature of all political parties in Romania. Although it embraced the neo-liberal principles to a greater extent than other parties, the democratic opposition also had its own nationalist concerns, in spite of attempts to associate nationalism strictly with the former Securitate and their neo-communist opponents (Verdery 1996, 104–129). They argued against a treaty with Ukraine and Russia by accusing the PDSR of 'abandoning' Moldova and the nationalist ideal of recreating the Romanian state as it existed before the Second World War (Andreescu 1996). On a different plane of theory and sophistication, the relationship between the national and European identities of the Romanian culture has always contained an element of reticence towards what was perceived as the excessively technical and instrumental culture of western capitalism (Pleşu 1997, Laignel-Lavastine 1998).

But certain political groups, such as the PUNR and the PRM linked their name to a form of extreme nationalism. The rhetoric of their publications is often rabidly anti-Semitic and anti-western. However, their political actions were opportunistic. In spite of the nuisance value of their nationalistic antics, antics that have been taken very seriously sometimes by domestic commentators anxious to establish Romania's democratic credibility abroad, they agreed to subordinate their rhetoric to national interest in several key moments. They signed the Snagov declaration of 1995 which was the basis for Romania's application for membership to the EU and the strategies for medium-term development which underpinned the invitation by the EU to open accession negotiations with Romania in December 1999. In this sense, their stance can be described as parasitic. Members of parliament representing these parties struggled to represent Romania in international fora and were proud of being allowed to participate (PRM 2000, chapter 4). The political programme of the Greater Romania Party considers that national interest is paramount and it can only be realised through political action within the wider world. Their view of the world community is romantic and cultural, and their model is one of heroical transcendence of current limitations (PRM 2000, chapter 1).

It has been shown in this section that the identity claims of the major Romanian political parties were played out in their attitude towards the West and their foreign policy stances. A degree of consistency as well as contradiction characterised these political identities, a reflection of the complexity of the pressures to which they had to respond. The presence of contradictions was seen as a failure of the political parties to create coherent platforms and to lead the reform effectively (Pasti, Miroiu and Codiţă 1997, 129–164). At the same time, it is perhaps remarkable that in spite of the recognised gap between the tasks of reform and the initial weakness of agency (Elster, Offe and Preuss 1998), some degree of coherence was achieved at all.

The role of the IFIs and the EU in steering marketisation in Romania

An often-repeated comment about the role of the IFIs and the EU in Romania's post-communist marketisation is that the activities of these organisations were the only element of continuity that bridged the reform efforts of the different governments during the 1990s (OECD 1998, 3; Stolojan 1999, 5–6). The rivalry between the major political parties in Romania led them to underestimate each other's achievements on the one hand and to present their own efforts as the 'new' or 'true' beginning of radical change on the other. It is argued here that the gradual deepening of the relationship between Romania and the IFIs and the EU could not have taken place without progress in the domestic reform and the accumulation of experience and expertise in carrying out these collaborative activities. At the same time, it is recognised that the staying power of these organisations was a crucial element in this development.

At the beginning of the marketisation process, Romania, uniquely among the former Soviet bloc countries, did not have any foreign debt and had discontinued its relations with the IFIs. This potential for self-reliance was quickly lost in 1990, when the eruption of the pent-up consumer demand in the economy led the provisional government to free imports of foodstuffs and energy. From a position of balance of payments surplus and a respectable level of hard currency reserves, by the end of 1990 the current account was in deficit.

To cover for this deficit, given the deterioration of trade conditions after the dismantling of the CMEA and the declining availability of aid funds after the events of June 1990, the Romanian authorities approached the World Bank and the IMF with requests for assistance. The first stand-by agreement with the IMF was signed in April 1991 and the first (Technical Assistance and Critical Imports – TACI) loan from the World Bank was agreed in June 1991, followed by a Structural Adjustment Loan (SAL) in June 1992. Together, these two loans 'marked the rebirth of the Bank-Romania partnership in the post cold war era' (World Bank 1996, 11). More importantly, 'SAL became the centerpiece of the Bank's dialogue with Romania on issues of stabilisation and systemic reform for a period of almost three years' (World Bank 1995a, ii).

During this period of tentative renewal of relations, both the IMF and the World Bank showed an inclination for the small scale and 'emergency' intervention. Thus, the first two loans from the World Bank were modest in their purpose and the conditionalities attached. For instance, the aim of the TACI ($180 million) was to help Romania stop the decline in industrial production by providing funds for technical assistance and for a list of urgent imports. This list and the required standard contracting procedure, in which the borrower did not have suitable experience, delayed the disbursement of the loan (World Bank 1996, 13). It did not close until December 31, 1996.

The performance of the SAL ($400 million) was also patchy. The SAL was not based on a coherent view of reform but brought together disparate conditions from seven policy areas: stabilisation, price liberalisation, elimination of consumer subsidies, trade liberalisation, privatisation, enterprise, financial discipline, public sector reforms and social safety net. Macro-economic stabilisation was achieved in 1994, when inflation was brought under control. Prices were liberalised before the SAL became effective, but the loan contributed to the deepening of the process and the elimination of the 30 per cent limit in mark-ups. Export restrictions were removed for up to 90 per cent of items thus contributing to trade liberalisation. The sale of 3,000 assets and the 'pilot privatisation programme', as already mentioned, were part of the conditions of the loan and were achieved by the end of 1993. The level of arrears had similarly decreased by 1993, compared to 1991, although their absolute level was still very high. In the public sector, the SAL contributed to the reduction of the number of SOEs accorded *regie autonome* status and initiated a review of public investment projects. The change in the social safety net promoted by SAL was the introduction of universal child allowance, as opposed to child allowance being paid through state enterprises only to state-workers (World Bank 1995a, iii–iv).

Similarly, the first stand-by agreements with the IMF reflected a concern for the stability of the country and rather modest expectations about the depth of the reform. The fund accepted the argument for gradual reform given the inherited imbalances in the economic structure and conceded the government's request for a narrow agreement. Targets for the control of money and credit supply, a small budget deficit, and a tax-based, partial indexation of wages were the main instruments for achieving stabilisation (OECD 1993, 53–56). However, interest rates were excluded from this agreement. These became the bone of contention in 1993, when the next stand-by agreement was discontinued by the IMF because the rates had become negative and the exchange rate was appreciated. Decisive measures in these areas were required before the IMF agreed to the third stand-by agreement in April 1994, a package that finally led to macro-economic stabilisation.

Gradually, the relationship between the Romanian governments and these two organisations became more extensive. The requirements on the part of the IMF and the World Bank deepened. Initially, the remit of the IMF's surveillance and intervention was balance of payments problems and conditionalities regarding the size and financing of the budget deficit. This expanded to reforms in the enterprise and financial sectors. The 1997 stand-by agreement put the focus squarely on accelerating privatisation, the closure of loss-making enterprises and the restructuring of the Agriculture Bank and

Bancorex (Done 1997). But the IMF-approved shock therapy of 1997 was based on over-optimistic expectations of growth and (reduced) inflation. The GDP was expected to contract by 2.2 per cent in 1997; the actual decrease was 6.9 per cent. Inflation was supposed to reach 90 per cent in the same year but it overshot by more than 60 per cent, at 154.8 per cent.[1]

Domestically, this was blamed not so much on the content of the shock therapy programme, or its appropriateness for the Romanian economy at the time, but on the inability of the Ciorbea government to develop autonomous domestic policies to complement the liberalisation and stabilisation measures (Pasti 1998a; Stolojan 1999). For the IMF the disappointing results of the stabilisation and liberalisation programmes were due to the failure to implement the structural reforms (IMF 1998). Unfortunately, the Ciorbea government did not use the experience with stabilisation developed under the previous regime when much of the programme of 1993–94 was generated by the BNR. They put their trust in IMF expertise instead in an attempt to validate the claims they had held throughout the 1990s that they were the true – and thus neo-liberal – reformers. The programme proved catastrophic for Romania, who could ill afford another three years of steep recession. This episode doubled the number of people living below the national poverty line, to reach a total of 41 per cent of the population (World Bank 2001, chapter 6, 2–3). The combination of a Romanian government too eager for international recognition and thus willing to comply with neo-liberal precepts and an IMF led only by neo-liberal ideology put back the development of the Romanian economy by a few years.[2]

Overall, the adjustment between a partner with strict imperatives, the IMF, and another that had to respond both to institutional and political constraints, the Romanian governments, took the form of a pattern of 'buying time'. All six stand-by agreements with the IMF during 1991–2000 were closed after the first or second review of the loan. Thus, the most effective periods from the point of view of compliance of the Romanian government with IMF prescriptions were those before the actual disbursement of the loan. After the first disbursement, policy usually slackened and the IMF would discontinue the agreement.

But subsequent agreements usually picked up the issues where they had been left off. For instance, in the negotiations for a new agreement in August 1999, the Isărescu government had a strong case because it had passed policies requested in the past. These included a new privatisation law, budget modifications, preparation of Bancorex for closure, audit of Romanian Commercial Bank, and participation in the IMF pilot programme for bailing-in private creditors (GR 1999a, annex A). As with the shock therapy, the consequences of some of these policies were counterproductive. For instance, the privatisation law increased the difficulties of finding buyers by raising the environmental standards and delayed the process by adding the costs of frequent legislative changes (GR 2000a).

After the Asian Crisis in 1997 the IMF created new contractual forms between sovereign borrowers and their lenders that would oblige the latter to shoulder some of the responsibility in case of default. Romania was asked to participate in this pilot programme in 1999. This entailed getting the holders of two 1996 bond issues to agree to roll over 80 per cent of the debt. These efforts were unsuccessful and in the end the debt crisis was resolved by independent means, i.e. by using the BNR reserves, a rise in domestic public debt and devaluation (Eichengreen and Ruhl 2000, 22–25). The IMF then agreed to sign the stand-by agreement in August 1999, despite the fact that Romania had not used their prescribed strategy for dealing with this peak in foreign debt servicing.[3]

The same trend towards deeper co-operation can be identified in the relationship with the EU. Initially, EU assistance consisted primarily of aid. An association agreement was signed in 1995 and this led to the gradual liberalisation and reorientation of trade towards the EU. In 2000, Romania's trade with the EU represented more than 60 per cent of both imports and exports. Another turning point was the invitation in December 1999 to open accession negotiations. From then on, all domestic policies were scrutinised for compatibility with EU legislation, in view of meeting the requirements for accession. Between February 2000 and September 2004, Romania closed temporarily twenty-eight of the thirty-one chapters of the acquis, the body of EU legislation that is shared by all its members. The ambitious objective of the Năstase government, to complete negotiations by the end of 2004, was met and the country is on schedule to become a full member of the organisation in 2007.

In parallel with these changes in the political relations, after 1997, the disbursement of EU aid through Phare changed from a demand-driven basis to co-ordination with the accession process. Phare funds were directed to areas and projects identified in the annual evaluation process of the progress towards accession and the reports published by the EU Commission on each of the applicant countries. The distribution of funds was also corroborated with the objectives identified in the National Programme for the Adoption of the Acquis (NPAA) agreed between the EU and the applicants. In 1998, Romania received support for the privatisation of state-owned banks and the insurance sector (6 million ECU), and the reconstruction of mining areas (10 million). This was part of the catch-up facility created by the EU to enable the five countries that were not yet invited at that time to negotiate accession (Bulgaria, Slovakia, Latvia, Romania, and Lithuania) to speed up the process of reform (Programme code RO9809 in EC-GDE database).[4] Another 10.1 million ECU was allocated for the support of Romania's integration in the internal market. This included activities leading to the preparation of the public utilities for privatisation and the clarification of their regulatory environment, strengthening the capacity of the National Bank, and restructuring one of the main savings banks, Casa de economii și consemnațiuni (CEC)

(Programme code RO9805 in EC-GDE database). Five other projects for institutional building in different areas of public administration and privatisation approved in 1998–2000 received about 200 million ECU (programme codes RO9804, RO9910, RO9906, RO0005, RO0006 in EC-GDE database).

The 2000 evaluation report on Phare also recommended the transition to multi-annual contracting, to strengthen the sense of long-term commitment of the Commission to certain projects (EC-DGE 2000, 1–10). Beginning in 2000, Phare was supplemented by two other major aid programmes, SAPARD (Structural Adjustment Programme for Agriculture and Rural Development) worth 500 million euro a year, and ISPA (Pre-Accession Structural Instrument) with a budget of 1 billion euro. Together with an increased budget for Phare of 1.5 billion euro a year, this represents a doubling of the pre-accession assistance provided by the EU to Romania, to 3 billion euro a year (EC 2000a, 10).

The IFIs and the EU reacted to the instability of the Romanian political scene by requesting all parties or the parliament to endorse certain agreements. This was the case with the 1994 stand-by agreement with the IMF, for instance. In 1999, the EU asked that all Romanian political parties participate in the elaboration and sign up to a medium-term national development strategy. This facilitated the cross-party dialogue and the strategy materialised in March 2000 (GR 2000a).

The effect of this pressure on the part of external partners to receive assurance that all significant parties were committed to particular foreign policy goals was amplified by the fact that the positions of the IFIs and the EU were systematically linked to each other, especially after 1997. For instance, the 1997 World Bank country assistance strategy for Romania included this aim specifically and tied the objectives of the strategy to the EU's expectations (World Bank 1997, 1998a). The IMF, the World Bank and the EU contributed to the elaboration of Romania's medium-term economic strategy and the action plan based on it. The objectives of this strategy were in accordance with commitments in the stand-by agreements with the IMF (IMF 2000, 20). The 2001 World Bank country assistance strategy for Romania contains two lending scenarios, the more generous of which is conditional upon the conclusion of an agreement between Romania and the IMF (World Bank 2001a, 2001b).

Thus, during the 1990s, the Romanian governments entered into a number of agreements with these international organisations. As the presentation of the succession of these agreements in the context of the policy decisions of the governments has shown, the policies actually taken by the Romanian government converged towards a liberal pole at those points in time when the agreements were negotiated or reviewed. Within this cycle of compliance, relapse and renewed commitment, the World Bank, the IMF, and the EU were willing to give the Romanian authorities another chance and the latter pursued reform in spite of temporary reversals. Due to this attitude on the part of the IFIs and the EU and the Romanian governments, the process of liberalisation and conversion to market economy in Romania has deepened and the problems slowly cleared. Although much remains to be done, the external partners represented a significant driving force in the development of a market economy in Romania.

Learning by doing: the role of the IFIs and the EU in the socialisation of 'good practice'

In addition to exercising influence over choices of macro-economic policy and general design of the reforms, the activities of these international organisations have also hand an impact on the development of the institutional infrastructure of the state and market. Implementation procedures, as well as policies, were transferred. Through this the IFIs and EU-supported programmes presented a challenge to the existing organisational culture, and this section outlines the most significant patterns of resistance to their influence across the public administration.

Perhaps the most basic observation that has to be made about the relationship between the Romanian Government and these international organisations is that the level of contact between them has deepened during the 1990s. Having started in 1990 from a position of relative isolation, by the end of the decade the visits and missions in both directions had become commonplace. The IMF opened a local mission in 1991 and produced the first staff country report on Romania in 1996. From then on, the amount of information generated by the fund increased steadily. In 1994, the World Bank country assistance strategy for Romania was included as mere commentary to one of the loans. In 2001 this framework document was discussed widely within official and civil society circles.[5] Since 1998, the EU Commission has also produced annual reports on the progress of the country on every aspect of the accession process, most crucially the degree of integration in the Romanian legislation of the thirty chapters of the *Acquis Communitaire*.

The development of agreements also reflected increased co-operation. Some of these agreements started from a need identified by the Romanian government. Sectoral strategies for restructuring the railways and the provision of social services were elaborated prior to approaching the lenders (World Bank 1994c, annexes 4 and 5; 1995c, annex 1). Most of the projects funded under the Phare scheme until 1997 also fall into this category. In the area of privatisation, Phare money was used in 1991–92 for technical assistance for the evaluation of enterprises and the setting up of the FPS and FPPs: their structure, recruitment and personnel policies, computer networks, staff training, and privatisation procedures (ANP 1993a, 14). Similarly, in 1993–96, 70 million ECU provided the capital for three investment funds to finance privatisation deals, for the restructuring of non-viable enterprises, the reform of the banking system and other technical assistance programmes.[6]

Other projects evolved out of joint activities of data gathering and assessments of necessary investment in the capacity of the public administration to implement agreed programmes. The IMF, for instance, sent forty technical assistance missions to Romania, most of them before 1996, to advise on monetary and fiscal policy, bank supervision and statistics. The Romanian governments accepted some of their suggestions about profit tax, investment tax allowances, the introduction of value-added tax, and a global personal income tax. Similarly, the BNR improved its capacity to generate statistics about money and the real economy sectors. Other Romanian agencies, however, were more sluggish in their response. As mentioned already, the Ministry of Finance did not develop its department for macro-economic projections until 1999 (IMF 2000, 45–54).

Similarly, most World Bank loans had important technical assistance components designed to enable the local recipients to utilise the loans according to plan. In the area of privatisation, a Private Sector Institution Building Loan (PSIBL) worth $25 million, approved in 1999, supplemented the main Private Sector Adjustment Loan (PSAL) ($300 million). PSIBL paid the up-front fees for the agents for privatisation contracted to sell sixty-four large companies, and several preparation studies for the privatisation of other SOEs. Also, it facilitated the setting up of the Asset Resolution Agency, to which the bad loans of the Agricultural Bank and Bancorex were transferred in 1999. This loan also provided funds for the setting up of market institutions: the central depository for the secondary market in treasury bills, the auditing industry, bankruptcy courts, training programmes related to corporate restructuring, work-outs, and liquidations, and an assessment of the regulatory environment for public utilities (World Bank 1999b, 20–23).

These details give an idea of the extent and depth of the technical assistance programmes and their objectives. They enhanced the capacity of the public administration and supported the emergent market institutions. This record also showed that the Romanian authorities became able to administrate the loans and the aid to the requirements of their partners. There was significant progress over time. The first loan to Romania agreed by the World Bank in 1990, TACI, was disbursed very slowly due to lack of local expertise in the procedures of procurement (World Bank 1996, 13). By 1999, the project appraisal document for the mine closure and social mitigation project could claim that the prospects for speedy implementation were good. The project management units were established and had adequate personnel and financial systems infrastructure (World Bank 1999c, 11).

Where the difficulties of implementation proved significant, they could be attributed, as the World Bank recognised, not only to the relative lack of experience of the Romanian authorities, and resistance from certain industrial sectors, but also to features of the lending instruments. In cases where the lender attached conditionalities broader than the agreed sectoral strategies, there were delays in the implementation. For instance two projects in the energy sector, for the rehabilitation of the petroleum and the power industries, concluded in 1994 and 1995 respectively, were rated as unsatisfactory from the point of view of their implementation in 1999 (World Bank 1999c, 16). The latter project recovered by the last portfolio review in 2001 (World Bank 2001a, annex 2). Similarly, the Financial and Enterprise Restructuring Loan (FESAL), agreed in 1995, was restructured in 1997 after the adoption of a new country assistance strategy, and eventually abandoned. The lesson drawn by the Bank was to avoid in the future the 'Christmas tree' approach and to identify straightforward benchmarks for performance (World Bank 2001a, chapter 4).

The record of the Phare programme confirms these observations. The overall performance of Phare, including all country beneficiaries, was that of the total commitments of 8,890.9 million euro between 1990 and 1998, 75.3 per cent (6,697.3 million) were contracted . A total of 5,589.1 million euro was paid out, representing 62.9 per cent of all committed funds (EC-DGE 1999a, 21). The commitments for Romania during the same period were 971.85 million euro, of which 675.75 million (69.53 per cent) were contracted and 598.13 million (61.54 per cent of committed funds) were actually paid out (EC-DGE 1999a, 84). Thus, in Romania, fewer funds were contracted but the figures for disbursed funds compare well with the regional average.

The complexity of the bureaucratic machinery in Brussels caused delays in the utilisation of Phare aid. In 1997 a major overhaul of the programme became necessary in order to address the low rates of contracting across the region. Decision-making was deconcentrated by giving local EU missions increased responsibility for approving projects (EC-DGE 1999b, 4–6). In the near future, some of this responsibility will be transferred to national governments.

It is quite clear that not only policies but also ideas and procedures, a whole 'technology of government' and 'good practice' were transferred from these international organisations to the Romanian bureaucracy. The transfer of policies is possible when there exists a common way of defining what the problems are and what is the best way to resolve them (Dolowitz 2000). In the process of building institutional capacity, the depth of this assumed commonality of vision, understanding, and commitment to certain values increases. Most details of institutional procedure, informational infrastructure, such as management and financial systems, training of personnel and evaluation of outcomes were part of the collaboration.[7]

To their credit, the IFIs used their comparatively secure position and far superior resources to absorb some of the risks involved in their relationship with the Romanian governments. Committed from the start to certain policy solutions to economic problems, the IFIs were willing to show a measure of flexibility in their negotiations. They appreciated the difficulties faced by the

Romanian authorities, the gravity of the distortions in the economy, and the skill deficiencies in both the economy and the public administration. For instance, the recent draft country assistance strategy of the World Bank comments:

> Many economic deficiencies in Romania's society are not the result of ill will but of lack of knowledge. To continue the dialogue with the Government, other interested parties, and society at large therefore carries a high pay-off. Whether connected to specific lending operations (e.g., new privatisation methods, bank restructuring) or to the design of reform (CAS, Public Expenditure Review, Country Economic Memorandum), these investments in people have proven to help build a consensus and momentum for reform. (World Bank 2001a, chapter 4)

But the relationship between these international organisations and the Romanian state bureaucracy was more complex that these broad observations suggest. The Romanian senior civil servants had to balance contradictory pressures. On the one hand, although formally equal, they were in a junior position in relation to foreign experts. The latter were, of course, better paid and more secure in their institutional position and knowledge. This represented a relative loss of status that had to be carefully managed. While Romanian civil servants had fewer skills, they certainly had more responsibility for the impact of such programmes. The IFIs and the EU do not have to bear directly the consequences of failed policies in Romania, even when they might incur some costs in terms of loss of reputation. For this reason, delays in the implementation of loans or aid agreements can be seen not as simple failures but as necessary cushions within which these pressures could be managed. The strategy of buying time helped the Romanian actors to deal with these discrepancies.

Variations in performance across the central bureaucracy point to another factor that played a role in the relative success or failure of the different programmes: the orientation of the public servants, whether technocratic or traditionalist. In some quarters of the state administration, especially in those that had more technocratic experience, compliance with the new norms proved easier. The BNR and certain departments in the Ministry of Finance and the Ministry of Industry are cases in point. In other parts of the public administration, the loyalties to older notions about the importance of preserving certain industries of 'strategic importance', or the ideal of self-sufficiency in coal and food production, for instance, were stronger. This was reflected in the greater resistance to change on the part of certain public utilities, the restructuring of state-owned farms, and the mining sector.

There is also some evidence that certain bureaucrats used international agreements to push for change and to overcome the opposition of their colleagues. According to one participant in a cabinet meeting where the closure of Bancorex was decided, the representatives of the BNR and the Commercial Bank framed the discussion in a way that eliminated options contrary to the agreement with the IMF. The timing of the meeting was also crucial, as the decision was due by the next day.[8] Similarly, Aurel Ciobanu-Dordea, the Romanian chief negotiator with the EU in 2000 tried to engage his more conservative colleagues by emphasising their crucial role in carrying through the very complex negotiation process and the implementation of policies resulting from it. He observed that resistance to the accession process was substantial and pointed to the low rate of take-up of training courses in EU law and procedures (Ciobanu-Dordea 2000, 19).

Thus, the participation in international programmes by Romania led to changes in practices and improved institutional capacity across the civil service. At the same time, it created a distinction between those who could take part and those who could not. Work for World Bank programmes was much better paid: 'market rates' were introduced in recognition of superior skills and training (World Bank 1999c). In spite of these tensions, democratic practices, such as consultation with civil society organisations in the elaboration of policy, became more common. One example was the consultation over the World Bank country assistance strategy, which involved a few thousand people and organisations (World Bank 2001a, 2001b). Similarly, the Department for European Integration initiated consultations about the consequences for Romania of opening negotiations over new chapters of the acquis.

Conclusion

This chapter has documented the different avenues through which international actors, and the IFIs and the EU more directly, have contributed to democratisation and marketisation in Romania. Their influence is mediated by the relatively autonomous dynamics of the domestic political process, institutional and bureaucratic resistance to change as well as structural constraints in the economy. For this reason, while it is reasonable to claim that they have played a significant role in Romania's post-communist transformations, they were neither the sole consistent promoter of these transformations nor their only champion. Rather, the strength of their influence can be attributed to the ability to be flexible and pragmatic in their actual activities even while their ideological pronouncements have been seen by some, at different times, as unequivocal statements of condemnation of the perceived failings of the Romanian governments.

Pragmatism has often been the most productive course of action for the Romanian counterparts as well. Excessively ideological identification with the neo-liberal norms, especially in the adoption of the shock therapy package in 1997, proved extremely costly politically and economically, both for the country and for the domestic promoters of this course of action.

Notes

1 See for instance the articles in the *Financial Times* 'Lex Column: Romania' (18 February 1997), 'Romania to slash state subsidies' (18 April 1997), and 'Romania '97: Economy: Shock therapy is prescribed' (25 June 1997).
2 See for instance IMF (1996, 1997, 2000 and 2001).
3 Issues of institutional capability are presented in Chapter 5.
4 These countries were invited to begin negotiations for accession in December 1999.
5 In 1998, the Romanian government requested that Romania should be included in the comprehensive development framework. This is a World Bank pilot programme in which the deliberation over the country assistance strategy includes extensive consultation with non-governmental organisations and individuals.
6 The internet address for the database of Phare-funded projects is http://europa.eu.int/phare-cgi/plsgl.
7 This is attested by the operational documents of the World Bank and all the other official documents mentioned in this section.
8 The source of this information was a senior official in the Romanian government between 1996 and 2000.

CONCLUSION

This book has presented the process of marketisation and democratisation in Romania as a process of parallel reconstitution of the political and economic spheres and a process of redefinition of their relationship as one of relative autonomy. These processes were driven by domestic and international factors and the interplay between these factors is also documented here. This analysis represents a departure from mainstream neo-liberal and neo-institutionalist approaches to the study of economy and politics. Thus, neo-liberal theories in economics, politics and international relations share common assumptions about actors – as self-interested, rational individuals – and base their explanations on the existence of spontaneous mechanisms of co-ordination such as the market, democratic pluralism or the structure of the international system (Di Palma 1990; Sachs 1993; Linz and Stepan 1996). However, these theories say very little about the connections between the political and economic spheres, domestic and international.

Neo-institutionalist theories improve on the assumptions of the neo-liberal theories by taking into account the role of institutions. Institutions exist prior to the calculations of the actors and provide accepted ways of doing things that shape the decisions of the individual actors. Rational calculation of interests still plays a role, but institutions determine what elements enter into calculations and their relative significance (North 1990; Olson 1996). Some authors, such as Elster, Offe and Preuss (1998) also suggested that institutions become established through an act of political delegation, and they assessed the progress in post-communist transformations of different countries by the extent to which institutions specific to the different social spheres have become autonomous.

However, neo-institutionalist theories cannot explain how certain ideas and values become established as institutions and do not address the question of the relationship between the economic and political spheres fully. Economic sociology, the politics of interests and symbols and critical international relations on the other hand attempt to understand how economic and political phenomena are embedded in social life through a discussion of structure and agency and an appreciation of the situated and historical character of social phenomena.

Thus, a few working hypotheses about the relationships between the economic and political spheres derived from all of these theories have been used tentatively throughout this analysis. The economic and political spheres are in a relationship of relative autonomy. They each have an autonomous structuring principle that varies historically. In contemporary Western Europe, a model that the countries of the CEE, including Romania, wish to emulate, these are the market and democratic pluralism. The starting point for these transformations was, of course, a close integration of the economy and politics and there was a direct connection between the plan, as the co-ordination mechanism in the economy and the communist political ideology.

The links between the two spheres derive from the fact that power accrued within each can be used, to a certain extent, for acquiring power in the other. Weber (1994) posited that there could be tension and misalignment between the dominant groups in economy and politics, but there is also a tendency for alignment. In their identities, actors seek to bring together material (economic) interests, ideas and symbols and for this reason 'identity' is a useful middle-range concept for understanding how the relationship between the two spheres is negotiated at particular junctures in time and space. Actors, their assets and their images of themselves are influenced by objective structures but are not entirely determined by them.

Thus, at one level, economic interests impact on the political field through voting or direct participation in policy-making. Economic structures are also recognised as objective constraints by policy-makers and are taken into account in arguments over policy. Additionally, the democratic principles on which the polity rests have a purchase on the public imagination and on the behaviour of political actors because there is a level of material co-optation, a prima facie coincidence between principles and distribution of material benefits. At the same time, politics consists of a symbolic universe, rituals and practices in which the public participates thorough its projections, fears and aspirations. This understanding of the relationship between the economy and politics, between material benefits and forms of integration and political symbolism allows us to appreciate why it is possible for political elites as well as the dispossessed to act in ways that might be in contradiction with their economic interests.

Chapter 1 set the historical context for the post-communist transformations in Romania after 1989, by looking at the structural imbalances in the economy, the patterns of economic governance under the plan, the crisis of authority and the dissolution of the communist social pact and the political significance of the regime breakdown as the mode of transition from communism. Romania entered the 1990s with an economic structure biased towards heavy industries and exhausted by the shortages and lack of basic technological imports and upgrades in the previous decade. Corporate governance under the plan was part of a bureaucratic and administrative structure that linked the many economic ministries to every state-owned enterprise in the land and encouraged misinformation and nepotism. The cognitive dissonance created by the contrast between the promises made by the regime and the failure to meet these promises were compensated though informal cultural work, *blat* networks and double consciousness. In spite of resistance to and criticism of the communist ideology, the patterns of judgement and the extraordinary expectations inculcated by the heroic myth of transcending material limitations to achieve the desired, 'multilaterally developed' society persisted and will continue to shape assessment of action in the public sphere for at least another decade. Politically, the structuring of political identities resulted out of a radicalisation of the opposition between sections of the public concerned by the need for moral purification after the failure of communism and those who had felt far too implicated in that regime to be able to contemplate this kind of radical judgement and evaluation.

Chapter 2 took up this question of the slow change in the language of politics, in the patterns of understanding used to make sense of reform, of ownership and privatisation. Strong identification with ideals and a lack of appreciation of the virtues of the middle ground were cultural biases that accentuated the opposition between political players, the dominance of certain industrial interests in the economic sphere and the slowness of institutional change. At the same time, the weak inheritance of technical knowledge in the social sciences also hampered the development of policy and the change in the tone of public debates.

These features were linked to the continued influence of the communist heroic model of action. Experience under the communist regime was moulded by regime-led bouts of mobilisation to transcend dire economic, social and political circumstances. This, and the need at the core of the party's identity to reconcile charisma and rational organisation, led to a continuous search for enemies. Thus, the absolute standards could be, and they were, cast around a great variety of objectives. Indeed, the Party wanted nothing less than to shape the whole of society, and human nature, according to its ideology.

The failure by the PCR to take responsibility for the consequences of its government and its ignominious end compounded the difficulties of leaving the heroic model of action behind. Informal practices of adaptation and resistance to the communist regime persisted, often leading to a confused negotiation of boundaries between the media and the judiciary, and the politicians and the media. The difficulty in forging and imposing a vision for reform was also linked to this dictate of absolute standards and inability to frame the discussion of issues as one of choice between alternatives and inevitable trade-offs. Also, the inability to reconcile to a certain extent the conflicting interests of the state, the capital and labour is a symptom of this.

At the same time, the freedom to experiment and reflect on these cultural norms, after 1989, led to a significant accumulation of first-hand, reliable experience that could be used to challenge these patterns. This has begun to erode the primacy of the heroic cultural model, as actors become more confident in their technical knowledge, and some of the economic and political insecurities that characterised the beginning of the transition have been partially resolved.

Chapter 3 used insights from neo-institutional and theories of symbolic politics to explain phenomena characteristic of and autonomous to the political sphere: the ethical and identity choices of the political parties, the resulting pact between them and the institutional embodiment of this pact. It also showed that the relationships between parties influenced the elaboration and enactment of economic and foreign policy.

Neo-institutionalist theorists identified the conditions under which political agency became possible after the fall of communism in CEE countries. In general, post-communist political elites were civilian, and did not have a past of struggle against the communist regime, or a comprehensive plan for the future. The collapse of the system from within did not generate a distinct or powerful social force to lead the society into the new era.

In Romania, this weakness was even more pronounced due to the uncertainty that attended the sudden breakdown of the communist regime and the widespread and diffuse grass roots political mobilisation. Even though the rejection of the communist regime was general, in the absence of pacting with the outgoing regime or any form of negotiated transfer of power, the political process for defining the transition to a democratic political system was fraught. The political forces that emerged after December 1989 had to address contradictory needs and pressures. Through direct action countless changes were implemented immediately: a shorter working week, freeing of imports and travel abroad, opening of the cities for residence, freedom of the press, private initiative, and political organisation. The spontaneous character of these sweeping changes, paradoxically, fuelled contradictory needs and anxieties about the past and the future. The need for reassurance that the break with the communist regime was irreversible co-existed with security concerns for the groups directly responsible for the regime – such as the security forces – but also for other members of society. The political parties that emerged after the revolution politicised these needs in the form of an apparently irreconcilable conflict. The historical parties wanted a process of moral purification, the exclusion from political life of the former communists, and the punishment of the members of the former political police. Others, the National Salvation Front in particular, were willing to compromise with the former establishment to buy social peace and pursue marketisation more slowly.

This antagonism between parties was accentuated by the choice of the democratic opposition to treat its ideals of democracy and decisive break with communism as ends in themselves. This ethics of principled conviction, as explained by Weber, has the effect of subordinating immediate practical concerns to ideals that are almost impossible to meet. It was a rigid stance that did not allow its supporters to formulate a political position that could appeal to sections of the public who were more concerned about immediate survival.

The need of the democratic opposition in Romania to be recognised as the morally pure survivors of communism, and the moral prosecutors of their adversaries who were deemed tainted by their association with that regime, was difficult to satisfy through compromise.

The institutional design of the political system also reflected this antagonism and lack of trust between parties. The electoral system was based on proportional representation, the legislative had broad powers and the two chambers of the parliament had identical duties. The review of privatisation policies also showed that all political parties had contradictory views on the different aspects of the role of the state and market in the economy and transformation. The democratic opposition was pleading more consistently for individual freedoms, but wanted to eliminate the possibility that a free market system might favour the former communist nomenklatura. The FSN was more concerned with ensuring equality of outcomes for citizens entitled to free shares. At the same time, FSN did not want to increase the overall share of state property that was to be distributed freely. Beyond this confrontation of ideas, the antagonism between parties surfaced in the shock tactics of stalling the passing of the law and de-legitimatising the parliamentary procedures.

This tension between assertions and actions, inevitable to a certain extent for all actors, proved extremely detrimental to the long-term political appeal of some of the parties in the democratic coalition. Absolute, uncompromising views of who they were led them to take decisions contradictory to the values they espoused, simply because those decisions were promoted by their adversaries. This tension at the core of their identity did not survive the test of being in office. The inability to govern effectively undermined their claim that moral purity was the most important qualification for good political leadership.

In spite of these tensions, the democratic system proved robust during this decade. As parties went in and out of power, their claims were tested and this led to a restructuring of the party system. The failure of the PNŢCD to gain seats in the 2000–2004 parliament, the consolidation of the nationalistic left in the PRM, and the fusion between the PDSR and PSDR to form a stronger and possibly more legitimate social-democratic party, the PSD, indicate that there the electoral system is exerting a significant structuring pressure. The PNL and PD are the main centre-right parties. They formed a successful alliance in the 2004 elections, which constituted the basis for merger talks in 2005.

It was the robustness of the democratic system itself that allowed this evaluation to take place and offered a correction to the politics of absolute identity. In this sense, the liberal cautionary tale that identity politics is intrinsically dangerous does not hold. More generally, the PNŢCD's tale of hubris and tragedy suggests that actors who do not depend on self-definitions based on a radical exclusion of others, but are able to negotiate difference without losing their distinctiveness, are more resilient.

Chapter 4 developed the argument about the role of the economic structure as a factor autonomous to the economic sphere in the marketisation of the Romanian economy after 1990. Neo-liberal and evolutionary economics and economic sociology contributed to this account of economic reform in Romania in different ways. Neo-liberal assessments of economic reform usually find that there has been unequal progress across different sectors, and the heavy industries are the major laggards. The analysis offered here agrees with this evaluation but rejects the expectation that structural changes in the economy could be executed through a change in environmental conditions. The market is itself shaped by the major economic players and these players cannot be displaced without assistance from the state and without compensation.

Thus, while the shift of resources from the industrial sector to trade and services is necessary, the difficulties of the reform can be better understood by using the framework of evolutionary economics and economic sociology. The real-time dimension of changes, the need to maintain a degree of stability in the economy while changes are taking place, and the relationship between the size of enterprises and sectors and their willingness or ability to change are all important factors in the economic reform in Romania. In addition, relational assets within networks represent another key mechanism through which actors can undermine governmental policy.

The review of privatisation in post-communist Romania showed that the change in the mechanism of economic co-ordination, from plan to market, was accompanied, and perhaps facilitated, by the change in the social structure and the modalities of insertion of the citizens in the economy. These citizens moved from being employees in the command economy to being shareholders and players in other markets, such as labour, land and housing markets. On balance, the gradualist programme of reform in Romania also had a slightly better record than shock therapy. Gradualism achieved a return to growth by 1993, macro-stabilisation by 1994, and the setting up of some indirect mechanisms for the management of the economy. It also encouraged a degree of spontaneous restructuring of enterprises. However, the liberalisation of prices was partial and in 1995–96 the management of inflationary pressures and of the current account deficit was becoming difficult. The shock therapy of 1997, on the other hand, led to a steep three-year recession. It is unclear whether the resumption of growth in 2000 and the successes with privatisation in 1997–2000 were the result of shock therapy. It is likely that the active restructuring of public utilities and the financial sector as well the effective institutional structure built in the previous years contributed to these positive developments.

Chapter 5 looked at how the state set the tone for the change in economic institutions and how the relationship between the economy and politics was institutionalised. In Romania, for most of the 1990s, political parties did not recognise that it was in their common interest, as political actors, to strengthen the administrative capacity of the state. The record was one of patchy delegation of authority and decree-ism, as expected by Elster, Offe and Preuss (1998).

The ability of the state administration to model and impose changes in the rules of the economic game for enterprises – from reliance on the state to self-reliance and competition in the open markets – was relatively weak. Greater changes occurred in the banking sector, where, over time, the BNR increased its capacity to act as the regulatory authority in the system. This process also contained phases of retreat on the part of the Bank, under the pressure of the government or the failing banks. This evolution was similar in the stock markets.

The governance role of the FPS was also weakened by the delay in the reform of the public administration. The FPS relied on information and personnel from the line ministries, and it could not impose, by itself, a new market ethos. On the contrary, its attempts to introduce new regulatory procedures for enterprises – contracts and performance indicators for managers, for instance – were undermined by collusion between FPS representatives and managers. However, these initial institutional weaknesses were corrected as the privatisation process progressed. Overall, the increase in the size of the private sector in the economy has led to the emergence of hard budget constraints, even though state intervention and especially the lenience towards bad debtor to the budget and the state-owned energy utilities persists.

As Chapter 6 documents, international factors, documented here especially through the activities of the international financial organisations, the IMF, the World Bank and the EU, have also exerted a correcting, disciplining effect on Romanian economy and politics. Culturally, these institutions were initially viewed within the patterns of perception and understanding characteristic to the heroic model as having overwhelming power to determine what constitutes a credible political programme or even a credible democratic polity. On the whole, the presence of these international organisations in the Romanian public space introduced an element of technical detachment, and a care to avoid the excessive politicisation of issues that was beneficial. Some of the values of liberal individualism that underpin western market economies, such as self-confident actualisation but also fairness and co-operation have now become more common.

The pattern of antagonism prevalent in Romanian politics in the 1990s was also reflected in economic and foreign policy. The need to assert their difference from their opponents led the democratic opposition to vote against marketisation measures that it had supported initially and were part of its programme simply because they were put forward by a government they found distasteful. Once in government after 1996, their decisions reflected conflicting pressures. The IMF-inspired stabilisation and liberalisation programme of 1997 was implemented, but associated restructuring decisions were postponed in order to ensure social peace and to increase the chances of Romania joining NATO.

The trend towards deeper reform during the 1990s was reflected in more extensive relations with the IFIs and the EU. All Romanian governments, irrespective of their ideological preferences, had to balance domestic constraints with the expectations of swift and deep market reform coming from these organisations. The accommodation between these two pressures took the form of a pattern of 'buying time'. While the Romanian authorities remained committed to the overall objectives of marketisation and, later, EU accession, their concessions to domestic pressures led to temporary reversals in external agreements.

The IFIs and the EU had an important role in bolstering the institutional capacity of the Romanian state. In time, the ability of the Romanian authorities to assume obligations and carry them through was strengthened and the relations with the IFIs and the EU deepened. At the same time this was a complex relationship. Formal equality could not mask the discrepancies in skill and knowledge between the parties and the asymmetry of responsibility. As a consequence, the pattern of buying time provided the necessary leeway for absorbing these tensions. In spite of temporary reversals and delays, the relationships were maintained and deepened.

The empirical findings presented above permit some observations about the interplay between agency and structure in the particular circumstances of the post-communist transformations in Romania. For instance, the consistency over time of the orientation towards market reform – although in doubt at particular moments in time – could be seen as a structural effect determined by the dominance of the neo-liberal ideology internationally and the power of certain domestic groups domestically. But the leeway of actors was also evident in the different ways in which these pressures were played out in policy. In the case of the social-democratic governments of 1990–96, this balancing act consisted of more reform that they might have desired on their own. For the right-of-centre governments of the Democratic Convention, their initial disregard for domestic constraints led to a severe downturn in economic activity and later a change of tack in their policy, from stabilisation and liberalisation to direct restructuring of certain public utilities.

The asymmetry in the structural position of the IFIs and the EU on the one hand and that of the Romanian Governments on the other was in practice negotiated through a strategy of 'buying time'. This strategy reflects more than mere failure to reform or to keep to contracts and agreements. It represented a realistic adjustment to the different power positions and priorities of the partners in this relationship.

The study of the institutional dimension of post-communist transformations also shed light on institutions as a particular kind of structure. As defined by neo-institutionalists, institutions as rules of the game have the power to shape the transactions between individuals and groups, and thus, they have a structuring quality. The study of post-communist institutional change revealed that at one level this change depends on ideational work, in the sense that new values and appropriate procedures need to be generated. To a certain extent, this could be a voluntaristic activity or could rely on imitative policy-transfer. But the test for the development of ideas into institutions is their ability to structure to a certain extent the activities of the actors. This efficacy assumes that their assumptions and requirements are already internalised by these actors. Behind this efficacy is the effective deployment of authority – in the examples presented in Chapter 5, the authority of the state administration, the BNR, and the FPS. It is worth observing that Romania's institutional development became possible after certain economic structures were eroded or displaced. Initially, vested interests were able to put a great deal of pressure on the state to cushion the impact of changed economic conditions of competition in the world markets and to allow them to delay restructuring. The theoretical implication is that institutions can exert their structuring pressure when underlying power relations between actors support them.

Finally, the role of cultural patterns of perception and understanding can also be linked to a specific issue in the agency and structure debate. Certainly, the existence of certain ideal (mental) structures – set ways of perceiving and framing issues around notions about action, what can be achieved and what should be expected – is an important element of post-communist reality. At the same time, it is not possible to trace, at this stage of the research, the exact influence of these structures on discrete events. The reasons why they persist and change are explained in relation to the dynamic and logic of cultural phenomena although it might be possible to establish, in the future, some connections between these ideal structures and structures of material interest.

The common methodological thread in the exploration of events, facts and information was the understanding of the dynamic relationship between agency and structure. For instance, in Chapter 3, the analysis reconstructed the perceptions political parties had of themselves, of each other, and of the conditions in the economy and society. These perceptions depend on the position of the actors in the political field, their strengths and weaknesses, and the conditions in the economy as structural elements beyond their immediate control.

In Chapter 4, the dominance of heavy industries in the economic structure was seen as a material factor that hampered the attempts to reform. Its action was through the direct resistance to reform of the economic interests that had structural power – the strikes, the pressure on the government to satisfy their requests. At the same time, the action of this structural feature was mediated by the perceptions that politicians had of the economy and what was possible or desirable to achieve.

In general, material constraints, actors' perceptions of their choices, and of each other, were integrated into an account that preserved the dynamic character of their interactions, as shown by the changes identified during this period. The salient structural constraints for the post-communist transformations in the economy and society were the breakdown of the central authority in December 1989, the broad grass roots mobilisation for democracy and economic rights, the relative weakness of the political classes, and the lack of interest of foreign investors. These constraints were clearly perceived as such by the relevant actors and thus they shaped the course of events in Romania. The outcome has been a form of 'popular capitalism' that resulted from extensive mass privatisation and the use of the MEBO method of privatisation.

The results of this research could be usefully evaluated in a broader comparative context. The CEE countries may be placed along a continuum describing the strength and particular mixture of these structural conditions. At one end would be countries where strong neo-liberal normative commitment and the relatively more secure economic and institutional bases of the elites, such as in Poland or Hungary, were conditions favourable to swift reform and economic growth. In such cases the disciplining of labour was more effective, as the values of neo-liberalism were more widely shared. This was reflected for instance by greater social acceptance of high unemployment.

At the other end of the spectrum, in Russia, the greater solidarity of the nomenklatura, which acted as a social class against a weak state, weaker elite and social commitment to rules-based capitalism led to the capture of the state by private interests. Capitalism there is characterised by great inequality and weaker rules and economic performance. In Romania, intra-elite conflict between factions that embraced neo-liberal reform and conservative interests that were not hostile to capitalism but insisted on social democratic provisions was very strong. This slowed down neo-liberal reform but it also led to the development of broader forms of social inclusion. Regulatory institutions emerged more slowly and the variable economic performance reflected this intra-elite conflict. An interesting and puzzling case is that of the Czech Republic, which managed a swift transition to a market economy without major costs in terms of unemployment. It is possible that the more technologically advanced industry, closeness to western markets, and strong normative commitment both of elites and the population to neo-liberal ideals led to a form of social inclusion based on the market.

A second avenue for further research is the question of the integration of the social spheres. A few tentative connections were used as working hypotheses in this book. The consequences of the structural conditions mentioned above cut across the different social spheres. Grass roots mobilisation created significant pressure both for the constitution of political parties and for their assertion in the economic sphere through their respective economic policies. In turn, the importance of this feature was connected with the structural imbalances in the economy, and the breakdown of the central political authority.

But more importantly, the connections between social and political change on the one hand and cultural change on the other could be explored further. It has been shown that the values of individualism could cut through the moral dilemmas and conflicts of post-communist culture by vesting responsibility onto the individual. The major question is what kind of social developments would have to happen before this sort of cultural change could become possible. One hypothesis, derived from Bourdieu's (Bourdieu and Wacquant 1992) notion of the homology between objective and subjective structures, would be that the vast processes of wealth creation and redistribution in the post-communist period were possibly helped by the confusion of standards, norms, and institutions. By the same token, the gradual consolidation of the new upper classes should motivate and allow them to introduce gradually a new formal system in which their history and the sources of their power would be concealed by the decorum and respectability of a cultural system based on individualism and the myth of individual achievement.

Bârlădeanu, Alexandru was a member of the Central Committee of the Romanian Communist Party until 1965, when he retired to avoid confrontation with Nicolae Ceauşescu, whose economic policies he criticised openly. In 1989 he was one of the six signatories of a widely publicised 'open letter' to Ceauşescu. The letter condemned Ceauşescu's rule and asked for liberal reforms in politics and the economy. In 1990 he was a member of the CNFSN, and later the President of the Senate for the 1990–92 legislature.

Băsescu, Traian is currently the President of Romania and a former leader of the Democratic Party. See *Partidul Democrat.*

Brucan, Silviu is a political scientist of international reputation, an influential commentator and opinion maker. He was one of the members of the CNFSN and advised President Iliescu and Prime Minister Roman during the first weeks after the revolution. He refused to accept political office, but continued to have a public presence through his media appearances.

Câmpeanu, Radu returned from exile in France after the revolution of December 1989 and re-established the National Liberal Party in January 1990. He was his party's presidential candidate in the May 1990 elections, when he lost in favour of Ion Iliescu. He supported the decision that his party should join the Democratic Convention in 1990, but at other times he advocated a more independent line, such as the PNL presenting its own list of candidates in national elections. He played a marginal role in Romanian politics for the rest of the decade.

Ceauşescu, Nicolae was the communist leader of Romania between 1964 and 1989. Initially an advocate of liberalisation and ideological openness, after 1971 he started a Cultural Revolution inspired by the Chinese and South Korean communist regimes. He eliminated his rivals to the position of Secretary of the PCR and in the last two decades of his rule his influence was virtually unchecked within the Party. In 1981, in reaction to a debt crisis, he decided to pay Romania's foreign debt in full ahead of time, which was the beginning of increasing restrictions on imports and food and energy scarcities. He was hostile to Mikhail Gorbachev's *perestroika* and *glasnost* and re-affirmed his commitment to communism. In November 1989 he was re-elected unanimously as the Party leader, but only a month later he failed to quell mass uprisings against his regime in spite of mobilising the army against the demonstrators. Ceauşescu fled the Party Headquarters on 22 December 1989, but was captured, tried, sentenced to death and executed three days later by the new revolutionary regime together with his wife, Elena.

Ciorbea, Victor was a prominent member of the PNŢCD. A former leader of one of the major national labour unions, in 1996 he was elected mayor of Bucharest. Ciorbea gave up that post for the role of Prime Minister in the Democratic Convention government, between November 1996 and March 1998. After the failure of the PNŢCD to enter parliament in the 2000 elections, Ciorbea won the leadership contest against Andrei Marga, a former Secretary of State for Education.

Consiliul Naţional al Frontului Salvării Naţionale (National Council of the National Salvation Front – CNFSN) emerged as the revolutionary post-communist government, and ruled between December 1989 and the end of January 1990. The Council was the ruling body of an organisation, the FSN, that was, at that stage, yet to emerge. It was replaced by the CPUN in February 1990, after the FSN registered as a political party.

Consiliul Provizoriu al Unităţii Naţionale (Provisional Council of National Unity CPUN) replaced the CNFSN as the provisional government, on 1 February 1990. The FSN retained half of the seats and the presidency. The rest of the seats were divided between the twenty-seven parties that emerged in January 1990. It ruled until the first free general elections in May 1990.

Constantinescu, Emil is a former President of Romania (1996-2000). A geology professor at the University of Bucharest, Constantinescu started his political career as the CDR presidential candidate in the 1992 elections. During his Presidency he was instrumental in the nomination of Victor Ciorbea and Mugur Isărescu as CDR Prime Ministers, but was hostile to the ascendancy of Radu Vasile. He was active in promoting the Romanian case in negotiations for membership of NATO and the EU.

Convenţia Democrată din România (Democratic Convention of Romania) was an umbrella organisation constituted in late 1990 as a coalition between the main opposition forces against the rule of the FSN and later PDSR. Its prominent members were the PNŢCD, PNL and PSDR. It won the 1996 elections and ruled until 2000. It dissolved prior to the 2000 elections.

Coposu, Corneliu was the leader of the Youth Organisation of the PNŢCD before 1947 and a personal secretary to the legendary PNŢCD leader Iuliu Maniu. Coposu was a political prisoner of the communist regime in the

1950s. He re-established the PNŢCD after the revolution of 1989 and advocated democratisation, restitution of property confiscated by the communist regime, and stern opposition to the FSN and later PDSR. He died in 1995 at the age of 79.

Cunescu, Sergiu was a member of the old Social Democratic Romanian Party (PSDR), and a political prisoner of the communist regime. In 1989 he re-established the PSDR and acted as its leader until 2000 when a younger generation of leaders decided to participate in elections on a common list with the PDSR. The merger of the two parties and the establishment of the Social Democratic Party (PSD) took place in June 2001.

Dăianu, Daniel is a former Chief Economist to the National Bank of Romania and Secretary of State for Finance (1998). He lost his job in the Vasile Cabinet when he refused to endorse a privatisation deal with the American company Bell Helicopters who had made the purchase conditional on the Romanian Army buying over $1 billion worth of helicopters.

Dimitriu, Sorin was the head of the State Ownership Fund and Secretary of State for Privatisation in 1997–98. Prime Minister Vasile dismissed him in October 1998 because of the slow pace of privatisation.

Frontul Salvării Naţionale (National Salvation Front – FSN) emerged out of the CNFSN in February 1990. It was the major force in the CPUN and won the first free elections of May 1990. The FSN was responsible for the first pro-market reforms in the economy. After the demise of the Roman government, in September 1991, conflicts within the party led to a split between the Roman and Iliescu factions in early 1992. The Roman faction used the name until January 1996 when it became the Democratic Party, while Iliescu's faction was named the Democratic FSN and later became the PDSR and recently the PSD.

Funar, Gheorghe. See *Partidul Unităţii Naţionale Române (PUNR)*.

Historical parties is a generic term for the political parties that existed before the beginning of the communist regime in Romania in 1947 and were resurrected by their old members after December 1989. The most prominent of these parties were the PNŢCD, PSDR and PNL. Most of the leaders of these parties perished in political prisons between 1946 and 1964. The survivors of this onslaught remained bitter about the way they were treated by the communist regime. They saw the revolution of December 1989 as an opportunity for making public these grievances against the PCR and what they saw as its reincarnation, the FSN and PDSR.

Iliescu, Ion was a Minister for Youth between 1967 and 1971 and briefly a member of the Central Committee of the PCR in 1971 but he was demoted for criticising the policies of Nicolae Ceauşescu. He remained in different positions in the PCR until 1989 when he organised the CNFSN. Iliescu served as the president of the CNFSN and then the CPUN and was elected President of Romania in 1990, 1992 and 2000. His connections with PCR were a major handicap in his co-operation with the historical parties, but they did not harm his standing with the Romanian electors. He was an advocate for moderation in political competition, supported the rules of democracy and sought to act as a facilitator for inter-party co-operation during his terms as president.

Ionescu Quintus, Mircea is a prominent member of the older generation of liberals. See *National Liberal Party (PNL)*.

Isărescu, Mugur has been the Governor of the Bank of Romania since 1990, with a short interruption in 1999-2000 when he served as the Prime Minister. In the 2000 elections, he ran as the Democratic Convention 2000 candidate for President but he lost in the first round.

Năstase, Adrian, a lawyer, is the current Prime Minister of Romania and leader of the Social Democratic Party (PSD). He was vice-president and president of the PDSR, and a president of the senate in 1992–96. He is the first party leader to accept the position of Prime Minister.

Paleologu, Alexandru is a prominent figure in the Romanian public culture and a liberal. See *Partidul Naţional Liberal (PNL)*.

Partidul Comunist Român (Romanian Communist Party – PCR) ruled Romania between 1947 and 1989. By the end of the period it had about 3.5 million members, but after the December 1989 it disappeared from the Romanian political scene. Under popular pressure, the FSN officially dissolved the PCR by decree at the end of January 1990.

Partidul Democrat (Democratic Party – PD), a centre-left reformist party, was known as the FSN-Roman between 1992 and January 1996. The PD has been the leading member of the Social Democratic Union, an alliance with a minor social-democratic party from January 1996 to the present. It partici-pated in the government with the Democratic Convention in 1996-2000. Current leader is Traian Băsescu, a former Secretary of State for Transport and present mayor of Bucharest.

Partidul Democraţiei Sociale din România (Romanian Party of Social Democracy – PDSR) was the conservative splinter of the original FSN. Between early 1992 and July 1993 it was known under the name of the

Democratic FSN. The PDSR was in power between 1992–1996, when it ruled in intermittent coalition with the PRM, PUNR and PSM. It won almost 40 per cent of the votes in the 2000 elections and rules as a minority government.

Partidul Naţional Liberal (National Liberal Party – PNL) is one of the three major historical parties revived after the revolution. It had numerous splinters. Some factions operated within the Democratic Convention, such as the National Liberal Party – the Youth Wing, and the National Liberal Party 1993. Others, under the leadership of Radu Câmpeanu, contested some of the local and national elections on their own. Prominent parliamentarians, liberals of the old guard who were members of the party prior to 1947 and served sentences as political prisoners under the communist regime include Alexandru Paleologu, Radu-Renée Policrat and Mircea Ionescu Quintus. Current leader is Valeriu Stoica.

Partidul Naţional Tărănesc Creştin şi Democrat (National Peasant Party – Christian and Democrat – PNŢCD) was one of the main opposition parties in post-communist Romania. It was the dominant member of the Democratic Convention and nominated the first two Prime Ministers of the Democratic Convention stint in power, in 1996-2000, Victor Ciorbea and Radu Vasile. In 2000 it organised a smaller coalition of democratic forces in order to participate in the elections, called the Democratic Convention 2000. It failed to gain enough votes to enter parliament in 2000 and its political future is now in question.

Partidul România Mare (Greater Romania Party – PRM) held its first congress in March 1993. It was an ally of the Văcăroiu government at different times in the 1992–96 legislature and won a surprise 20 per cent of the vote in the 2000 elections. Its ideology is nationalistic and it is regarded as an extremist party.

Partidul Social – Democrat al României (Social Democratic Romanian Party – PSDR) was one of the three main historical parties revived in January 1990. It was an active member of the democratic opposition, within and outside of the Democratic Convention. A member of the Socialist International, in 2001 it merged with the PDSR to form the Social Democratic Party (PSD).

Partidul Social Democrat (Social Democratic Party – PSD) is the new name of the ruling party in Romania, which resulted from the merger in June 2001 of the PDSR and the PSDR.

Partidul Socialist al Muncii (Socialist Party of Labour – PSM) was the official successor to the PCR. Ilie Verdeţ, a former prime minister under Nicolae Ceauşescu, led it until March 2001. In 1992–96 it participated in the Văcăroiu government, in coalition with the PUNR, PRM and PDSR. It promoted extreme left policies and was a reluctant supporter of privatisation. It ceased to play a role in Romanian politics after the 1996 elections.

Partidul Unităţii Naţionale Române (Party of Romanian National Unity – (PUNR) first participated in national elections in 1990. Its leader, Gheorghe Funar, was a presidential candidate in 1992 and 1996, and was the mayor of Cluj-Napoca, one of the major cities in Transylvania during this period. Before the 2000 elections, the PUNR merged with a smaller party led by Virgil Măgureanu, a former Romanian Intelligence Service chief, to form the National Alliance. It failed to obtain the necessary number of votes to enter parliament.

Pleşu, Andrei is a philosopher, member of the 'Păltiniş Group' of anti-communist cultural resistance led by the legendary Constantin Noica (1909–87), a prominent intellectual who survived political prison and enjoyed almost cult-like status in the Romanian culture. Pleşu served as Secretary of State for Culture in the provisional government of Petre Roman until May 1990 and as Foreign Secretary in 1997–98.

Policrat, Radu-Renée is a member of the older generation of liberals. See *Partidul Naţional Liberal (PNL)*.

Roman, Petre was the first prime minister of post-communist Romania and led the provisional government between December 1989 and May 1990. After the victory of the FSN in the May 1990 elections, he remained in the post and presided over the beginnings of the economic reform programme, launched in November 1990. After his resignation in September 1991 under apparent pressure from President Iliescu, the conflicts between his reformist faction and the conservatives in the FSN led to a split at the beginning of 1992. Roman remained the leader of the party during the 1990s, was the President of the Senate in 1996–99 and the Secretary of State for Foreign Affairs in 1999–2000. In the 2000 elections he was his party's candidate in the presidential elections but garnered fewer votes than the party. He lost the leadership elections in early 2001.

Sârbu, Radu was the manager of the Cluj office of the State Ownership Fund before serving as the head of the State Ownership Fund between October 1998 and November 2000. He is currently under investigation for the legality of some of the privatisation sales conducted during his time in office.

Şerbănescu, Ilie is an economist and publicist. Without political affiliation, he was appointed Secretary of State for Reform in the Ciorbea and Vasile Cabinets.

Severin, Adrian was the first president of the National Agency for Privatisation in 1990 and was one of the main architects and supporters of the privatisation law of 1991. After the FSN broke up in early 1992, he sided with the Roman faction and in 1997 he served as Secretary of State for Foreign Affairs. He was dismissed in December 1997, when his claims that certain politicians and journalists were spies for foreign powers were found groundless.

Stoica, Valeriu, a former Secretary of State for Justice in the Democratic Convention governments, is currently the leader of the National Liberal Party (PNL).

Stolojan, Theodor was a civil servant in the Ministry of Finance prior to the 1989 revolution. In July 1991 he was a speaker for the government in the debates around the privatisation law in the senate and served briefly as the Director of the National Agency for Privatisation. In September 1991 Stolojan was appointed Prime Minister, with the mandate to prepare the first general election in accordance with the new post-communist constitution. He worked for the World Bank for a few years before returning to Romanian politics in 2000 when he was the candidate of the Liberal Party in the presidential elections.

Uniunea Democrată a Maghiarilor din România (Democratic Union of the Hungarians in Romania – UDMR) has had consistent representation in parliament since 1990. It promotes the interests of the Hungarian minority in Romania and has taken a position favourable to market reform in the coalition with the Democratic Convention in 1996–2000, and is currently supporting the Năstase government.

Uniunea Social Democrată (Social Democratic Union – USD) has been a coalition between the Democratic Party and a minor social democratic party from January 1996 to the present.

Văcăroiu, Nicolae was a civil servant in the Planning Commission prior to the 1989 revolution. In 1992 he was appointed to lead the PDSR government and, in spite of general scepticism, he managed to hold on to his mandate for four years. He was elected as an MP in 1996 and 2000 and served in the commission for privatisation and economic reform of the Senate.

Vasile, Radu, an economist, was a vice-president of the PNȚCD and became a Prime Minister between March 1998 and December 1999. After leaving office he established a far-right party that failed to enter parliament in the 2000 elections.

Results for parliamentary elections in Romania in 1990, 1992, 1996 and 2000

Results of the parliamentary elections in Romania in 1990 and 1992 (percentages)

Parties	1990		1992		Percentage change	
	Chamber	Senate	Chamber	Senate	Chamber	Senate
FSN	66.31	67.02	10.18	10.38		
DFSN[a]	–	–	27.71	28.29		
FSN+DFSN	66.31	67.02	37.89	38.67	–28.42	–28.35
PNL[b]	6.41	7.06	2.44	2.68		
New Liberal Party[a]	–	–	0.58	0.52		
Liberals	6.41	7.06	3.02	3.20	–3.39	–3.86
PNTCD[a]	2.50	2.56	–	–		
PER[c]	1.62	1.38	–	–		
PSDR[c]	0.53	0.50	–	–		
CDR[a]	4.65	4.44	20.01	20.16	+ 15.36	+ 15.72
UDMR	7.23	7.20	7.45	7.58	+ 0.22	+ 0.38
PUNR[d]	2.12	2.15	7.71	8.12	+ 5.59	+ 5.97
PDA[e]	1.83	1.55	2.99	3.30	+ 1.16	+ 1.75
PRM[a]	–	–	3.89	3.85		
PSM[a]	–	–	3.03	3.18		
Other parties	11.45	10.58	14.01	11.94		
Total	100.00	100.00	100.00	100.00		

a Did not run in 1990.
b Did not pass the 3% hurdle in 1992.
c In 1992 ran on CDR lists, which included 18 parties and associations.
d In 1990 ran jointly with the Republican Party
e Did not pass the 3% hurdle for the Chamber of Deputies in 1992.
Source: Adapted from Shafir (1992g).

Results of the parliamentary elections in Romania, November 1996 (percentages)

	Chamber	Senate
CDR	30.17	30.70
PDSR	21.52	23.08
USD	12.93	13.16
UDMR	6.64	6.81
PRM	4.46	4.54
PUN	4.36	4.22

Source: Adapted from Popescu (1997, 181).

Results of the parliamentary elections in Romania, November 2000 (percentages)

Party	Chamber	Senate
PDSR	36.61	37.09
PRM	19.48	21.01
PD	7.03	7.58
PNL	6.98	7.48
UDMR	6.80	6.90
CDR	5.04	5.29
ApR	4.07	4.27

Source: www.politics.ro/alegeri26nov2000_official.php, visited on 2/12/00.

Party acronyms: elections 1990 and 1992

FSN	National Salvation Front (Roman)
DFSN	Democratic National Salvation Front (Iliescu)
PNL	National Liberal Party
PNL-AT	National Liberal Party – Young Wing
PNTCD	National Peasant Party-Christian Democratic
PER	Romanian Ecologist Party
PSDR	Social Democratic Party of Romania
CDR	Democratic Convention of Romania
UDMR	Democratic Union of Hungarians in Romania
PUNR	Party of Romanian National Unity
PDA	Democratic Agrarian Party
PRM	Greater Romania Party
PSM	Socialist Party of Labour

Elections 1996 (new names or new parties)

PDSR	Party of Social Democracy of Romania, changed name (July 1993) of DFSN

USD   Social Democratic Union, an alliance of the PD and a small social-democratic Party.

PUN   National Unity Party, changed name of PUNR

Elections 2000 (new names or new parties)

PD   Democratic Party

ApR   Alliance for Romania

Romania: Macro-economic indicators 1989–2001

Main indicators of economic performance (percentage change)

	1989	1990	1991	1992	1993	1994	1995	1996	1997	1998	1999	2000 (est.)
Real GDP	−5.8	−5.6	−12.9	−8.7	1.5	3.9	7.1	3.9	−6.9	−5.4	−3.2	1.5
Inflation (CPI annual average)	1.1	5.1	161.1	210.4	256.1	136.7	32.3	38.8	154.8	59.1	45.8	45.9
Wages (nominal annual average)	3.9	10.5	121.3	170	202.1	129.5	n/a	n/a	n/a	31.9	−16.1	3.3
Unemployment	n/a	n/a	n/a	6.2	9.5	9.5	9.5	6.6	8.9	10.3	11.5	11.17[a]
General government balance (per cent of GDP)	8.4	1.2	3.3	-4.6	-0.4	−1.9	−4.1	−4.9	−3.6	−2.8 (BNR) −5.0 (IMF)	−2.6 (BNR) −3.8 (IMF)	−4.2 IMF

[a] Calculated based on monthly averages given in the BNR Statistical Bulletin, Dec. 2000, p. 24.

Sources: The data for 1989 and 1990 are from Kasper Bartholdy (1996, 544).

For 1991–1994 the data are from Raiser and Sanfey (1998, 272).

For 1995–1999 the data are from BNR (1999, 28–29). The estimates for 2000 are from IMF (2000, 16, 36, 43).

Indicators of external vulnerability (in US billion)

	1989	1990	1991	1992	1993	1994	1995	1996	1997	1998	1999	2000 (proj.)
External debt[a]	−0.8	0.6	2.1	3.2	4.2	5.5	5.48	7.20	8.58	9.30	8.43	9.34
Current account balance (US billion)	2.9	−1.8	−1.18	−1.51	−1.23	-0.51	−1.77	−2.57	−2.13	−2.96	−1.28	−1.5
Trade balance (US billion)	2.6	−1.8	−1.25	−1.37	−1.13	−0.48	−1.57	−2.47	−1.98	−2.62	−1.09	−1.44
Exchange rate (leu to USD, av.)	14.9	22.4	76.3	308	760	1,580	2,033	3,083	7,167	8,874	15,332	21,693[b]

Sources: The data for 1989 and 1990 are from Kasper Bartholdy (1996, 544).
For 1991–1994 the data are from Raiser and Sanfey (1998, 272).
For 1995–1999 the data are from BNR (1999, 28–9). The estimates for 2000 are from IMF (2000: 16, 36, 43).

a The external debt for 1989 and 1990 is given as net of reserves, end of year. For the rest of the period, the figures are for the total external debt.
b Calculated based on monthly averages given in the BNR Statistical Bulletin, Dec. 2000, p. 24.

Private sector share of the GDP (per cent)

1990	1991	1992	1993	1994	1995	1996	1997	1998	1999
16.40	23.60	26.40	34.80	38.90	45.00	52.00	58.00	61	62

Sources: IMF (2000, 31); World Bank: Public Enterprise Reform and Privatisation Database

Cultural factors in economic and political transformations: a detailed example

In Chapter 2, I made the argument that schemes of perception and interpretation socialised as part of the formal political culture of the communist regime in Romania survived during the 1990s. Their influence will be documented here in relation to a heated political moment in Romanian post-communist history: the resignation of Prime-Minister Victor Ciorbea, fifteen months into his mandate, as a result of political conflict within the ruling coalition. After winning the elections in November 1996, the Democratic Convention, led by the National Peasant Party – Christian and Democrat (PNŢCD), with the participation of the National Liberal Party (PNL) and the Democratic Party (PD), pronounced the end of the 'democratic transition'. It claimed that at last the country had made a break with communism by voting out of power the 'neo-communist' government of Nicolae Văcăroiu and the President Ion Iliescu (Make 1998).

The new prime minister, Victor Ciorbea, a member of PNŢCD, launched early in 1997, with the support of the IMF, the World Bank and the EU, an ambitious stabilisation and liberalisation programme. It led, however, to recession and higher than expected inflation (151 per cent year on year, compared with a projection of 90 per cent). As the consequences of the programme were becoming clear, disputes within the coalition centred on the failure of Ciorbea to implement the restructuring and privatisation measures necessary to secure the long-term macro-economic stability sought by this programme. Attempts to close certain loss-making enterprises, in the summer of 1997, were stalled by opposition from the enterprises concerned and controversy over their financial situation.[1] Politically, this conflict took the form of public declarations by the members of the Democratic Party, especially Traian Băsescu, criticising the record of the government, in December 1997. As this was an explicit breach of a an earlier rule made public by Ciorbea, that ministers should not make public statements about policy without consultation in the cabinet, Băsescu was forced to resign. He was the second PD minister to leave the government, after Adrian Severin, the foreign affairs minister who made accusations of espionage against some journalists and politicians that were found baseless.

The obstructive politics initiated by the PD against the coalition government they were part of lasted until the end of March 1998. After its two ministers resigned, the PD refused to endorse the budget for 1998 and pressed for the resignation of Ciorbea. The unfruitful visit by the IMF negotiator to Bucharest and the negative assessment on the release of the third instalment from the stand-by loan also undermined the credibility of Ciorbea (Pasti 1998a). Against this background, at the end of March 1998, just as Prime Minister Ciorbea was about to present his resignation, three of his ministers went public with an appeal to public opinion. They were Daniel Dăianu, Finance Minister, Andrei Pleşu, Foreign Affairs Minister, and Ilie Şerbănescu, Minister for Reform (1998). Their appeal went like this:

> We feel obliged, in our capacity as members of the government, uncommitted to any party structures and consequently free of political ambitions, to make a collegial appeal to all the segments of the public life – be they the civil society, the governing coalition or the opposition – and to all the institutions responsible for the administration of the country, for an adequate and prompt approach to the prolonged crisis we are traversing. Each of us, in our respective domains of specific competence, notices every day a worrying aggravation of the situation, liable to lead to a blockage that would be difficult to reverse. At this late hour, it is not about people, programmes and ideologies. It is about profound, structural ills which no subsequent government, irrespective of its political colour and competence, could remedy other than in time, through a patient investment of pragmatism, ingenuity, professionalism and continuity. There are no providential individuals and no miraculous recipes. Frankness, lucidity, and disinterested effort are needed. This is exactly what, at this moment, we lack. At this very moment, when the acceleration of reforms in the economy is vital and requires firm and resolute measures, that would benefit from a solid political support, at this very moment the political discourse allows itself to be confiscated by populism, demagoguery, and electoral excitement. The reform seems to have become a simple pretext for the negotiation of certain power positions. The probability for early elections increases, and this paralyses reformist thought and daring effectiveness. The real economic context is ignored and its importance is minimised. The small euphoria of 'let's not dramatise' is preferred. To signal the evil, to tell the truth, is, for some, a banal form of defeatism or ill will. Those who can take decisions hesitate, those who do not hesitate, are not allowed to take decisions. Telling for the confusion caused by the superficial political agitation is, for instance, the arbitrary ungrounded dispute around the budget.
>
> The human capital available to us is not used. The bad rewards make it difficult to mobilise the specialists, and those who still want to get involved are often rejected, according to criteria that put the political file or personal interests above competence. The right tone in communication with the citizens is not found. The

institutions function with difficulty, against a background of resistance to change that is discouraging. At all levels we encounter managerial incompetence. It is impossible to enter into the damaging fortresses that are the *regies autonomes* and the loss-making enterprises. Drastic, unavoidable intervention is postponed, for fear of social reactions that might endanger 'the stability' of one's post that has become a fetish. The national wealth – precarious in any case – tends to be squandered through negligent or occult distribution. The lag of our country in relation to processes of globalisation and technological advancement becomes more pronounced. Against this background our legitimate desire to become integrated in the European and Euro-Atlantic structures risks losing its arguments. It is not possible to build an offensive and convincing diplomatic action in a context of prolonged instability, indecision and corruption. A country with remarkable potential and a significant strategic position looks condemned to miss once again its historic chance for development. All of these should give us insomnia, or, if we managed to fall asleep, to wake us up. It is not a simple political crisis that we have to resolve, but a deeper one: a crisis of principles, of mentalities, and, ultimately, a crisis of identity. (Dăianu, Pleşu and Şerbănescu 1998).[2]

This appeal is interesting at a number of levels. Messages to do with pragmatic self-interest mingle with cultural props belonging to the code of heroism, imminent danger, and the need for transcendence. The main point they wanted to put across was that early elections, a perceived threat at a time of inconclusive negotiations for a political solution to the conflict between the PNŢCD and the PD, would be a mistake. Firstly, this was because the causes of the difficulties were long-term and they could not be solved immediately, irrespective of the government. Secondly, instability frustrated or paralysed 'reformist thought and daring effectiveness', was a reference to their agenda. The appeal also denounced their adversaries: the resistance to change was reflected in personnel policies in the public administration and the 'impossibility of entering' into the *regies autonomes*.

This relatively straightforward message was however heavily overlaid by confusing characterisation of their own intentions, those of their adversaries, the diagnosis of the current situation and their own gesture of coming to the public with a direct appeal. Precisely because these ministers were among the most credible and most technically competent forces in the government it is interesting to note that they unwittingly dressed their appeal in the cultural language of the time.[3]

Thus, the authors, ministers in some of the crucial ministries of the country, made the choice of appealing directly to the public to do something they could not do on their own. They seemed to be able to notice, to worry, and to take decisions, but, unaccountably, their efforts were hampered as 'those who do not hesitate, are not allowed to take decisions'. The sense that solutions to the problems they identified could not be found even by well-meaning people in high positions of authority. This admission of powerlessness undermined the conventional assumptions about government:

was it the case that although nominally in power, they did not have power? Or was it rather that they did not want to assume its responsibilities?

At a minimum, this appeal was a breach of a convention within the democratic pact: those elected to rule are doing so in the name of and for the people. They may do it badly or not at all, but then they have the choice of resigning or waiting for the judgement reserved for the electorate on the day of the election. By coming to the public with this admission they failed to take any of these honourable solutions and blurred the definitions of these two roles, the electors and the elected. They seemed to want to plead for sympathy by pre-empting the electors' evaluation of their performance and drawing them into shouldering responsibility for the outcome of their performance in office. They did not frame their ministerial positions in a technical way, as a job. By stepping out of the prescriptions of their public role, they confused the boundaries between the discipline of that role and their private emotional needs.

Nothing short of heroic transcendence of difficulties was called for in this appeal, and perhaps this was the scale on which they assessed their own performance. The way they framed it confirms the power of this reference point. To launch the appeal was an extreme measure, justified by the pathos of the situation, a continuous 'worrying aggravation of the situation', and purified of selfish reasons. The implication, reinforced later by derogatory remarks on the assumed 'selfish' motivation of others suspected of being interested primarily in their posts, is that only pure motives are allowed in politics. Self-interest, the motor of progress in liberal ideology, is here made illegitimate. No connection seemed possible between 'frankness, lucidity and disinterested effort', the qualities considered necessary to resolve the crisis, and self-interest. On the contrary, they are granted effectiveness of their own accord, once embedded in a motivation of heroic dedication to the public cause. This is perhaps another facet of avoiding responsibility, a common cultural prop. The refusal to stay within the discipline of the public role is doubled here by unwillingness to concede to having selfish reasons.

Some of the assessments contained in the appeal can be defended as reasonable and true. The perception of political instability is indeed costly for the credibility of the Romanian governments and their ability to negotiate with NATO and the EU. The lack of consistency in economic policy also creates difficulties. However, these observations do not serve in this appeal a clear strategy for action or, at a minimum, a list of clear objectives to be realised through specific policies. Those called to help are a diffuse mass, asked to transcend the limitations of the present for the sake of a problem-free if not idealised future.

This conception of politics as a question of heroism, and the notion of altruism as the moral guarantee of the politicians, were also at the forefront of Ciorbea's mind. In his long resignation speech pronounced in front of the TV cameras on 30 March 1998 and published next day by the press, his main concern seemed to be to establish that he was an honest man, that he did not profit materially from his position. After deploring his forced departure, which was the result of a sophisticated 'mineriada',[4] he said in his defence:

> Perhaps I lack in the instinct for conservation, but I did not consider necessary the fear, the suspicion and the other manifestations of the 'political manhood' so cherished in certain places: the fist on the table, the shrewdness, the swindling, the blackmail, the lack of common sense, the getting rich overnight at the expense of the citizens and so on. I was not avid for power or its external accoutrements, and for this reason I believed and believe sincerely that it is possible to work as a team, that the government programme is sufficient proof of faith to silence rivalries. I had hoped that at the end of this process we would all have won, i.e. the country, the citizens, the parties and the politicians. I could not conceive that the common good would be valued less by some than an illusory momentary victory. The popularity built on these methods and with this price does not last, and, in the end, the people and history will sanction this popularity, as it deserves. (Ciorbea 1998)

The role of the politician is again cast in purist terms, and the confusion between the actor and his actions forms the basis of his judgement of his colleagues' actions. This refusal to 'dirty his hands' and engage in tough, pragmatic politics was according to some analysts the cause of Ciorbea's downfall. The lack of pragmatism and authority in forging a common line within a divided coalition led to a prolonged stalemate in government, which in turned caused a slowing down of reforms at the end of 1997 and the beginning of 1998 (Pasti 1998c). His inability to offer leadership in difficult circumstances was also linked to the fact that while in opposition, during 1990–96, the Democratic Convention as a whole chose an uncompromising moral stance, rather than active engagement with pragmatic policies and responsible governance (Pasti 1998b, 1998d). It was thus possible for them to substitute the agreement for a stand-by loan with the IMF for their economic policy, with the effect of causing a deep, unexpected recession that lasted until 2000.

This situated analysis of political statements, at a moment of change and crisis, has shown that cultural props belonging to the communist culture were mobilised, as late as 1998, to justify actions and decisions of great consequence. That politicians, a mere nine years into a democratic regime, were still struggling to find the appropriate definitions of their roles and the values around which to rally the public was perhaps not surprising. The crucial developments that would have to happen, if more efficient governance is to become possible in Romania, are to do with the understanding of politics as the legitimate and orderly pursuit of self-interest, of boundaries around public roles, and the appropriate assumption of responsibility for one's actions.

Notes

1   One analyst claimed that implementation of plans for plant closure was judged by the
    government as likely to lead to social unrest. This outcome would have hampered
    their attempt to portray Romania as a factor of stability in the region, which in turn
    was a crucial argument in Romania's campaign to join NATO prior to the organisa-
    tion's Madrid meeting of July 1997 (Secăreş 1998).

2   This author's translation.

3   In decoding this message, issues of methodology arise. Among them is the question of
    the authors' intention in projecting their message, the extent to which they identified
    with all the contents of their communication. To ask this question is to ask the ques-
    tion of the interplay between subjective (what the authors think they are saying, as
    gleaned from what they say explicitly) and objective, i.e. social elements (what the
    authors communicate unwittingly). The interpretation here is based on the idea that
    both intended and unintended components of the message are important, an issue
    recognised in social psychology (Argyle 1992) and sociology (Goffman 1969). In
    other words, by 'objectifying' the message, by treating it as an 'object' for analysis, the
    aim is not only to make a statement about the subjective views of the three authors in
    question, but also to point out the ways in which what they say unwittingly reflects
    their participation in the broader social context. This is possible because, according
    to Bourdieu, 'social agents are knowing agents who, even when they are subjected to
    determinism, contribute to producing the efficacy of that which determines them in
    so far as they structure what determines them. And it is almost always in the "fit"
    between determinants and the categories of perception that constitute them as such
    that the effect of domination arises' (Bourdieu and Wacquant 1992, 167).

4   This is a reference to the invasion of Bucharest by the miners from Valea Jiului, which
    led to the resignation of Petre Roman in 1991.

$\mathcal{R}$EFERENCES

Note: All internet sites were active at the time of the research. Hard copies of web documents and manuscripts are available from the author.

Abbott, Kenneth, W, Robert O. Keohane, Andrew Moravczik, Anne-Marie Slaughter and Duncan Snidal. 2000. The concept of legalisation. *International Organisation* 54:3. 401–419.

Adam, Christopher, William Cavendish and Piercy S. Mistry. 1992. *Adjusting privatization. Case studies from developing countries.* London: James Currey.

Adevărul economic. 1997. Managementul întreprinderilor mici – în derută! 6–12 June. http://adevarul.kappa.ro/eco273–04.html.

Adler, Emanuel. 1997. Seizing the middle ground: constructivism in world politics. *European Journal of International Relations* 3: 319–363.

Agenţia Naţională de Privatizare (ANP). 1993a. Buletin informativ 1. Bucharest: ANP.

————. 1993b. Buletin informativ 2. Bucharest: ANP.

————. 1993c. Buletin informativ 3. Bucharest: ANP.

————. 1993d. Buletin informativ 4. Bucharest: ANP.

————. 1994. Buletin informativ 1. Bucharest: ANP.

Aligică Paul Dragoş. 2001. Romania's economic policy: before and after the elections. *East European Constitutional Review.* www.law.nyu.edu/eecr /vol10num1/features/romaniaeconomicpolicy.html

Almond, Mark. 1990. Romania since the revolution. *Government and Opposition* 25: 484–496.

————. 1992. *The rise and fall of Nicolae and Elena Ceauşescu.* London: Chapmans.

Andarache, Radu. 1996. Avertisment: Industria de celuloză şi hârtie în pragul colapsului. *Economistul,* November: 18–19.

Anderson, Benedict. 1991. *Imagined communities: reflections on the origin and spread of nationalism.* Revised edition. London: Verso.

Andreescu, Gabriel (with Alexandru Paleologu, Fey Laszlo, Daniel Vighi, Liviu Andreescu, Laurentiu Ulici and Dan Oprescu). 1996. *Nationalişti, antinationalişti: O polemică în publicistica românească.* Iaşi: Polirom.

————. 1998. *Solidaritatea alergătorilor de cursă lungă: jurnal tematic.* Iaşi: Polirom.

Antohe, Cătălin. 2000. Acţionarii de la Global Muntenia Finance s-au ingrăşat pe banii SIF Muntenia. *Curentul,* 11 May.

Antohi, Dorina. 1995. Situaţia financiară a întreprinderilor cu capital de stat în condiţiile tranziţiei. *Oeconomica* No. 1: 31–40.

Antohi, Sorin. 2001. România după 11 ani. Interview by Rodica Palade. *22,* 4–8 January: 6–9.

Antonescu, Cristian. 1997. Rezistenţa la reformă. *Adevărul,* 5 August.

Antonesei, Liviu. 1995. *Jurnal din anii ciumei 1987–1989: încercări de sociologie spontană.* Iaşi: Polirom.

Argyle, Michael. 1992. *The social psychology of everyday life.* London: Routledge.

Ash, Timothy Garton. 1983. *The Polish revolution: solidarity 1980–1982.* London: Jonathan Cape Ltd.

Ashley, Richard. 1987. The geopolitics of geopolitical space: toward a critical social theory of international politics. *Alternatives* XII: 403–434.

————. 1991. The state of the discipline: Realism under challenge. In *International relations: global and Australian perspectives on an evolving discipline,* ed. R. Higgott and J. L. Richardson, 37–69. Canberra: Australian National University Press.

Baer, Werner and Annibal V. Villela. 1994. Privatisation and the changing role of the state in Brazil. In *Privatization in Latin America: new roles for the public and private sectors,* ed. Werner Baer and Melissa H. Birch, 1–19. Westport, Connecticut: Praeger.

Baldwin, David A. 1993. Neoliberalism, neorealism and world politics. In *Neorealism and neoliberalism: the contemporary debate,* 5–25. New York: Columbia University Press.

Banca Naţională a Romaniei (BNR). 1997a. *Annual reports, 1991–1995.* Bucharest: BNR.

————. 1997b. *Annual report, 1996.* Bucharest: BNR.

————. 1999a. *Annual report, 1998.* Bucharest: BNR.

————. 1999b. Declaraţie de Presă a Consiliului de Adminstraţie: golirea băncilor de valori, o afirmaţie falsă. *Curentul,* 31 May: 13.

————. 2000. *Annual report, 1999.* Bucharest: BNR.

Barber, Bernard. 1995. All economies are 'embedded': the career of a concept and beyond. *Social Research* 62: 387–413.

Barbu, Daniel. 1997. *Şapte teme de politicâ românească.* Bucharest: Antet.

Bar-On, Daniel. 1999. *The indescribable and the undiscussable: reconstructing human discourse after trauma.* Budapest: Central European University Press.

Bartholdy, Kasper. 1996. Statistical review. *Economics of Transition* 4: 527–550.

Batt, Judy. 1991. The end of communist rule in East-Central Europe: a four-country comparison. *Government and Opposition* 26: 368–390.

————. 1994. Political dimensions of privatization in Eastern Europe. In

Privatization in Central and Eastern Europe, ed. Saul Estrin, 83–91. London: Longman.

———. 2001. *Reinventing Banat*. Centre for the Russian and Eastern European Studies. University of Birmingham: Mimeo.

Bauer, Michael. 1994. An example of enterprise restructuring in the context of privatisation: Vranco S.A. Romania. *Trends and policies in privatisation* 2: 123–145. Paris: OECD Publications.

Bauman, Zygmunt. 1992. *Intimations of post-modernity*. London: Routledge.

———. 1994. After the patronage state: a model in search of class interests. In *The new great transformation? Change and continuity in East-Central Europe*, ed. Christopher G. A. Bryant and Edmund Mokrzycki, 14–35. London: Routledge.

———. 1995. Searching for a centre that holds. In *Global modernities*, ed. Mike Featherstone, Scot Lash and Roland Robertson, 140–154. London: Sage.

Baylis, Thomas A. 1994. 'Plus ça change?' Transformation and continuity among East European elites. *Communist and Post-Communist Studies* 27: 315–328.

Băban, Adriana. 1996. Viaţa sexuală a femeilor: o experienţă traumatizantă în România socialistă. In *Cine suntem noi? Despre identitatea femeilor din România modernă*, ed. Mădălina Nicolaescu, 51–68. Bucharest: Anima.

Băieşu, Ion. 1990. Cui i-e frică de Virginia Woolf? *Adevărul*, 30 January.

Bărbulescu, Adrian. 2001. Faţa neagră a privatizării: întreprinderi considerate producători unici au dispărut sau au fost transformate în depozite. *Curentul*, 20 March.

Behr, Edward. 1999. '*Sărută mîna pe care n-o poţi muşca*' *Românii şi Ceauşeştii: investigaţia unui blestem al istoriei*. Bucharest: Humanitas.

Ben-Ner, Avner and John Michael Montias. 1991. The introduction of markets in a hypercentralized economy: the case of Romania. *Journal of Economic Perspectives* 5: 163–170.

———. 1994. Economic system reforms and privatization in Romania. In *Privatization in Central and Eastern Europe*, ed. Saul Estrin, 279–310. London: Longman.

Bennett, Anthony. 1997. The measurement of privatisation and related issues. In *How does privatization work? Essays on privatization in honour of Prof. V.V. Ramanadhan*, 3–22. London: Routledge.

Berg, Andrew. 1994. The logistics of privatisation in Poland. In *The transition in Eastern Europe*. Vol. 2. *Restructuring*, ed. Olivier Jean Blanchard, Kenneth A. Froot and Jeffrey D. Sachs, 165–188. Chicago: Chicago University Press.

Berki, R. N. 1982. The state, Marxism, and political legitimation. In *Political legitimation in communist states*, ed. T. H. Rigby and Ferenc Feher, 146–169. London: Macmillan.

Betea, Lavinia. 1997. *Alexandru Bârlădeanu despre Dej, Ceauşescu şi Iliescu*. Bucharest: Evenimentul Românesc.

Biersteker, Thomas J. 1992. The 'triumph' of neoclassical economics in the developing world: policy convergence and bases of governance in the international economic order. In *Governance without government: order and change in world politics*, ed. James N. Rosenau and Ernst-Otto Czempiel, 102–131. Cambridge: Cambridge University Press.

Blaga, Ionel. 1994a. Însemnări pe marginea scrisorii de intenţie şi a memorandumului guvernului adresate Fondului Monetar Internaţional. *Oeconomica* No. 1: 69–72.

________. 1994b. Privatizarea: probleme şi soluţii în România. *Oeconomica* No. 2: 59–68.

Blanchard, Olivier. 1997. *The economics of post-communist transition.* Oxford: Clarendon Press.

Blanchard, Olivier, Rudiger Dornbusch, Paul Krugman, Richard Layard and Lawrence Summers. 1991. *Reform in Eastern Europe.* Cambridge Ma: The MIT Press.

Blanchard, Olivier, Maxim Boycko, Marek Dornbusch, Richard Layard and Andrei Schleifer. 1993. *Post-communist reform: pain and progress.* Cambridge Ma: The MIT Press.

Boot, Arnoud W. A. and Sweder van Wijnbergen. 1995. Financial sector design, regulation and deposit insurance in Eastern Europe. In *Banking reform in Central Europe and the Former Soviet Union*, ed. Jacek Rostowski, 42–57. Budapest: Central European University Press.

Borc, Costin. 1999. Why are domestic interest rates so high? Paper presented at the conference 'Romania 2000 – 10 years of transition: past, present and future', Bucharest: 21–22 October.

Borocz, Joszef and Akos Rona-Tas. 1995. Small leap forward: Emergence of new economic elites. *Theory and Society* 24: 751–781.

Botcheva, Liliana and Lisa L. Martin. 2001. Institutional effects on state behavior: Convergence and divergence. *International Studies Quarterly* 45:1. 1–26.

Botez, Mihai. 1997. *Lumea a doua.* Bucharest: Du Style.

Bourdieu, Pierre. 1990. *The logic of practice.* trans. Richard Nice. London: Polity Press.

________. 1991. *Language and symbolic power.* ed. and intro. John B. Thompson, trans. Gino Raymond and Matthew Adamson. London: Polity Press.

Bourdieu, Pierre and Loic J. D. Wacquant. 1992. *An invitation to reflexive sociology.* London: Polity Press.

Brada, Josef C. 1996. Privatization is transition – or is it? *Journal of Economic Perspectives* 10: 67–86.

Brandys, Kazimierz. 1984. *A Warsaw diary, 1978–1981.* trans. Richard Lourie. London: Chatto and Windus, The Hogarth Press.

Breban, Nicolae. 1997. *Riscul în cultură.* Iaşi: Polirom.

Brucan, Silviu. 1996. *Stâlpii noii puteri în România.* Bucharest: Nemira.

______. 1998a. De la party hacks la nouveaux riches – schimbarea socială în Rusia şi Europa de Est. *Sfera Politicii*, April. www.dntb.ro/sfera/arhiva /nr59a/articole/articol3text.htm.

______. 1998b. *De la capitalism la socialism şi retur: o biografie între două revoluţii.* Bucharest: Nemira.

Brunner, Georg. 1982. Legitimacy doctrines and legitimation procedures in East European systems. In *Political Legitimation in Communist States,* ed. T. H. Rigby and Ferenc Feher, 27–44. London: Macmillan.

Bruszt, Laszlo. 1990. 1989: the negotiated revolution in Hungary. *Social Research* 57: 365–387.

Bulai, Alfred. 1999. Arta supravieţuirii. *Curentul,* 4 August. http://curentul.logicnet.ro/curentul/arhiva/05aug99/080499/op01.htm.

Bunce, Valerie. 1995. Comment: should transitologists be grounded? *Slavic Review,* Spring. www.econ.uiuc.edu/~slavrev/upenn/spring95/bunce .html.

Burawoy, Michael. 2003. For a sociological Marxism: the complementary covergance of Antonio Gramsci and Karl Polanyi. *Politics and Society* 31: 193–261.

Burch, Kurt. 1997. Constituting IPE and modernity. In *Constituting IPE,* ed. K. Burch and R. Denemark, 21–40. Boulder: Lynne Rienner Publishers.

Buzura, Augustin. 1974. *Feţele tăcerii.* Bucharest: Cartea Românească.

Campbell, David. 1992. *Writing security: US foreign policy and the politics of identity.* Manchester: Manchester University Press.

Campbell, John L. 1996. An institutional analysis of fiscal reform in post-communist Europe. *Theory and Society* 25: 45–84.

______. 1998 Institutional analysis and the role of ideas in political economy. *Theory and Society* 27: 377–409.

Capital. 1999a. Sub biciul Fondului Monetar Internaţional, premierul Radu Vasile mai promite o dată. 7 January.

______. 1999b. Ajutoarele financiare externe s-au vânturat în numele reformei: în opt ani, cinci guverne au cheltuit nouă miliarde ECU. 29 January.

______. 1999c. Sindicatele braşovene au învăţat lecţia minerilor: chemările la reformă ale Guvernului nu-i impresionează pe salariaţii de la Roman şi Tractorul. 1 February.

______. 1999d. Uriaşul Sidex se rupe în bucăţi. 13 February.

______. 1999d. Capitala e prea departe de Resiţa şi Hunedoara. 13 February.

______. 1999f. Salariaţii din siderurgie sunt o marfă pe stoc. 13 February.

______. 1999g. Tractorul aşteaptă ca statul să-i vândă marfa: Braşovenii mizează pe subvenţionarea dobânzii la creditele pentru cumpărarea de maşini agricole. 15 April.

Carey, Henry F. 1996. From big lie to small lies: state mass media dominance in post-communist Romania. *East European Politics and Societies* 10: 16–45.

Carlin, Wendy and Colin Mayer. 1994. The Treuhandastalt: privatisation by state and market. In *The transition in Eastern Europe. Volume II: Restructuring,* ed. Olivier Jean Blanchard, Kenneth A. Froot and Jeffrey D. Sachs, 189–213. Chicago: Chicago University Press.

Carlin, Wendy, Saul Estrin and Mark Schaffer. 1999. Measuring progress in transition towards EU accession: a comparison of manufacturing firms in Poland, Romania, and Spain. EBRD Working paper No. 40.

Carlin, Wendy, Steven Fries, Mark Schaffer and Paul Seabright. 2000. Barter and non-monetary transactions in transition economies: evidence from a cross-country survey. Centre for Economic Reform and Transformation, Heriot-Watt University, Edinburgh. Discussion Paper 2000/04.

Carr, Edward Hallett. 1940. *The twenty years' crisis 1919–1939: an introduction to the study of international relations.* London: Macmillan.

Castells, Manuel. 1997. *The information age: economy, society and culture.* Volume II: *The power of identity.* Oxford: Blackwell Publishers.

Călinescu, Matei and Vladimir Tismăneanu. 1992. The 1989 revolution and Romania's future. In *Romania after tyranny* ed. Daniel N. Nelson, 11–44. Boulder: Westview Press.

Câmpeanu, Pavel. 1990. Prima criză politică. *22* February, No 3: 10.

________. 1999. Ceauşescu: anii numărătorii inverse 1989–1999. *Sfera Politicii* 66: 42–46.

Centrul pentru Sociologie Urbană şi Regională (CURS). 1997. *National Public Opinion Poll.* Soros Foundation for an Open Society. Bucharest, 9–15 June.

________. 1999. Impactul social al privatizării de masă: percepţia schimbărilor sociale şi politice din România în perioada de tranziţie, consecinţe sociale manifeste şi latente ale privatizării de masă. Mimeo. Bucharest, May.

________. 2000. *Barometrul de opinie publică.* Fundaţia Soros pentru o Societate Deschisă. Bucharest, November.

________. 2001. Percepţia schimbărilor şi atitudinilor populaţiei faţă de reforma economică în perioada de tranziţie: sondaje de opinie realizate pe provincii istorice. Mimeo. Bucharest, April.

Cercelescu, Gheorghe. 1998. Impasul economic şi conspiraţia mondială. *Adevărul,* 23 June.

Cerna, Silviu. 1996. Banca Naţională: independenţă şi legitimitate. *Oeconomica* No. 3: 43–52.

Cerny, Philip G. 2000. Political globalization and the competition state. In *Political economy and the changing global order,* 2nd edition, ed. Richard Stubbs and Geoffrey Underhill, 300–309. Toronto: Oxford University Press.

Chandler, Alfred D. Jr. 1992. The emergence of managerial capitalism. In *The sociology of economic life,* ed. Mark Granovetter and Richard Swedberg, 131–158. Boulder: Westview Press.

Ciobanu-Dordea, Aurel. 2000. Relaţiile României cu Uniunea Europeană: contextul şi starea lor actuală. Mimeo.

Ciorbea, Victor. 1998. Victor Ciorbea a demisionat: fragmente din textul demisiei prezentate ieri de premierul Victor Ciorbea. *România Liberă*, 31 March.

Clague, Christopher. 1992. The journey to a market economy. In *The emergence of market economies in Eastern Europe*, ed. Christopher Clague and Gordon G. Rausser, 1–22. Cambridge Ma: Blackwell.

Coase, R. H. 1993. 1991 Nobel Lecture: the institutional structure of production. In *The Nature of the Firm*, eds. Oliver Williamson and Simon Winter, 227–235. Oxford: Oxford University Press.

Cojanu, Valentin. 1994. Avantajele comparative şi restructurarea economiei româneşti. *Oeconomica* No. 3–4: 87–92.

Comisia Naţională a Valorilor Mobiliare (CNVM). 2001. Raport de activitate pe anul 2000. Bucharest, April. http://cnvm.rdsnet.ro/legislatie /trimislaRasdaq/RapCNVM2000.htm.

Comisso, Ellen. 1986. Introduction: State structures, political processes, and collective choice in the CMEA states. *International Organization* 40: 195–238.

Commander, Simon, Mark Dutz and Nicholas Stern. 1999. Restructuring in transition economies: ownership, competition and regulation. Paper prepared for the Annual World Bank Conference on Development Economics, Washington D.C., 28–30 April.

Connolly, William E. 1987. *Politics and ambiguity*. Madison: University of Wisconsin Press.

Constantin, Maria. 1998. Banca Naţională a primit puterea să taie şi să spânzure: noua lege bancară acordă instituţiei din strada Doamnei autoritatea cuvenită unei bănci centrale, însă bancherii se tem că sancţiunile vor fi aplicate în mod subiectiv. *Capital* 16 April: 32–33.

Constantinescu, Emil. 1997. Interviu de Dumitru Tinu. *Adevărul*, 28 November. http://adevarul.kappa.ro/a2340–02.html.

Coşea, Mircea 1993. Interviu de Ionuţ Popescu. *Capital* 2:2, 15 January.

Coşea, Mircea and Cecilia Vlăsceanu. 1993. Dificultăţi ale previziunii produsului intern brut în economia de tranziţie. *Oeconomica* No. 4: 95–110.

Cox, Robert W. 1999. Civil society at the turn of the millennium: prospects for an alternative world order. *Review of International Studies* 25: 3–28.

________. 2000. Political economy and world order: problems of power and knowledge at the turn of the millenium. In *Political economy and the changing global order*, ed. Richard Stubbs and Geoffrey Underhill, 25–38. Toronto: Oxford University Press.

Crăiuţu, Aurelian. 1995. A dilemma of dual identity: the Democratic Alliance of Hungarians in Romania. *East European Constitutional Review* Spring: 43–49.

________. 1996. Ucenicia dificilă a libertăţii: note asupra consolidării democraţiei în România. *Polis* 3/2: 140–161.

Croitoru, Lucian. 1993. Probleme ale mecanismului ratei de schimb. *Oeconomica* No. 4: 25–42.

________. 1994a. Politica de stabilizare şi impunerea restricţiilor financiare tari într-o economie în tranziţie. *Oeconomica* No. 1: 21–50.

________. 1994b. Liberalizările financiare şi funcţionarea sistemului bancar românesc in perioada 1991–1993. *Oeconomica* No. 3–4: 55–81.

Croitoru Lucian and Cornel Tărhoacă. 1999. Fiscal policy in Romania. Paper presented at the conference 'Romania 2000. Ten years of transition: past, present and future', Bucharest: 21–22 October.

Dahl, Robert A. 1976. *Modern Political Analysis*. 3rd edition. New Jersey: Prentice-Hall.

David, Simona. 1999a. Menghina FMI. *Adevărul*, 16 July.

________. 1999b. România nu se mai închină la zeul FMI. *Adevărul*, 11 December.

Davidică, Gratziella. 1998. Ingineria financiară a capilor CNSRL-Frăţia. *România Liberă*, 28 March: 7.

Dăianu, Daniel. 1993a. Arieratele intra-întreprinderi în economia de tranziţie. *Oeconomica* No. 4: 9–23.

________. 1993b. Dinamica dezechilibrelor într-o economie de tranziţie: cazul românesc. *Oeconomica* No. 5: 23–38.

________. 1994. Europa în faţa unei duble provocări. *Oeconomica* No. 3–4: 43–54.

________. 1994a. Disolvarea şi construirea drepturilor de proprietate în regimuri post-comuniste. *Oeconomica* No. 1: 11–20.

________. 1995. Banking in Romania. In *Banking reform in Central Europe and the former Soviet Union*, ed. Jacek Rostowski, 212–226. Budapest: Central European University Press.

________. 1996a. Stabilization and exchange rate policy in Romania. *Economics of Transition* 4: 229–248.

________. 1996b. *Transformarea ca proces real: de la comandă la piaţă*. Bucharest: IRLI.

________. 1996c. Marea provocare pentru politica monetară în 1997. *Oeconomica* No. 4: 5–10.

________. 1999. Structure, *strain* and macroeconomic dynamic in Romania. Paper presented at the conference 'Romania 2000 – 10 years of transition: past, present and future', Bucharest: 21–22 October.

Dăianu, Daniel, Andrei Pleşu and Ilie Şerbănescu. 1998. În lupta pentru putere, 'reforma a devenit un simplu pretext'. *Adevărul*, 28 March.

Dijmărescu, Eugen. 1993a. Liberalizarea preţurilor şi controlul inflaţiei în perioda de tranziţie. *Oeconomica* No. 4: 57–69.

________. 1993b. Opţiunile economice între politică şi pragmatism. *Oeconomica* No. 5: 77–86.

________. 1994. Limite şi alternative ale tranziţiei. *Oeconomica* No. 1: 5–10.

Dimofte, Cătălin. 1997. Lumea afacerilor între logoreea politicianistă şi pragmatismul întreprinzătorilor. June 20–26. http://adevarul.kappa.ro /eco275–04.html.

Di Palma, Giuseppe. 1990. *To craft democracies: an essay on democratic transitions.* Berkeley: University of California Press.

________. 1991. Legitimation from the top to civil society: politico-cultural change in Eastern Europe. *World Politics* 44: 49–80.

Djankov, Simeon. 1999. The enterprise isolation program in Romania. Mimeo.

Djilas, Milovan. 1957. *The new class: an analysis of the Communist system.* London: Thames & Hudston.

Dobrogeanu-Gherea. 1910. *Neoiobăgia.* Bucharest: Editura Librăriei SOCEC & Comp.

Dochia, Aurelian. 1994. Unele consideraţii asupra programului de privatizare în masă. *Oeconomica* No. 2: 69–74.

________. 1999. New private firm contributions to structural change in the Romanian economy. Paper presented at the conference: 'Romania 2000. 10 years of transition: past, present and future', Bucharest: 21–22 October.

Dolowitz, David P. 2000. Policy transfer: a new framework of policy analysis. In *Policy transfer in British social policy: learnings from USA?* with Rob Hulme, Mike Nellis and Fiona O'Neill, 9–37. Buckingham: Open University Press.

Doltu, Claudiu. 1999. The evolution of the banking system in Romania. Paper presented at the conference 'Romania 2000 – 10 years of transition: past, present and future', Bucharest: 21–22 October.

Done, Kevin. 1997. Survey: Romania '97: Economy: Shock therapy is prescribed. *Financial Times*, 25 June.

Douglas, Mary. 1987. *How institutions think.* London: Routledge and Kegan Paul.

Drăgotescu, Corina. 1999. Reforma legislativă. *Adevărul,* 14 December.

Drăgulin, Ion and Eugen Rădulescu. 1999. Politica monetară: Provocări şi perspective. Paper presented at the conference 'Romania 2000 – 10 years of transition: past, present and future', Bucharest: 21–22 October.

Durandin, Catherine. 1998. *Istoria românilor.* Trans. from French by Liliana Buruiană-Popovici, with a foreword by Al. Zub. Iaşi: The European Institute.

Earle, John S. and Dana Săpătoru. 1994. Privatizarea într-o economie hipercentralizată: Cazul României. *Oeconomica* No. 2: 85–100.

Earle, John S. and Almos Telegdy. 1998. The results of 'mass privatization' in Romania: A first empirical study. *Economics of Transition* 6: 313–332.

East European Constitutional Review (EECR). 1995a. Constitutional Watch: Romania. Spring: 21–24.

________. 1995b. Constitutional Watch: Romania. Summer: 21–23.

________. 1996a. Constitutional Watch: Romania. Winter: 19–20.

________. 1996b. Constitutional Watch: Romania. Spring/Summer: 19–21.

________. 1997a. Constitutional Watch: Romania. Winter: 22–24.

________. 1997b. Constitutional Watch: Romania. Spring/Summer: 28–30.

________. 1998a. Constitutional Watch: Romania. Winter: 27–30.

________. 1998b. Constitutional Watch: Romania. Spring: 23–25.

________. 1998c. Constitutional Watch: Romania. Fall: 27–29.

________. 1999a. Constitutional Watch: Romania. Winter/Spring: 29–32.

________. 1999b. Constitutional Watch: Romania. Summer www.law.nyu.edu
/eecr.vol8num3/constitutionwatch/romania.html.

________. 1999c. Constitutional Watch: Romania. Fall www.law.nyu.edu/eecr
/vol8num4/constitutionwatch/romania.html

Edelman, Murray. 1974. *The symbolic uses of politics.* Urbana: University of
Illinois Press.

Eichengreen, Barry and Christof Ruhl. 2000. The bail-in problem: systematic
goals, ad hoc means. National Bureau of Economic Research. Working
Paper 7653. www.nber.org/papers/w/7653.

Eliasoph, Nina. 1997. 'Close to home': the work of avoiding politics. *Theory
and Society* 26: 605–647.

Elster, Jon. 1996. The role of institutional interest in East European constitu-
tion-making: explaining legislative dominance. *East European
Constitutional Review.* Winter: 63–65.

Elster, Jon, Claus Offe and Ulrick K. Preuss. (with Frank Boenker, Ulrike
Goetting, and Friedbert W. Rueb) 1998. *Institutional design in post-
communist societies: rebuilding the ship at sea.* Cambridge: Cambridge
University Press.

Ettori, Francois. 1998. Interviu de Stelian Tănase. *Sfera Politicii*, April.

European Bank for Reconstruction and Development (EBRD). 1999.
Transition report: Ten years of transition. London: EBRD.

________. 2000. *Transition report: Employment, skills and transition.* London:
EBRD.

The European Commission (EC) 2000a. *Enlargement strategy paper: report on
the progress towards accession by each of the candidate countries.*
November.

________. 2000b. *Romania 2000 regular report from the Commission on
Romania's progress towards accession.* November.

________. 2004. *Regular report on Romania's progress towards accession.*
October.

The European Commission. Directorate General Enlargement (EC-DGE).
1999a. The Phare Programme: annual report 1998. Mimeo.

________. 1999b. Overview of the Phare Programme and the new Pre-
Accession Funds. Proceedings of a seminar held in September 1999 at
the EU Information Centre in Budapest. Mimeo.

________. 2000. Phare 2000 review. Strengthening preparations for membership. Communication from Mr Verheugen (Commissioner for Enlargement). C(2000)3103/2. 27 October. Mimeo.

Evangelista, Matthew. 1996. Stalin's revenge: institutional barriers to internationalisation in the Soviet Union. In *Internationalisation and domestic politics*, ed. Robert O. Keohane and Helen V. Milner, 159–185. Cambridge: Cambridge University Press.

Eyal, Gil and Eleanor Townsley. 1995. The social composition of the Communist nomenklatura: a comparison of Russia, Poland, and Hungary. *Theory and Society* 24: 723–750.

Eyal, Gil, Ivan Szélenyi and Eleanor Townsley. 1998. *Making capitalism without capitalists: class formation and elite struggles in post-communist central Europe.* London: Verso.

Fearon, James D. and David D. Laitin. 2000. Violence and the social construction of ethnic identity. *International Organisation* 54: 845–877.

Fehér, Ferenc. 1982. Paternalism as a mode of legitimation in Soviet-type societies.In *Political legitimation in communist states*, ed. T. H. Rigby and Ferenc Fehér, 64–81. London: Macmillan.

Feigenbaum, Harvey B. and Jeffrey R. Henig. 1994. The political underpinnings of privatization: a typology. *World Politics* 46: 185–208.

Fischer, Mary Ellen. 1989. *Nicolae Ceauşescu: a study in leadership.* Boulder: Lynne Rienner Publishers.

__________. 1992. The new leaders and the opposition. In *Romania after tyranny* ed. Daniel N. Nelson, 45–65. Boulder: Westview Press.

__________. 1996. Romania: the anguish of post-communist politics. In *Establishing democracies*, 178–212. Boulder: Westview Press.

Fischer, Stanley. 1992. Privatisation in East European transformation. In *The emergence of market economies in Eastern Europe*, ed. Gordon C. Rausser and Christopher Clague, 227–243. Cambridge Ma: Blackwell.

Fischer, Stanley, Ratna Sahay and Carlos A. Vegh. 1996. Stabilisation and growth in transition economies: the early experience. *Journal of Economic Perspectives* 10: 45–66.

Fish, M. Steven. 1998. The determinants of economic reform in the post-communist world. *East European Politics and Societies* 12: 31–78.

Fodor, Eva, Edmund Wnuk-Lipinski and Natasha Yershova. 1995. The new political and cultural elite. *Theory and Society* 24: 783–800.

Fondul Proprietăţii de Stat (FPS). 1999a. Evoluţia procesului de privatizare în perioada 1999 – 30.06.1999. Mimeo. www.sof.ro/romania /comunicat.html.

__________. 1999b. Contractul Dacia-Renault. Mimeo. www.sof.ro/romania .Dacia_Renault.html.

__________. 2000a. Privatizări de succes din perspectiva analizelor postprivatizare. Mimeo. www.sof.ro/fps/contsucc.html.

__________. 2000b. Privatizarea în România: Decembrie 1992 – Septembrie 2000. Mimeo. www.sof.ro/fps/privatizarea%20in%20romania.

Frieden, Jeffry and Ronald Rogowski. 1996. The impact of the international economy on national policies: an analytical overview. In *Internationalisation and domestic politics*, ed. Robert O. Keohane and Helen V. Milner, 25–47. Cambridge: Cambridge University Press.

Friedman, Milton. 1962. *Capitalism, freedom, and democracy*. Chicago: University of Chicago Press.

Frydman, Roman, Cheryl Gray, Marek Hessel and Andrzej Rpaczynski. 1997. Private ownership and corporate performance: evidence from transition economies. EBRD Working Paper No. 26.

Frydman, Roman, Kenneth Murphy and Andrzej Rapaczynski. 1998. *Capitalism with a comrade's face: studies in post-communist transition*. Budapest: Central University Press.

Fukuyama, Francis. 1992. *The end of history and the last man*. New York: Avon Books.

Gallagher, Tom. 1992a. Ultranationalists take charge of Transylvania's capital. *RFE/RL Research Report*, 27 March: 23–30.

———. 1992b. Electoral breakthrough for Romanian nationalists. *RFE/RL Research Report*, 13 November: 15–20.

———. 1993. Ethnic tension in Cluj. *RFE/RL Research Report*, 26 February: 27–33.

———. 1994. The rise of the Party of Romanian National Unity. *RFE/RL Research Report*, 18 March: 25–32.

———. 1995. *Romania after Ceauşescu: the politics of intolerance*. Edinburgh: Edinburgh University Press.

Garrett, Geoffrey and Peter Lange. 1996. Internationalization, institutions and political change. In *Internationalisation of domestic politics*, ed. Robert O. Keohane and Helen Milner, 48–75. Cambridge: Cambridge University Press.

Gerschenkron, Alexander. 1992. Economic backwardness in historical perspective. In *The sociology of economic life*, ed. Mark Granoveter and Richard Swedberg, 111–130. Boulder: Westview Press.

Gheorghe, Gabriela, and Adelina Huminic. 1999. Istoria mineriadelor din anii 1990–1. *Sfera Politicii* 67.

Gheorghiu, Lucian. 2001. O simplă formalitate: PNL a divorţat de PDSR. *Cotidianul*, 12 May.

Giddens, Anthony. 1984. *The constitution of society: outline of the theory of structuration*. Cambridge: Polity Press.

Gilberg, Trond. 1992. Romanians and democratic values: socialisation after communism. In *Romania after tyranny*, ed. Daniel N. Nelson, 83–94. Boulder: Westview Press.

Gill, Graeme. 1982. Personal dominance and the collective principle: individual legitimacy in Marxist-Leninist systems. In *Political legitimation in communist states*, ed. R. H. Rigby and Ferenc Fehér, 94–110. London: Macmillan.

Gilpin, Robert. 1987. *The political economy of international relations.* Princeton NJ: Princeton University Press.

Glăvan, Diana. 1999. Senatorul PD Teodor Hauca, secretarul Comisiei economice: BNR duce o politică necorespunzătoare. *Curentul,* 1 June: 12.

Goffman, Erving. 1969. *The presentation of self in everyday life.* London: Allen Lane.

————. 1986. *Frame analysis: An essay on the organisation of experience.* Boston: Northeastern University Press.

Goldfarb, Jeffrey C. 1989. *Beyond Glasnost: the post-totalitarian mind.* Chicago: University of Chicago Press.

Goldstein, Judith and Robert O. Keohane. 1993. Ideas and foreign policy: an analytical framework. In *Ideas and foreign policy: beliefs, institutions, and political change,* ed. Judith Goldstein and Robert O. Keohane, 3–30. Ithaca: Cornell University Press.

Goldstein, Judith and Lisa L. Martin. 2000. Legalisation, trade liberalisation, and domestic politics. *International Organization* 54: 603–632.

Goodwin, Barbara. 1997. *Using political ideas.* Fourth edition. Chicester: John Wiley & Sons.

Granovetter, Mark. 1985. Economic action and social structure: the problem of embeddedness. *American Journal of Sociology* 91: 481–510.

————. 1992. The sociological and economic approaches to labor market analysis: a social structural view. In *The sociology of economic life,* ed. Mark Granovetter and Richard Swedberg, 233–264. Boulder: Westview Press.

Granovetter, Mark and Richard Swedberg (eds). 1992. *The sociology of economic life.* Boulder: Westview Press.

Green, Peter S. 2001. Eastern Europe Exchanges consider merging operations. *The New York Times,* 16 April. www.nytimes.com/2001/04/17/business/17BOUR.html.

Grieco, Joseph M. 1995. Anarchy and the limits of co-operation: a realist critique of the newest liberal institutionalism. In *Controversies in international relations theory,* ed. C. Kegley, 151–171. New York: St. Martin's Press.

Gross, Peter. 1998. Orbii conducându-i pe orbi: mass-media şi democraţia în Europa de Est. *Sfera Politicii* No. 64. http://dntb.ro/sfera/64/gross.htm.

Grunberg, Isabelle. 1990. Exploring the 'myth' of hegemonic stability. *International Organization* 44: 431–477.

Gunther, Richard, Nikiforos P. Diamandouros, and Hans-Jurgen Puhle. 1996. O'Donnell's 'Illusions': a rejoinder. *Journal of Democracy* 7: 151–159.

Guvernul României (GR). 1999a. Letter of intent and memorandum of policies. 26 July. www.imf.org/external/np/loi/1999/072699.html.

————. 1999b. Supplementary letter of intent. 5 August. www.imf.org/external/np/loi/1999/080599.htm

________. 2000a. Strategia naţională de dezvoltare economică a României pe termen mediu. Mimeo.

________. 2000b. Letter of intent and memorandum of the government of Romania on economic policies. 16 May. www.imf.org/external /np/loi/2000/rom/01/index.htm.

________. 2001. Programul de guvernare. Mimeo. http://domino.kappa.ro /guvern/programul.

Hall, Edward T. 1959. *The silent language.* New York: Anchor Books.

Halpern, Nina P. 1993. Creating socialist economies: Stalinist political economy and the impact of ideas. In *Ideas and foreign policy: beliefs, institutions, and political change,* ed. Judith Goldstein and Robert O. Keohane, 87–110. Ithaca: Cornell University Press.

Halpert, Adriana, Mihail Gălăţeanu and Alin Iacob. 1998. Parlamentarii se bat şi ei fiecare pentru mămăliga lui: deputaţii PDSR arată cu degetul spre colegii lor de la PNL şi UDMR. *Capital,* 16 April: 9.

Hankiss, Elemer. 1990. *Eastern European alternatives.* Oxford: Clarendon Press.

Havel, Vaclav. 1991. *Open letters.* ed. Paul Wilson. London: Faber and Faber.

Hayek, Friedrich August. 1944. *The road to serfdom.* London: Routledge.

Held, David, Anthony McGrew, David Goldblatt and Jonathan Perraton. 1999. *Global transformations: Politics, economics, and culture.* London: Polity Press.

Helleiner, Eric. 1995. Explaining the globalization of financial markets: bringing states back in. *Review of International Political Economy* 2: 315–41.

Heller, Agnes. 1982. Phases of legitimation in Soviet-type societies. In *Political legitimation in communist states,* ed. T. H. Rigby and Ferenc Fehér, 45–63. London: Macmillan.

Hellman, Joel. 1996. Constitutions and economic reform in the postcommunist transitions: a case for constitutional precommitment. *East European Constitutional Review* Winter: 46–56.

Hellman, Joel S., Geraint Jones and Daniel Kaufmann. 2000. Seize the state, seize the day: state capture, corruption and influence in the transition. World Bank Policy Research Working Paper No. 2444.

Henig, Jeffrey R. 1990. Privatization in the United States: theory and practice. *Political Science Quarterly* 104: 649–670.

Herman, Judith Lewis. 1994. *Trauma and recovery: from domestic abuse to political terror.* London: Pandora.

Herman, Robert G. 1996. Identity, norms and national security: the Soviet foreign policy revolution and the end of the Cold War. In *The culture of national security: norms and identity in world politics,* ed. Peter J. Katzenstein, 271–316. New York: Columbia University Press.

Higgott, Richard. 2000. Contested globalization: the changing context and normative challenges. *Review of International Studies* 26: 131–153.

Higgott, Richard and Simon Reich. 1998. Globalisation and sites of conflict: towards definition and taxonomy. Centre for the Study of Globalisation and Regionalisation Working Paper No. 01, February 1998.

Higley, John, Judith Kullberg and Jan Pakulski. 1996. The persistence of post-communist elites. *Journal of Democracy* 7: 133–147.

Hitchins, Keith. 1994. *Romania 1866–1947*. Oxford: Clarendon Press.

Huntingdon, Samuel P. 1968. *Political order in changing societies*. New Haven: Yale University Press.

Hunya, Gabor. 1998. Romania 1990–2002: Stop-go transformation. *Communist Economies and Economic Transformation* 10: 241–258.

Iancu, Aurel. 1994. Tranziţia ca proces de schimbare instituţională (I). *Oeconomica* No. 3–4: 24–41.

———. 1995. Tranziţia ca proces de schimbare instituţională (II). *Oeconomica* No. 1: 5–17.

Iliescu, Ion. 1990. Revoluţia înseamnă, acum, muncă. *Adevărul*, 9 January.

International Institute for Democracy and Electoral Assistance (IIDEA). 1997. *Democraţia in Romania*. Bucharest: Nemira.

International Monetary Fund (IMF). 1996. Romania: Recent economic developments and selected background studies. Staff country report no. 96/9. Washington DC: IMF.

———. 1997. Romania: Recent economic developments. Staff country report no. 97/46. Washington DC: IMF.

———. 1998. IMF Concludes Article IV consultation with Romania. Public Information Notice No. 98/79, 6 October. www.imf.org/external/np/sec/pn/1998/pn9879.html.

———. 2000. Romania: 2000 article IV consultation – Staff country report no. 00/159. Washington DC: IMF.

———. 2001. Romania: Selected issues and statistical appendix. Country Report No. 01/16. Washington DC: IMF.

Ion, Teodor. 2000. Preşedintele FPS, Radu Sârbu, îşi arată muschii 'Cartea albă' a privatizărilor 'negre'. *Adevărul economic* 15–21 November: 3.

Ionescu, Dan. 1992a. Romania: testing large-scale privatization. *RFE/RL Research Report* 10 January: 33–35.

———. 1992b. Social tension threatens frail Romanian economy. *RFE/RL Research Report* 6 March: 32–36.

———. 1992c. Romania's ruling party splits after congress. *RFE/RL Research Report* 17 April: 8–12.

———. 1992d. Romania's public war over secret police files. *RFE/RL Research Report* 17 July: 9–15.

———. 1992e. Another Front for Romania's salvation. *RFE/RL Research Report* 21 August: 17–23.

———. 1993a. Romania's cabinet in search of an economic strategy. *RFE/RL Research Report* 22 January: 45–49.

________. 1993b. Romania signs association accord with the EC. *RFE/RL Research Report* 5 March: 33–37.

________. 1993c. Romania's quandary. *RFE/RL Research Report* 19 March: 13–37.

________. 1993d. Romania's liberals. *RFE/RL Research Report* 28 May: 22–27.

________. 1993e. Strike wave in Romania. *RFE/RL Research Report* 17 September: 23–27.

________. 1993f. Romania admitted to the Council of Europe. *RFE/RL Research Report* 5 November: 40–45.

________. 1994a. Romania's privatization programme: who is in charge? *RFE/RL Research Report* 4 February: 28–34.

________. 1994b. Romania adjusting to NATO's Partnership for Peace Program. *RFE/RL Research Report* 9 March: 43–47.

________. 1994c. Romania's standby agreement with the IMF. *RFE/RL Research Report* 6 May: 21–26.

________. 1994d. Personnel changes in the Romanian intelligence service. *RFE/RL Research Report* 8 July: 22–25.

________. 1994e. UM0215: a controversial intelligence service in Romania. *RFE/RL Research Report* 29 July: 27–30.

Ionescu, Dan and Michael Shafir. 1994. Romanian government reorganized. *RFE/RL Research Report* 1 April: 14–19.

Ionete, Constantin. 1993. *Criza de system a economiei de comandă şi etapa sa explozivă*. Bucharest: Editura Expert.

________. 1996. Privatizarea, barometru al tranziţiei şi reformei. *Oeconomica* No. 3: 31–41.

Ioniţă, Sorin. 1996. Capitalismul românesc: O dezbatere fără sfirşit. *Revista de cercetări sociale*. No. 1, 155–166.

Isărescu, Mugur. 1994. Despre reforma sistemului bancar şi politica B.N.R. *Oeconomica* 1: 113–116.

________. 2001. Prezentarea Guvernatorului Băncii Naţionale a României Mugur Isărescu in şedinţa Guvernului din 18 ianuarie 2001. www.bnro.ro/Ro/Pubs/Prez/20010118guv.pdf.

Ishiyama, John T. 1995. Communist parties in transition: structures, leaders and processes of democratisation in Eastern Europe. *Comparative Politics* 27: 147–166.

Janos, Andrew C. 1991. Social science, communism, and the dynamics of political change. *World Politics* 44: 81–112.

Jela, Doina. 1997. *Telejurnalul de noapte*. Iaşi: Polirom.

Johnson, Simon, John Mcmillan, and Christopher Woodruff. 1999. Entrepreneurs and the ordering of institutional reform: Poland, Romania, Russia, the Slovak Republic and Ukraine compared. EBRD Working Paper No. 44. London: EBRD.

Jowitt, Kenneth. 1978. The socio-cultural basis of national dependency in peasant countries. In *Social change in Romania 1860–1940: a debate on development in a European nation,* 1–30. Berkeley: University of California Press.

————. 1992. *New world disorder: the Leninist extinction.* Berkeley: University of California Press.

————. 1998a. Foreword: In praise of the 'ordinary'. In *Adam Michnik: letters from freedom. Post-Cold War realities and perspectives,* ed. Irena Grudznska Gross, with new translations from the Polish by Jane Cave, xiii–xxxiii. Berkeley: University of California Press.

————. 1998b. Challenging the 'correct' line: reviewing Katherine Verdery's *What was socialism and what comes next? East European Politics and Societies* 12: 87–106.

Katzenstein, Peter J. 1996. *The culture of national security: norms and identity in world politics,* ed. New York: Columbia University Press.

Keohane, Robert O. 1986. Realism, neorealism and the study of world politics. In *Neorealism and its critics,* ed. Robert O. Keohane, 1–26. New York: Columbia University Press.

————. 1989. *International institutions and state power: essays in international relations theory.* Boulder, Colorado: Westview Press.

Kharkhordin, Oleg. 1995. The Soviet individual: genealogy of a dissimulating animal. In *Global modernities,* ed. Mike Featherstone, Scot Lash and Roland Robertson, 209–226. London: Sage.

Kideckel, David A. 1992. Peasants and authority in the new Romania. In *Romania after tyranny,* ed. Daniel N. Nelson, 67–81. Boulder: Westview Press.

Kiss, Yudit. 1994. Privatisation Pardoxes in East Central Europe. *East European Politics and Societies* 8: 122–152.

Kligman, Gail. 1998. *The politics of duplicity: controlling reproduction in Ceauşescu's Romania.* Berkeley: University of California Press.

Kochanowicz, Jacek. 1998. Frustration of the liberals. *East European Politics and Societies* 12: 132–144.

Kohut, Heinz. 1971. *The analysis of the self.* New York: International Universities Press.

Kolodko, Grzegorz W. 1993. From recession to growth in post-communist economies: Expectations versus reality. *Communist and Post-Communist Studies* 26: 123–143.

Kornai, Janos. 1992. *The Socialist system: the political economy of communism.* Oxford: Clarendon Press.

————. 2000. What the change of system from socialism to capitalism does and does not mean. *Journal of Economic Perspectives* 14: 27–42.

Krasner, Stephen D. 1982a. Structural causes and regime consequences: regimes as intervening variables. *International Organization* 36:2. 1–21.

————. 1982b. Regimes and the limits of realism: regimes as autonomous variables. *International Organization* 36: 2. 355–368.

Kubik, Jan. 1994. The role of decentralisation and cultural revival in post-communist transformations: the case of Cieszyn Silesia, Poland. *Communist and Post-Communist Studies* 27: 331–355.

Laignel-Lavastine, Alexandra. 1998. Filosofie şi naţionalism: Paradoxul Noica. Trans. Emanoil Marcu. Bucharest: Humanitas.

Leander, Anna. 2000. A nebbish presence: undervalued contributions of sociological institutionalism to IPE. In *Global political economy: contemporary theories*, ed. Ronen Palan, 184–196. London: Routledge.

Ledeneva, Alena V. 1998. *Russia's economy of favours: blat, networking and informal exchange.* Cambridge: Cambridge University Press.

Lefort, Claude. 1986. *The political forms of modern society: bureaucracy, democracy, and totalitarianism.* London: Polity Press.

Lieberman, Ira W. 1995. Mass privatisation in Central and Eastern Europe and the Former Soviet Union: a comparative analysis. In *Mass privatisation: an initial assessment*, OECD, 13–33. Paris: OECD.

Lifton, Robert Jay. 1963. *Thought reform and the psychology of totalism: a study of 'brainwashing' in China.* New York: W.W. Norton & Company Inc.

Linden, Ronald H. 1986. Socialist patrimonialism and the global economy: the case of Romania. *International Organization* 40: 347–380.

Linz, Juan J. and Alfred Stepan. 1996. *Problems of democratic transition and consolidation: Southern Europe, South America, and post-communist Europe.* Baltimore: The Johns Hopkins University Press.

List, Friedrich. 1991 [1885]. Political and cosmopolitan economy. In *Theoretical evolution of international political economy*, ed. G. Crane and Abla Amowi, 48–54. Oxford: Oxford University Press.

Livezeanu, Irina. 1998. Cultură şi naţionalism în România Mare. Bucharest: Humanitas.

Luca, Mirela. 2001. PDS(R), spre clubul de elită al stăpânilor Europei. *Ziarul Financiar* 18 June.

Lupşan, Pompei. 2001a. România, în faţa 'Înaltei Porţi' a Fondului Monetar Internaţional. *Adevărul Economic* February: 3. 31–36.

______. 2001b. Corupţia în România: Material de lucru pentru Banca Mondială. *Adevărul Economic* March: 16. 14–20.

Lupu, M. A. 1968. *The economy of Romania.* Bucharest: Meridiane.

Make. 1998. Post tranziţia – stop tranziţia! *Bursa* 10 April: 1.

Manoliu, Maria. 1997. Potrivit Raportului Departamentului de Control al Guvernului 6000 de profitori cu funcţii au luat cu japca zeci de mii de hectare. *Adevărul* 18 July.

Marga, Andrei. 1993. Cultural and political trends in Romania before and after 1989. *East European Politics and Societies* 7: 14–32.

Markus, Maria. 1982. Overt and covert modes of legitimation in East European societies. In *Political legitimation in communist states*, ed. T. H. Rigby and Ferenc Fehér, 82–93. London: Macmillan.

Marsh, Virginia. 1998. Profile Radu Vasile: fighting inner demons. In *Financial Times Survey*, 28 September: 1.

Mărgărit, Ioan. 1999. Guvernul a uitat de ce vrea acord cu FMI: achitarea datoriilor ţine loc de reformă economică. *Capital,* 1 April.

Mcfaul, Michael. 1995. State power, institutional change, and the politics of privatization in Russia. *World Politics* 47: 210–243.

Michels, Robert. 1958 [1915]. *Political parties: a sociological study of the oligarchical tendencies of modern democracy.* Trans. Eden and Cedar Paul. Glencoe, Illinois: The Free Press.

Michnik, Adam. 1993. *The church and the left.* Ed., trans. and intro. David Ost. Chicago: The University of Chicago Press.

————. 1997. Interviu de Cristian Tudor Popescu. *Adevarul,* 14 May.

Mihăilescu, Ioan. 1993. Mental stereotypes in the first years of post-totalitarian Romania. *Government and Opposition* 28: 315–324.

Mihuţ, Liliana. 1994. The emergence of political pluralism in Romania. *Communist and Post-Communist Studies* 27: 411–422.

Milosz, Czeslaw. 1962. *The captive mind.* London: Mercury Books.

Miroiu, Adrian. 2000a. Ideile în spaţiul public românesc actual. University of Bucharest; Mimeo.

————. 2000b. Dreptatea restitutiva şi problema generaţiilor trecute. University of Bucharest; Mimeo.

————. 2000c. Cum va evolua sistemul de partide în România? University of Bucharest; Mimeo.

Miroiu, Mihaela. 1999. *Societatea Retro.* Bucharest: Editura Trei.

Monitorul Oficial al României (MOR). 33–34/1990. Hotărâre no. 201 din 3 martie 1990 pentru aprobarea normelor de aplicare a Decretului-lege nr.54/1990 privind organizarea şi desfăşurarea unor activităţi economice pe baza liberei iniţiative. Anexa 3. Partea 1. Bucharest: Imprimeria Naţională.

————. 98/1990. Lege nr. 15 din 7 august 1990 privind reorganizarea unităţilor economice de stat ca regii autonome şi societăţi comerciale. Part 1. Bucharest: Imprimeria Naţională.

————. 160/1991. Part 2. Dezbateri parlamentare: Camera Deputaţilor. Bucharest: Imprimeria Naţională.

————. 169/1991. Lege nr. 58 din 14 august 1991 privind privatizarea societăţilor comerciale. Part 1. Bucharest: Imprimeria Naţională.

————. 177/1991. Part 2. Dezbateri parlamentare: Camera Deputaţilor. Bucharest: Imprimeria Naţională.

————. 178/1991. Part 2. Dezbateri parlamentare: Senat. Bucharest: Imprimeria Naţională.

————. 179/1991. Part 2. Dezbateri parlamentare: Senat. Bucharest: Imprimeria Naţională.

————. 180/1991. Part 2. Dezbateri parlamentare: Camera Deputaţilor. Bucharest: Imprimeria Naţională.

————. 181/1991. Part 2. Dezbateri parlamentare: Senat. Bucharest: Imprimeria Naţională.

________. 182/1991. Part 2. Dezbateri parlamentare: Camera Deputaţilor. Bucharest: Imprimeria Naţională.

________. 184/1991. Part 2. Dezbateri parlamentare: Camera Deputaţilor. Bucharest: Imprimeria Naţională.

________. 186/1991. Part 2. Dezbateri parlamentare: Camera Deputaţilor. Bucharest: Imprimeria Naţională.

________. 188/1991. Part 2. Dezbateri parlamentare: Camera Deputaţilor. Bucharest: Imprimeria Naţională.

________. 190/1991. Part 2. Dezbateri parlamentare: Camera Deputaţilor. Bucharest: Imprimeria Naţională.

________. 192/1991. Part 2. Dezbateri parlamentare: Camera Deputaţilor. Bucharest: Imprimeria Naţională.

________. 195/1991. Part 2. Dezbateri parlamentare: Camera Deputaţilor. Bucharest: Imprimeria Naţională.

________. 200/1991. Criterii Nr. 1043 din 20 septembrie 1991 pentru selectarea societăţilor comerciale care se privatizează prin vânzare de acţiuni, înainte de organizarea Fondurilor Proprietăţii Private şi a Fondului Proprietăţii de Stat. Partea I. Bucharest: Imprimeria Naţională.

________. 121/1992. Hotărâre Nr. 254 din 8 mai 1992 pentru aprobarea Regulamentului-cadru privind organizarea şi funcţionarea Fondului Proprietăţii de Stat. Partea I. Bucharest: Imprimeria Naţională.

________. 208/1992a. Ordonanţa Nr.10 din 7 august 1992 pentru aprobarea Statutului-cadru al Fondului Proprietăţii Private. Partea I. Bucharest: Imprimeria Naţională.

________. 208/1992b. Hotărâre Nr. 443 din 7 august 1992 privind aprobarea statutelor proprii ale Fondurilor Proprietăţii Private. Partea I. Bucharest: Imprimeria Naţională.

________. 262/1992. Hotărâre Nr. 643 din 8 octombrie 1992 pentru aprobarea Regulamentului de organizare şi funcţionare a Fondului Proprietăţii de Stat. Partea I. Bucharest: Imprimeria Naţională.

________. 318/1992. Lege nr. 115 din 7 decembrie 1992 privind prelungirea termenului de încheiere a acţiunii de distribuire a certificatelor de proprietate, prevăzut de Legea privatizării societăţilor comerciale nr. 58/1991. Partea I. Bucharest: Imprimeria Naţională.

________. 12/1993. Norma Nr. 1 din 22 decembrie 1992 privind procedura-standard de privatizare a societăţilor comerciale mici prin vânzare de acţiuni. Partea I. Bucharest: Imprimeria Naţională.

________. 77/1993. Ordin Nr. 187 din 13 aprilie 1993 privind arondarea societăţilor comerciale cu capital de stat, în vederea distribuirii a 30% din capitalul social al acestora între cele cinci Fonduri ale Proprietăţii Private. Bucharest: Imprimeria Naţională.

________. 81/1994a. Hotărâre Nr. 3 din 16 martie 1994 privind aprobarea raportului de activitate al Fondului Proprietăţii de Stat în anul 1993. Partea I. Bucharest: Imprimeria Naţională.

________. 81/1994b. Hotărâre Nr. 4 din 16 martie 1994 privind aprobarea Programului de privatizare al Fondului Proprietăţii de Stat pentru anul 1994. Partea I. Bucharest: Imprimeria Naţională.

________. 209/1994. Lege Nr. 77 din 1 august 1994 privind asociaţiile salariaţilor şi membrilor conducerii societăţilor comerciale care se privatizează. Partea I. Bucharest: Imprimeria Naţională.

________. 21/1995. Norme metodologice Nr. 2 din 11 noiembrie 1994 pentru aplicarea Legii nr. 77/1994 privind asociaţiile salariaţilor şi membrilor conducerii salariaţilor comerciale care se privatizează. Partea I. Bucharest: Imprimeria Naţională.

________. 122/1995. Lege Nr. 55 din 15 iunie 1995 pentru accelerarea procesului de privatizare. Partea I. Bucharest: Imprimeria Naţională.

________. 138/1995. Hotărâre Nr. 476 din 1 iulie 1995 cu privire la funcţionarea Secretariatului naţional şi a secretariatelor judeţene pentru urmărirea aplicării Legii nr. 55/1995 pentru accelerarea procesului de privatizare. Partea I. Bucharest: Imprimeria Naţională.

________. 158/1995. Hotărâre Nr. 499 din 10 iulie 1995 pentru aprobarea Normelor metodologice privind distribuirea cupoanelor nominative de privatizare. Partea I. Bucharest: Imprimeria Naţională.

________. 190/1995. Hotărâre Nr. 626 din 16 august 1995 pentru aprobarea listei societăţilor comerciale care se privatizează potrivit Legii nr. 55/1995 pentru accelerarea procesului de privatizare. Partea I. Bucharest: Imprimeria Naţională.

________. 223/1995. Hotărâre Nr. 749 din 22 septembrie 1995 pentru aprobarea Normelor metodologice privind procedura schimbului carnetelor de certificate de proprietate şi/sau cupoanelor nominative de privatizare contra acţiuni la societăţile comerciale cu capital de stat care se privatizează în baza Legii nr. 55/1995, precum şi la Fondurile Proprietăţii Private, procedura de alocare a acţiunilor acestor societăţi comerciale şi de certificare a calităţii de acţionar ca urmare a schimbului. Partea I. Bucharest: Imprimeria Naţională.

________. 251/1995. Hotărâre Nr. 855 din 23 octombrie 1995 pentru aplicarea prevederilor art. 22 din Legea nr. 55/1995 cu privire la privatizarea societăţilor comerciale prestatoare de servicii pentru agricultură de tip 'Agromec,' 'Servagromec,' şi 'Agroservice.' Partea I. Bucharest: Imprimeria Naţională.

________. 50/1996. Republicată. Hotărâre Nr. 749 din 22 septembrie 1995 privind procedura schimbului carnetelor de certificate de proprietate şi/sau cupoanelor nominative de privatizare contra acţiuni la societăţile comerciale cu capital de stat care se privatizează in baza Legii nr. 55/1995, precum şi la Fondurile Proprietăţii Private, procedura de alocare a acţiunilor acestor societăţi comerciale şi de certificare a calităţii de acţionar ca urmare a schimbului, aprobate prin Hotărârea Guvernului nr. 749/1995. Partea I. Bucharest: Imprimeria Naţională.

________. 102/1996. Norme specifice nr. 20/291 din 6 mai 1996 privind privatizarea societăţilor comerciale de cercetare-dezvoltare. Partea I. Bucharest: Imprimeria Naţională.

________. 273/1996. Lege Nr. 133 din 28 octombrie 1996 pentru transformarea Fondurilor Proprietăţii Private în Societăţi de Investiţii Financiare. Partea I. Bucharest: Imprimeria Naţională.

________. 21/1997. Hotărâre Nr. 12 din 29 ianuarie 1997 pentru aprobarea Normelor metodologice privind regularizarea cotelor de capital social deţinute de Fondul Proprietăţii de Stat şi de Societăţile de Investiţii Financiare rezultate în urma transformării Fondurilor Proprietăţii Private în temeiul Legii nr. 133/1996 la societăţile comerciale prevăzute în articolul 2 din Legea 58/1991. Partea I. Bucharest: Imprimeria Naţională.

________. 51/1997. Hotărâre Nr. 76 din 15 martie 1997 privind publicarea rezultatului alocării acţiunilor, respectiv a indicelui de alocare la societăţile comerciale care au facut obiectul procesului de privatizare conform Legii nr. 55/1995 pentru accelerarea procesului de privatizare. Partea I. Bucharest: Imprimeria Naţională.

________. 88/1997. Ordonanţa de urgenăţ Nr. 15 din 5 mai 1997 pentru modificarea şi completarea Legii privatizării societăţilor comerciale nr. 58/1991. Partea I. Bucharest: Imprimeria Naţională.

________. 98/1997. Lege Nr. 83 din 21 mai 1997 pentru privatizarea societăţilor comerciale bancare la care statul este acţionar. Partea I. Bucharest: Imprimeria Naţională.

________. 125/1997. Ordonanţa de urgenţă Nr. 30 din 15 iunie 1997 privind reorganizarea regiilor autonome. Partea I. Bucharest: Imprimeria Naţională.

________. 381/1997. Ordonanţa de urgenţă Nr. 88 din 23 decembrie 1997 privind privatizarea societăţilor comerciale. Partea I. Bucharest: Imprimeria Naţională.

________. 515/1998. Ordonanţa de urgenţă Nr. 56 din 23 decembrie 1998 privind unele măsuri pentru restructurarea Guvernului. Partea I. Bucharest: Imprimeria Naţională.

________. 236/1999. Lege Nr. 99 din 26 mai 1999 privind unele măsuri pentru accelerarea reformei economice. Partea I. Bucharest: Imprimeria Naţională.

Montias, John Michael. 1967. *Economic development in communist Romania.* Cambridge, Ma: The MIT Press.

Moravcsik, Andrew. 1998. *The choice for Europe: social purpose and state power from Messina to Maastricht.* Ithaca: Cornell University Press.

Morgan, John P. 1994. The communist torturers of Eastern Europe: prosecute and punish of forgive and forget? *Communist and Post-Communist Studies* 27: 95–109.

Morgenthau, Hans J. 1985. *Politics among nations: the struggle for power and peace.* 6th edition, revised by Kenneth W. Thompson. New York: McGraw-Hill, Inc.

Mouffe, Chantal. 1993. *The return of the political.* London: Verso.

Mungiu, Alina. 1996. Correspondence from Bucharest: intellectuals as political actors in Eastern Europe: the Romanian case. *East European Politics and Societies* 10: 333–364.

Mungiu, Alina and Andrei Pippidi. 1994. Letter from Romania. *Government and Opposition* 29: 348–361.

Mungiu-Pippidi, Alina. 1999. *Transilvania subiectivă.* Bucharest: Humanitas.

________. 2001. For an institutional approach to post-communist corruption: analysis and policy proposal based on a survey of three central European states. Paper prepared for the Bertelsmann Conference on Accountability. Bucharest. 3–5 May.

Munteanu, Costea. 1994a. Despre ritmul şi metoda de privatizare. *Oeconomica* No. 2: 75–84.

________. 1994b. Din nou despre privatizare. *Oeconomica* No. 3–4: 93–98.

________. 1995. Politica de reformă în Romania între 1990–1993: Un caz de gradualism patologic. *Oeconomica* No. 1: 19–30.

Munteanu, Lelia. 1999. Pe linie moartă. *Adevărul,* 10 December.

Murrell, Peter. 1991. Can neoclassical economics underpin the reform of centrally planned economies? *Journal of Economic Perspectives* 5: 59–76.

________. 1992. Evolution in economics and in the economic reform of the centrally planned economies. In *The emergence of market economies in Eastern Europe,* ed. Christopher Clague and Gordon C. Rausser, 35–53. Cambridge Ma: Blackwell.

________. 1996. How far has the transition progressed? *Journal of Economic Perspectives* 10: 25–44.

________. 2001. Demand and supply in Romanian commercial courts: generating information for institutional reform. IRIS Centre, second draft 18 June. www.bsos.umd.edu/econ/murrell/Romania/Romania_judet_paper.pdf.

Năstase, Adrian. 2001. Teleconferinţa primului-ministru, domnul Adrian Năstase, cu prefecţii. 23 februarie. Bucharest: Government of Romania. www.domino.kappa.ro/guvern/discursuriPM.nsf/arhiva.

Neculau, Adrian. 1999. *Memoria pierdută: eseuri de psihosociologia schimbării.* Iaşi: Polirom.

Neculau, Adrian and Mihai Curelaru. 2000. Dislocarea 'latenţei ideologice' şi refacerea stimei de sine colective. University 'Al. I. Cuza', Iasi. Mimeo.

Negrescu, Dragoş. 1999. A decade of privatisation in Romania. Paper presented at the conference: 'Romania 2000. 10 years of transition: past, present and future', Bucharest: 21–22 October.

Negriţoiu, Mişu. 1996a. Despre economia de piaţâ şi tranziţie. *Revista de cercetări sociale* 1: 124–151.

________. 1996b. Modernizarea societăţii şi economiei româneşti: sistemul producţiei naţionale. *Revista de cercetări sociale* 2: 119–127.

Negulescu, Arabela Sena. 1999. Old and restructured firms. Paper presented at the conference: 'Romania 2000. 10 years of transition: past, present and future', Bucharest: 21–22 October.

Nelson, Daniel N. 1988. *Romanian politics in the Ceauşescu era.* New York: Gordon and Breach Science Publishers.

Nicolae, Caterina and Mihai Diac. 2000. Cazul Severnav nu e o întâmplare: pentru privatizarea Întreprinderii Optica Română, FPS nu a găsit decât un client: Ede Erderly, IOR este unicul furnizor român de optoelectrică pentru armată. *Adevărul,* 31 October.

Nodia, Ghia. 1996. How different are post-communist transitions? *Journal of Democracy* 7: 15–29.

North, Douglass C. 1990. *Institutions, institutional change and economic performance.* Cambridge: Cambridge University Press.

Nunberg, Barbara. 1999. *The state after communism: administrative transitions in Central and Eastern Europe,* with contributions by Luca and Hans-Ulrich Derlien. Regional and sectoral studies. Washington DC: World Bank.

O'Donnell, Guillermo. 1996a. Illusions about consolidation. *Journal of Democracy* 7: 35–51.

________. 1996b. Illusions and conceptual flaws. *Journal of Democracy* 7: 160–168.

O'Donnell, Guillermo, Philippe C. Schmitter and Laurence Whitehead. 1986. *Transitions from authoritarian rule: comparative perspectives.* Baltimore: The Johns Hopkins University Press.

OECD. 1993. *Romania: an economic assessment.* Paris: OECD Publications.

________. 1996. *Trends and policies in privatisation.* vol. 3, no. 1. Paris: OECD Publications.

________. 1998. *OECD economic surveys: Romania.* Centre for the Co-operation with non-members. Paris: OECD Publications.

Oeconomica. 1993. Un decalaj temporar. Interviu realizat cu dl Dr Lucian C. Ionescu Director general/rector al Institutului Bancar Român. 4: 111–112.

Offe, Claus. 1991. Capitalism by democratic design? Democratic theory facing the triple transition in East Central Europe. *Social Research* 58: 865–892.

________. 1996. *Varieties of transition: the East European and East German experience.* London: Polity Press.

________. 1997. Cultural aspects of consolidation: a note on the peculiarities of postcommunist transformations. *East European Constitutional Review* Fall: 64–68.

Oghan, Serdar. 1999. Interviu de Ionuţ Bălan. *Curentul,* 14 October.

Olson, Mancur Jr. 1992. The hidden path to a successful economy. In *The emergence of market economies in Eastern Europe,* ed. Christopher Clague and Gordon R. Rausser, 55–75. Cambridge Ma: Blackwell Press.

________. 1996. Big bills left on the sidewalk: why some natiôns are rich, and others poor. *Journal of Economic Perspectives* 10: 3–24.

Orenstein, Michael A. 2001. *Out of the red: building capitalism and democracy in postcommunist Europe*. Ann Arbor: The University of Michigan Press.

Osman, Oana. 1999. Akmaya ameninţă cu justiţia. *Curentul*, 7 June.

Ost, David. 1990. *Solidarity and the politics of anti-politics: opposition and reform in Poland since 1968*. Philadelphia: Temple University Press.

________. 1993. The politics of interest in post-communist East Europe. *Theory and Society* 22: 453–479.

Paic, Dan. 1999. Mafia alcoolului a păgubit statul roman cu încă 12 miliarde de lei. *Curentul*, 17 June.

Pais, Adrian. 1999. Curentul întreprinzătorilor. *Curentul*, 1 June: 14.

Paler, Octavian. 1999. Exerciţii de sinceritate: cu Grigore Gheba despre trădare. *Curentul*, 11 October.

Partidul România Mare (PRM). 2000. Coordonatele politicii externe ale Partidului România Mare. Chapter 1: Politica externă a PRM şi doctrina naţională www.romare.ro/partid/progext.html; Chapter 4: Partidul România Mare şi integrarea Europeană www.romare.ro/partid/progext /c4.html.

Pasti, Vladimir. 1995. *România în tranziţie: căderea în viitor*. Bucharest: Nemira.

________. 1998a. FMI a renunţat să mai sprijine guvernul Ciorbea. *Bursa*, 2 March: 1.

________. 1998b. Victor Ciorbea – santinela parăsită. *Bursa*, 12 March: 1.

________. 1998c. Cele patru motive ale lui Ion Diaconescu. *Bursa*, 18 March: 1.

________. 1998d. Moştenirea lui Victor Ciorbea. *Bursa*, 1 April: 1.

________. 1998e. Politica împotriva economiei: de la guvernarea ostilă la restructurarea politicii româneşti. Fundaţia 'Un Viitor pentru România'. Mimeo.

Pasti, Vladimir, Mihaela Miroiu and Cornel Codiţă. 1997. *România: starea de fapt*. Bucharest: Nemira.

Patapievici, Horia Roman. 1996. *Politice*. Bucharest: Humanitas.

Patrichi, Viorel. 1998. Daniel Nelson: nu este o criza a democraţiei în România. *România Liberă*. February 6. www.romanialibera.com/1POL /06sopcri.htm.

Păuna, Cătălin and Bianca Păuna. 1999. Output decline and labor reallocation in transitional economies: Where does Romania stand? Paper presented at the conference 'Romania 2000. 10 years of transition: Past, present, and future', Bucharest: 21–22 October.

Pârvu, Elena. 1997. Politica de distrugere a economiei româneşti continuă: Acum e rândul producătorilor de utilaj petrolier. *Adevărul Economic*, 9–15 May. adevarul.kappa.ro/eco269–03.html.

Perotti, Enrico C. 1994. A taxonomy of post-socialist financial systems:

decentralised enforcement and the creation of inside money. *Economics of Transition* 2: 71–81.

Perotti, Enrico C. and Octavian Carare. 1996. The evolution of bank credit quality in transition theory and evidence from Romania. Edinburgh: Centre for Economic Reform and Transformation, Heriot-Watt University.

Pierson, Paul. 1995. *Dismantling the welfare state? Reagan, Thatcher, and the politics of retrenchment.* Cambridge: Cambridge University Press.

Pilat, Vasile. 1993a. Domnul Vasile Pilat despre Bursa Română de Mărfuri. *Oeconomica* No. 4: 113–115.

________. 1993b. Despre tranziţie: însemnări pentru o schiţă de concepţie (I). *Oeconomica* No. 5: 39–46.

________. 1995. Restructurarea: o problemă centrală a economiei românesti. *Oeconomica* No. 1: 41–44.

________. 1996. Integrarea în structurile economice europene: o dură provocare pentru economia şi societatea românească. *Oeconomica* No. 2: 5–52.

Pleşu, Andrei. 1990. Interviu. *Adevărul,* 7 January: 1.

________. 1997. Towards a European patriotism: obstacles as seen from the East. *East European Constitutional Review.* Spring/Summer: 53–55.

Pogonaru, Florin and Camil Apostol. 1999. Romanian capital markets: a decade of transition. Paper presented at the Conference 'Romania 2000: 10 years of transition, past, present and future', Bucharest: 21–22 October .

Pohl, Gerhard, Robert E. Anderson, Stijn Claessens and Simeon Djankov. 1997. Privatization and restructuring in Central and Eastern Europe: evidence and policy options. World Bank Technical Paper No. 368. Washington DC: The World Bank.

Polanyi, Karl. 1957 [1944]. *The great transformation: The political and economic origins of our time.* Foreword by Robert M. MacIver. Boston: Beacon Press.

________. 1992 [1957]. The economy as instituted process. In *The sociology of economic life,* ed. Mark Granovetter and Richard Swedberg, 29–51. Boulder: Westview Press.

Pop, Doru. 1998. *Obsesii sociale.* Iaşi: The European Institute.

Pop, Liliana. 1993. Identitate, libertate, rezistenţă: Un studiu asupra detenţiei politice din România 1945–1964. Department of Sociology, University of Bucharest. Mimeo.

Popa, Răzvan. 2001. Cea mai mare captură a Poliţiei 1000 de blatişti într-un singur personal! *Adevărul,* 17 May.

Popescu, Cristian Tudor. 2001. Cabinetul de lucru al primului-ministru nu este ţara. *Adevărul,* 7 April.

Popescu, Ionuţ. 1992. În fond ce sânt Fondurile? Peste citeva zile Fondurile Proprietăţii Private îşi vor intra în atribuţii. *Capital,* 19 November.

Popescu, Liliana. 1997. A change of power in Romania: the results and significance of the November 1996 elections. *Government and Opposition* 32: 172–186.

Poznanski, Kazimierz. 1993. An interpretation of communist decay: the role of the evolutionary mechanisms. *Communist and Post-Communist Studies* 26: 3–24.

Prahoveanu, B. 1998. Magazinele duty-free închise pentru că sunt râvnite de alţii. *România Liberă* 28, March: 7.

Prizel, Ilya. 1998. *National identity and foreign policy: nationalism and leadership in Poland, Russia, and Ukraine.* Cambridge: Cambridge University Press.

Przeworski, Adam. 1993. Economic reforms, public opinion and public institutions: Poland in the Eastern European perspective. In *Economic reforms in new democracies: a social-democratic approach,* ed. Luiz Carlos Bresser Pereira, Jose Maria Maravall and Adam Przeworski, 132–198. Cambridge: Cambridge University Press.

Raiser, Martin and Peter Sanfey. 1998. Statistical review. *Economics of Transition* 6: 237–273.

Rapaczynski, Andrzej. 1996. The roles of the state and the market in establishing property rights. *Journal of Economic Perspectives* 10: 87–103.

Ratesh, Nestor. 1991. *Romania: the entangled revolution.* New York: Praeger.

Rausser, Gordon C. and Leo K. Simon. 1992. The political economy of transition in Eastern Europe: packaging enterprises for privatisation. In *The emergence of market economies in Eastern Europe,* ed. Gordon C. Rausser and Christopher Clague, 245–270. Cambridge Ma: Blackwell.

Rădulescu, Dina. 1997. Societatea informaţională: România îşi semnează condamnarea la statutul de ţară subdezvoltată. *Romania Liberă,* December.

Rădulescu, Eugen. 1993. Unele consideraţii privind politica monetară a Băncii Naţionale. *Oeconomica* No. 4: 71–78.

Rădulescu, Eugen and Ion Drăgulin. 1995. Politica monetară în România post-comunistă. *Oeconomica* No. 1: 69–91.

Rigby, T. H. 1982. Introduction: Political legitimacy, Weber and communist mono-organizational systems. In *Political legitimation in communist states,* ed. T. H. Rigby and Ferenc Fehér, 1–26. London: Macmillan.

Roberts, Henry L. 1951. *Romania: political problems of an agrarian state.* New Haven Conn: Yale University Press.

Ronnas, Per. 1991. The economic legacy of Ceausescu. In *Economic change in the Balkan states: Albania, Bulgaria, Romania and Yugoslavia,* ed. Orjan Sjoberg and Michael L. Wyzan, 45–68. London: Pinter Publishers.

__________.1992. Romania: ailing state firms may create a roadblock. *RFE/RL Research Report,* 24 April 85–90.

Rosamond, Ben. 1997. Political culture. In *Politics: an introduction,* ed. Barrie Axford, Gary K. Browning, Richard Huggins, Ben Rosamond, John Turner, with Alan Grant, 75–106. London: Routledge.

Rostowski, Jacek. 1995. Introduction. In *Banking reform in Central Europe and the former Soviet Union*, 1–15. Budapest: Central European University Press.

Rothschild, Joseph. 1993. *Return to diversity: a political history of East Central Europe since World War II*. 2nd edition. New York: Oxford University Press.

Ruggie, John Gerard. 1982. International regimes, transactions, and change: embedded liberalism in the postwar economic order. *International Organization* 36: 379–415.

__________. 1992. Multilateralism: the anatomy of an institution. *International Organization* 46: 561–598.

__________. 1993. Territoriality and beyond: problematizing modernity in international relations. *International Organization* 47: 139–174.

__________. 1998. *Constructing world polity*. London: Routledge.

Ruhl, Christof. 1999. Intervention in the panel discussion I: Structural change and macroeconomic policies. Conference 'Romania 2000. 10 years of transition: past, present, and future', Bucharest: 21–22 October. www.worldbank.org.ro/eng/news/conf/panel1.shtml.

Rus, Cristiana. 1997. O agresiune fără precedent asupra micilor întreprinderi private. *Adevărul Economic*, 9–15 May. http://adevarul.kappa.ro /eco269–04.html.

Rutland, Peter. 1995. On the road to capitalism: Reflections on East Europe and the global economy. Paper prepared for the ISA annual convention, Chicago.

Sachs, Jeffrey. 1993. *Poland's jump to market economy*. Cambridge, Ma: The MIT Press.

Sampson, Steven L. 1982. *The planners and the peasants: an anthropological study of urban development in Romania*. Monographs in East-West studies. University Centre of South Jutland, Denmark.

Sădeanu, Adina. 1999. Sistemul mafiot – pe cale de a îngenunchea guvernul în 'afacerea Bancorex'. *Adevărul*, 3 May.

Sălăgean, Viorel. 1997a. Scrisori către premier (IX): obsesia investitorilor străini. *Adevărul Economic* 2–8 May. http://adevarul.kappa.ro /eco268–02.html.

__________. 1997b. Scrisori către premier: sperietoarea celor 200 de zile. *Adevărul Economic* 16–22 May. http://adevarul.kappa.ro/eco270–01.html

__________. 1997c. Un ocean de vorbe pentru odihna poporului. *Adevărul Economic*, 6–12 June. http://adevarul.kappa.ro/eco273–01html.

__________. 1997d. Oare reforma a reânceput? *Adevărul Economic*, 13–19 June. http://adevarul.kappa.ro/eco274–01html.

Sârbu, Ion D. 1992. *Adio, Europa*. Bucharest: Cartea Românească.

Scholte, Jan Aart. 1997. Global capitalism and the state. *International Affairs* 73: 427–452.

__________. 1998. Globalization, governance and democracy in post-communist Romania. *Democratization* 5: 52–77.

Schumpeter, Joseph A. 1943. *Capitalism, socialism and democracy*. London: George Allen & Unwin Ltd.

Schwarz, Herman. 1997. Statul de drept şi guvernarea. In *Democraţia în România*, ed. International IDEA, 93–124. Bucharest: Humanitas.

Scott, James C. 1990. *Domination and the arts of resistance: hidden transcripts*. New Haven: Yale University Press.

Searle, John R. 1995. *The construction of social reality*. London: Penguin.

Secăreş, Vasile. 1998. România riscă să iasă pentru multă vreme de pe agenda SUA! Interviu de Irina Bârlă. *Naţional*, 15 April.

Shafir, Michael. 1985. *Romania: Politics, economics and society. Political stagnation and simulated change*. London: Frances Pinter.

————. 1986. Romania. In *Leadership and succession in the Soviet Union, Eastern Europe and China*, ed. Martin McCauley and Stephen Carter, 114–135. London: Macmillan.

————. 1992a. Romania's tortuous road to reform. *RFE/RL Research Report* 3 January: 96–99.

————. 1992b. 'War of the roses' in Romania's National Salvation Front. *RFE/RL Research Report* 24 January: 15–22.

————. 1992c. Romania: National Liberal Party quits Democratic Convention. *RFE/RL Research Report* 12 June: 25–30.

————. 1992d. The Movement for Romania: A party for 'radical return'. *RFE/RL Research Report* 17 July: 16–21.

————. 1992e. Romania: main candidates in the presidential elections. *RFE/RL Research Report* 4 September: 11–8.

————. 1992f. Romania's elections: why the Democratic Convention lost. *RFE/RL Research Report* 30 October: 1–7.

————. 1992g. Romania's elections: more change than meets the eye. *RFE/RL Research Report* 6 November: 1–8.

————. 1992h. Romania's new government. *RFE/RL Research Report* 27 November: 11–16.

————. 1993a. The HDFR congress: confrontations postponed. *RFE/RL Research Report* 26 February: 34–39.

————. 1993b. Growing political extremism in Romania. *RFE/RL Research Report* 2 April: 18–25.

————. 1993c. Romania: the rechristening of the National Salvation Front. *RFE/RL Research Report* 2 July: 22–26.

————. 1993d. Romanian Prime Minister announces cabinet changes. *RFE/RL Research Report* 24 September: 17–22.

————. 1993e. The Caritas affair: a Transylvanian 'Eldorado'. *RFE/RL Research Report* 24 September: 23–27.

————. 1993f. 'A Future for Romania' group: fish or fowl? *RFE/RL Research Report* 10 December: 9–14.

————. 1994a. Marshal Ion Antonescu and Romanian politics. *RFE/RL*

Research Report 11 February: 22–28.

————. 1994b. Romanian politics in turmoil. *RFE/RL Research Report* 22 July: 1–6.

————. 1994c. Ethnic tension runs high in Romania. *RFE/RL Research Report* 19 August: 24–31.

————. 1996. Opting for political change. *Transition*, 27 December.

Shafir, Michael and Dan Ionescu. 1993. Romania: political change and economic malaise. *RFE/RL Research Report* 1 January: 108–112.

————. 1994. Romania: a crucially uneventful year. *RFE/RL Research Report* 7 January: 122–126.

Slay, Ben. 1993. Roundtable: privatization in Eastern Europe. *RFE/RL Research Report* 13 August: 47–57.

Słomcyński, Kazimierz and Goldie Shabad. 1997. Systemic transformation and the salience of class structure in East Central Europe. *East European Politics and Societies* 11: 155–189.

Smith, Adam. 1997 [1776]. *The wealth of nations.* Books I–III. With an introduction by Andrew S. Skinner. London: Penguin Books.

Stan, Lavinia. 1995a. 'Romanian privatization: Assessment of the first five years. *Communist and Post-Communist Studies* 28: 427–435.

————. 1995b. Some aspects of post-communist privatization. Cahiers de Sociologie Economique et Culturelle No. 24. 95–100.

Staniszkis, Jadwiga. 1984. *Poland's self-limiting revolution,* ed. Jan T. Gross. Princeton: Princeton University Press.

————. 1991. *The dynamics of the breakthrough in Eastern Europe: the Polish experience.* Berkeley: University of California Press.

Stark, David. 1990. Privatization in Hungary: from plan to market or from plan to clan? *East European Politics and Societies* 4: 351–392.

————. 1992. Path dependence and privatization strategies in East Central Europe. *East European Politics and Societies* 6: 17–54.

Stark, David and Laszlo Bruszt. 1998. *Postsocialist pathways: transforming politics and property in East Central Europe.* Cambridge: Cambridge University Press.

Steen, Anton. 1997. *Between past and future: elites, democracy, and the state in post-communist countries.* Aldershot: Ashgate.

Stepan, Alfred. 1986. Paths towards redemocratization: theoretical and comparative considerations. In *Transitions from authoritarian rule: comparative perspectives,* ed. Guillermo O'Donnell, Philippe C. Schmitter and Laurence Whitehead, 64–84. Baltimore: The Johns Hopkins University Press.

Stiglitz, Joseph E. 1999. Whither reform? Ten years of the transition. World Bank: Annual Bank Conference on Development Economics, April 28–30.

Stoenescu, George Virgil. 1994. Gânduri la plecarea prietenului nostru. *Oeconomica* No. 1: 123.

Stolojan, Theodor. 1999. Elaborarea, coordonarea şi aplicarea politicilor guvernamentale în România. Working paper 18/1999. Bucharest: Romanian Centre for Economic Policy.

Strange, Susan. 1982. Cave! Hic dragones: a critique of regime analysis. *International Organization* 36: 2. 337–354.

———. 1987. The persistent myth of lost hegemony. *International Organization* 41: 551–574.

Striblea, Cătălin. 2001. Unii spun că avem o presa isterică: interviu cu Mihai Coman, decan al Facultăţii de Jurnalistică din cadrul Universităţii Media Bucureşti. *Opinia Studenţească* No. 84: 8–9.

Szélenyi, Iván and Szonja Szélenyi. 1995. Circulation and reproduction of elites during the post-communist transformation of Eastern Europe. *Theory and Society* 24: 615–638.

Szélenyi, Iván, Éva Fodor and Eric Hanley. 1997. Left turn in postcommunist politics: bringing class back in? *East European Politics and Societies* 11: 191–224.

Şandor, Dorel. 1999. Politics versus policies: How to succeed in blocking reforms. Paper presented at the Conference 'Romania 2000: 10 years of transition: past, present and future', Bucharest: 21–22 October.

Şerbănescu, Ilie. 1993. Reforma blocată. *Oeconomica* No. 4: 43–56.

———. 1994. *Jumatăţile de măsură dublează costurile sociale.* Bucharest: Staff.

———. 1999. Can the vicious circle be broken? Paper presented at the Conference 'Romania 2000: 10 years of transition: past, present and future', Bucharest: 21–22 October.

Ştefan, Stela. 1998. Partidele politice sunt umbrela care protejează ilegalităţile. Gorj: furturi de miliarde acoperite de tăcerea complicitară a RENEL. *România Liberă*, 1 August.

Ştefan-Scalat, Laurenţiu. 2001. Political elite recruitment and party development in post-communist Romania. Paper presented at the European Consortium for Political Research First General Conference, Canterbury, September.

Ştefoi-Sava, Elena. 1995. Romania: organizing legislative impotence. *East European Constitutional Review* Spring: 78–83.

Tal, Kali. 1996. *Worlds of hurt: reading the literatures of trauma.* Cambridge: Cambridge University Press.

Tănase, Stelian. 1993. *Şocuri şi crize.* Bucharest: Staff.

———. 1995. *Ora oficială de iarnă.* Iaşi: The European Institute.

———. 1996. *Revoluţia ca eşec: elite şi societate.* Iaşi: Polirom.

———. 1997. *Anatomia mistificării 1994–1989.* Bucharest: Humanitas.

Teleanu, Ion. 1999. Ali Baba şi… privatizarea la Ploieşti. *Curentul,* 1 June.

Teodorescu, Alin. 1991. The future of a failure: the Romanian economy. In *Economic change in the Balkan states: Albania, Bulgaria, Romania and Yugoslavia,* ed. Orjan Sjoberg and Michael L. Wyzan, 69– 82. London: Pinter Publishers.

Teodorescu, Vlad. 1997. Doi prim-miniştri, Petre Roman si Theodor Stolojan, şi o şleahtă de miniştri au semnat o hoţie de 12 milioane dolari din bugetul României – afacerea Megapower. *Adevărul,* 27 February.

Teşliuc, Cornelia Mihaela, Lucian Pop and Emil Daniel Teşliuc (2001). *Sărăcia şi sistemul de protectie socială.* Iaşi: Polirom.

Thom, Françoise. 1996. *Sfîrşiturile comunismului.* Trans. Gabriela Gavril. Iaşi: Polirom.

Thompson, John B. 1991. Editor's Introduction. In *Language and symbolic power,* by Pierre Bourdieu, trans. Gino Raymond and Matthew Adamson, 1–31. London: Polity Press.

Thomsen, Paul. 1997a. Interviu de Simona David. *Adevărul,* 8 August.

_______. 1997b. Interviu de Simona David. *Adevărul,* December.

Tismăneanu, Vladimir. 1989. Personal power and political crisis in Romania. *Government and Opposition* 24: 177–198.

_______. 1993. The quasi-revolution and its discontents: emerging political pluralism in post-Ceauşescu Romania. *East European Politics and Societies* 7: 308–347.

_______. 1996a. *Arheologia terorii.* 2nd edition. Bucharest: Alfa.

_______. 1996b. *Balul mascat: un dialog cu Mircea Mihăeş.* Iaşi: Polirom.

_______. 1998. *Fantasies of salvation: democracy, nationalism, and myth in post-communist Europe.* Princeton: Princeton University Press.

Tismăneanu, Vladimir and Dan Pavel. 1994. Romania's mystical revolutionaries: the generation of angst and adventure revisited. *East European Politics and Societies* 8: 402–438.

True, Jacqueline. 1997. Global life and the politics of temporality: Reconstructing tradition and history in post-communist times. Paper presented at the 38th Annual Convention of ISA. Toronto.

_______. 1999. Expanding markets and marketing gender: the integration of the post-socialist Czech Republic. *Review of International Political Economy* 6: 360–389.

Underhill, Geoffrey. 2000. Global issues in historical perspective. In *Political economy and the changing global order* 2nd edition, ed. Richard Stubbs and Geoffrey Underhill, 105–118. Toronto: Oxford University Press.

Vachudová, Milada Anna and Tim Snyder. 1997. Are transitions transitory? Two types of political change in Eastern Europe since 1989. *East European Politics and Societies* 11: 1–35.

Vainshtein, Grigory. 1994. Totalitarian public consciousness in a post-totalitarian society: the Russian case in the general context of post-communist developments. *Communist and Post-Communist Studies* 27: 247–259.

Varvara, Camelia. 1998. De ce moare industria textilă cu 23 la sută din exportul pe economie: România, ţara lui lohn. *Adevărul,* 18 July.

Vasilescu, Adrian. 1999. Adnotări la cazul 'Albina': între obsesia ingineriilor financiare şi sfidarea logicii. *Curentul,* 17 June: 12.

Vasiliu, Teodora and Ciprian Vasiliu. 1999. Critici dure la adresa sistemului bancar românesc. *Curentul,* 1 June: 12.

Verdery, Katherine. 1991. *National ideology under socialism: identity and cultural politics in Ceausescu's Romania.* Berkeley: University of California Press.

————. 1996. *What was socialism and what comes next?* Princeton: Princeton University Press.

————. 1999. Fuzzy property: rights, power, and identity in Transylvania's decollectivization. In *Uncertain transition: ethnographies of change in the postsocialist world,* ed. Michael Burawoy and Katherine Verdery, 53–81. Lanham: Rowman & Littlefield Publishers Inc.

Verdery, Katherine and Gail Kligman. 1992. Romania after Ceauşescu: post-communist communism? In *Eastern Europe in revolution,* ed. Ivo Banac, 117–147. Ithaca: Cornell University Press.

Veress, Robert. 2001. 'Negrii' de la stat. *Adevărul,* 7 April.

Vickers, John and George Yarrow. 1988. *Privatization: an economic analysis.* Cambridge Ma: The MIT Press.

Vlăsceanu, Lazăr. 2000. Tranziţie şi dezvoltare: aplicabilitatea 'Consensului de la Washington'. University of Bucharest, Mimeo.

Voicu, George. 1996. Sisteme de partide în Europa de Est. *Polis* 3/2: 116–136.

Vosganian, Varujan. 1994a. *Jurnal de front: articole economice.* Bucharest: Staff.

————. 1994b. Locul şi rolul profitului în perioada de tranziţie. *Oeconomica* No. 3–4: 99–105.

Voslenski, Michael. 1984. *Nomeklatura: anatomy of the Soviet ruling class.* London: The Bodley Head.

Wagstyl, Stefan and Virginia Marsh. 1998. Time to deliver promised land. *Financial Times Survey: Romania.* 28 September: 1.

Walicki, Andrzej. 1991. From Stalinism to post-communist pluralism: the case of Poland. *New Left Review* 185: 92–121.

Walker, R. B. J. 1993. *Inside/outside: international relations as political theory.* Cambridge: Cambridge University Press.

Wallerstein, Immanuel. 1979. *The capitalist world-economy.* Cambridge: Cambridge University Press.

Waltz, Kenneth N. 1979. *Theory of international politics.* Reading Ma: Addison-Wesley Publishing Company.

————. 1995. Realist thought and neorealist theory. In *Controversies in international relations theory,* ed. C. Kegley, 67–82. New York: St. Martin's Press.

Weber, Cynthia. 1990. Representing debt: Peruvian presidents Bealunde's and Gracia's reading/writing of Peruvian debt. *International Studies Quarterly.* 34: 353–365.

Weber, Eugen. 1965. Romania. In *The European right: a historical profile,* ed. Hans Rogger and Eugen Weber, 501–575. Berkeley: University of California Press.

Weber, Max. 1976. *The protestant ethic and the spirit of capitalism.* Tran. Talcott Parsons, introduction by Anthony Giddens. London: George Allen & Unwin.

————. 1994. *Political writings.* ed. Peter Lassman and Ronald Speirs. Cambridge: Cambridge University Press.

Wedel, Janine R. 1998. *Collision or collusion: the strange case of Western aid to Eastern Europe, 1989–1998.* London: Macmillan.

Wendt, Alexander. 1995 [1992]. Anarchy is what states make of it: the social construction of power politics (1992). In *International theory: critical investigations,* ed. James Der Derian, 129–177. London: Macmillan.

Wiatr, Jerzy J. 1995. The dilemmas of re-organizing the bureaucracy in Poland during the democratic transformation. *Communist and Post-Communist Studies* 28: 153–160.

Wijnbergen, Sweder van. 1998. Bank restructuring and enterprise reform. European Bank for Reconstruction and Development Working paper No. 29.

Williamson, John. 1990. *Latin American adjustment: how much has happened?* Wasghinton DC: Institute for International Economics.

————. 1994. In search of a manual for technopols. In *The political economy of policy reform,* 11–28. Washington DC: Institute for International Economics.

Winiecki, Jan. 1992. Privatisation in East-Central Europe: avoiding major mistakes. In *The emergence of market economies in Eastern Europe,* ed. Gordon C. Rausser and Christopher Clague, 271–277. Cambridge Ma: Blackwell.

Wojtyna, Andrzej. 1994. Stabilization versus privatization in Poland: a sequencing problem at the macro- and microeconomic levels. In *A fourth way? Privatization, property, and the emergence of new market economies,* ed. Gregory S. Alexander and Grazyna Skapska, 79–94. London: Routledge.

Woolcock, Michael. 1998. Social capital and economic development: toward a theoretical synthesis and policy framework. *Theory and Society* 27: 151–208.

The World Bank. 1994a. Romania: Petroleum sector rehabilitation project. Report No. 12026–RO. 14 March.

————. 1994b. Romania: Industrial development project. Report No. 11542–RO 26 April.

————. 1994c. Romania: Employment and social protection project. Report No. 12769–RO. 31 October.

————. 1995a. Romania: Structural adjustment loan. Implementation completion report. Report No. 14726. June.

________. 1995b. Romania: Power sector rehabilitation and modernization project. Report No. 13887–RO. 9 August.

________. 1995c. Romania: Railway rehabilitation project. Report No. 13857–RO. 15 December.

________. 1996. Romania: Technical assistance/critical imports loan (loan 3363–RO) and the structural adjustment loan (loan 3481–RO). Performance audit report. Report No. 15791. 25 June.

________. 1997. Memorandum and recommendation of the President of the International Bank for Reconstruction and Development to the Executive Directors on a Country Assistance Strategy of the World Bank Group for Romania. Report No. 16559–RO. 9 May.

________. 1998a. Romania: Telecommunications reform and privatization support project. Staff appraisal report. Report No. 16323–RO. 6 March.

________. 1998b. Romania: Public expenditure review. Part I: Public sector financial management. Part II: Civil service reform. Report No. 17743–RO. 26 June.

________. 1999a. Public enterprise reform and privatization database, ECSPF and DECRG. www.worldbank.org.ecspf/PSD-Yearbook/romania.html.

________. 1999b. Project appraisal document on a proposed loan in the amount of US$25 million to Romanian for a Private institution building loan. Report No: 19265–RO. 17 May.

________. 1999c. Project appraisal document on a proposed loan in the amount of US$44.5 million equivalent to the Government of Romania for a mine closure and social mitigation project. Report No: 19347–RO. 6 August.

________. 2001a. Romania. Draft country assistance strategy paper. http://worldbank.org.romaniacas.

________. 2001b. Summary of feedback on World Bank's draft Country Assistance Strategy for Romania. January 16–February 8, 2001. 9 February. Mimeo. http://worldbank.org.romaniacas.

Yeaple, Stephen and Warren Moskowitz. 1995. The literature on privatization. Research Paper #9514. Federal Reserve Bank of New York.

Young, Oran R. 1992. The effectiveness of international institutions: hard cases and critical variables. In *Governance without government: order and change in world politics*, ed. James N. Rosenau, Ernst-Otto Czempiel, 160–194. Cambridge: Cambridge University Press.

________. 1999. *Governance in world affairs*. Ithaca: Cornell University Press.

Zamfir Elena, Ilie Bădescu and Cătălin Zamfir. 2000. *Starea societăţii româneşti dupa 10 ani de tranziţie*. Bucharest: Expert.

Zamfir Elena, Marin Preda. 2000. *Diagnoza problemelor sociale comunitare*. Bucharest: Expert.

Zhang, Baohui. 1993. Institutional aspects of reforms and the democratisation of communist regimes. *Communist and Post-communist Studies* 26: 165–181.

Zilber, Herbert (Belu). 1997. *Actor în procesul Pătrăşcanu: prima versiune a memoriilor lui Belu Zilber*. Bucharest: Humanitas.
Zinoviev, Alexander. 1985. *The reality of communism*. London: Paladin Books.